MW00603709

pastor jack

THE
AUTHORIZED
BIOGRAPHY OF
JACK HAYFORD

pastor jack

S. DAVID MOORE

DAVID C COOK

transforming lives together

PASTOR JACK
Published by David C Cook
4050 Lee Vance Drive
Colorado Springs, CO 80918 U.S.A.

Integrity Music Limited, a Division of David C Cook
Brighton, East Sussex BN1 2RE, England

The graphic circle C logo is a registered trademark of David C Cook.

The website addresses recommended throughout this book are offered as a
resource to you. These websites are not intended in any way to be or imply an
endorsement on the part of David C Cook, nor do we vouch for their content.

Unless otherwise noted, all Scripture quotations are taken from the King James Version of the
Bible. (Public Domain.) Scripture quotations marked ESV are taken from the ESV® Bible (The
Holy Bible, English Standard Version®), copyright © 2001 by Crossway, a publishing ministry
of Good News Publishers. Used by permission. All rights reserved; NIV are taken from THE
HOLY BIBLE, NEW INTERNATIONAL VERSION®, NIV® Copyright © 1973, 1978,
1984, 2011 by Biblica, Inc.® Used by permission. All rights reserved worldwide; NKJV are
taken from the New King James Version®. Copyright © 1982 by Thomas Nelson. Used by
permission. All rights reserved; and NRSV are taken from the New Revised Standard Version
Bible, copyright 1989, Division of Christian Education of the National Council of the
Churches of Christ in the United States of America. Used by permission. All rights reserved.

Library of Congress Control Number 2020935411
ISBN 978-0-8307-8111-9
eISBN 978-0-8307-8112-6

Published in cooperation with The King's University Press and Gateway Press.

The Team: Michael Covington, Jeff Gerke, Stephanie Bennett, Megan Stengel,
Jack Campbell, Michael Fedison, Jon Middel, Susan Murdock
Cover Design: John Lucas
Cover photo used with permission by David J. Pavol
Interior photographs courtesy of The King's University,
The Church On The Way, and the Hayford family.

Printed in the United States of America
First Edition 2020

1 2 3 4 5 6 7 8 9 10

063020

Dedicated to H. Vinson Synan (1934 to 2020)
My doktorvater, *mentor, and dear friend.*

CONTENTS

FOREWORD

Pastor Jack is one of my closest and dearest friends and mentors. He has been a spiritual father to me for many years. His wisdom, books, messages, and songs have profoundly impacted my life and continue to today. I, along with many others, have experienced the benefit of spending one-on-one time with him. The results of his influence are evident in my life and in the lives of people all over the world.

Paul told the church at Corinth, "For though you might have ten thousand instructors in Christ, yet you do not have many fathers" (1 Corinthians 4:15 NKJV). While I have but few spiritual fathers, Pastor Jack is one of them. He is a tremendous example of a spiritual father who has loved me, nurtured me, encouraged me, and called out my destiny.

Dr. David Moore, who has written this book, is another man who has experienced the benefits of Pastor Jack's influence and mentorship. David has known Jack personally since 1984. When they first met, David was a young pastor with only thirty-five people attending his church. Within the next five years, his church grew to be one of the largest churches in the city with nearly a thousand people in attendance, which David wholeheartedly attributes to Jack's influence and mentorship. Over the years, they have enjoyed a long, fruitful journey as a spiritual father and son.

When David began putting this book together, Pastor Jack put his full trust in him to write an accurate and truthful biography telling his whole life story. He gave David complete access to all his journals, correspondence, and even financial statements. Nothing was held back. Truthfully, Jack has more integrity than most men I know and has nothing to hide, yet he allowed David to dive deep into his personal documents and discover the truth for himself.

David says that it has been one of his greatest and most humbling privileges to be trusted to write Jack's authorized biography. You may have read biographies in the past that seemed to focus only on the happy moments and didn't fully represent the person's real life and real struggles. I can assure you this book is different. While Pastor Jack's legacy is honored, there is no stone left unturned. His openness about his life and candidness about his own struggles and failures are what have always made him so relatable and loved by people everywhere. Starting with his fascinating entry into this world, you'll read about Jack's family and childhood, his submission to God's call on his life, the growing pains he experienced as a young pastor, and how he became a global leader in the body of Christ.

On the following pages, you'll learn intimate details about Pastor Jack, a man I've often said is the Apostle Paul of our generation. Paul was a man of the Spirit who knew the power of God, yet at the same time he was a man who knew the Scriptures. He was brilliant and could communicate to different people and different churches in many ways, which is represented by the letters he wrote. When I think of the Apostle Paul, I think of a man who has a diverse and rich background. A man who is an effective teacher of the Scriptures. A man who is of the Spirit, yet also a man of intellect. A man who's seen the power of God at work within him. A man like Pastor Jack.

Robert Morris
Founding Lead Senior Pastor, Gateway Church
Chancellor, The King's University
Bestselling Author of The Blessed Life, Frequency,
Beyond Blessed, and Take the Day Off

ACKNOWLEDGMENTS

In 2002 I was awarded a PhD fellowship in the School of Divinity at Regent University in Virginia. I knew from the outset that I hoped to write my dissertation on the life of Jack W. Hayford, one of the most highly regarded Pentecostal pastors in the world at the time. Having been associated with Hayford's ministry for years, I contacted him about the idea and was pleased—and wonderfully surprised—when he offered his enthusiastic support. That support included not only granting interviews but full access to his journals, correspondence, and all personal files. Nothing was held back despite the fact he was given no editorial voice in the project. Needless to say, his support was of inestimable worth to the completion of both the dissertation and this more popularly written biography. I offer my profound gratitude to "Pastor Jack" for his willingness to let his life be an "open book."

In many ways, this project began with a lengthy video interview I conducted with Hayford in 1993 for a graduate class at Oral Roberts University. Janet Kemp, Hayford's executive assistant at the time, deserves special thanks for helping arrange that seminal interview with Hayford and two interviews with Jack's mother, Dolores, and his early mentor, Vincent Bird. The interviews with his mother and Bird proved providential since both passed before I began my dissertation research a decade later.

I can't sufficiently thank the amazing team at David C Cook. My thanks to Michael Covington and Stephanie Bennett for your support and belief in this book. Special thanks to my editors, Jeff Gerke and Jack Campbell. Thanks for your hard work and patience when I missed due dates. Thanks to Craig Dunnagan and John Anderson at Gateway Publishing for your partnership in this project.

There are so many others that deserve thanks. This book would have been impossible without the help of Hayford's executive assistant, Lana Duim, and his personal assistant, Bob Caron. Both went far beyond the call of duty, coordinating interviews, providing documents, and answering innumerable questions. Jack's daughter Rebecca Bauer was an important advocate. Michael Lynch and the late Bill Shumate, who each directed Jack Hayford Ministries at different seasons, offered their full support. Kimberly Boschman and David Garza at Jack Hayford Ministries gave valuable assistance. Lee Mimms was essential in arranging celebrity interviews. Steve Zeleny, the archivist at the Foursquare Church's Heritage Archives, located key documents. I'm especially grateful for each person who so willingly gave their time for formal interviews (see the interview list near the end of the book).

Sincere thanks to my PhD dissertation committee chair, the late Vinson Synan, and committee members David Edwin Harrell and Frank Macchia. Their unflinching critiques shaped and refined my interpretation of Hayford's life. Dr. Synan's counsel helped in my decision to write Hayford's biography for a general audience. After all, the people who valued Hayford the most were pastors, leaders, and everyday Christians who read Jack's books and knew him through his teaching and preaching. "Write for them," Synan said.

I extend my thanks to The King's University for the release time afforded me through the M. G. Robertson Chair of Pneumatology I hold. Dr. David Cole, the university provost, championed my research and writing, providing valuable counsel on many occasions. My colleague Dr. Jonathan Huntzinger has been a constant dialogue partner on this project since I joined the university faculty in 2013. Thank you, Jon, for encouraging me when I complained—I'm good at that! My thanks to The King's University president, Dr. Jon Chasteen, and to all my faculty colleagues for their friendship and support.

Special thanks to Jackson Avenue Church, the congregation I serve as lead pastor. Your love and support are greatly appreciated. I'm forever grateful for the eight-week sabbatical you provided me in the summer of 2019 as I worked on the manuscript. Thanks to Dan Armstrong, Brian Mouw, and Gary Poovey for filling in for me many weekends.

Last, and certainly not least, heartfelt thanks to my wife of fifty years, dear Patty (we both look too young to be married that long!). She has been my constant companion and cheerleader throughout this project and has always offered invaluable editorial support. This book would have been impossible without her at my side.

S. *David Moore*
May 2020

Introduction

"IT IS WHAT YOU THINK IT IS"

Saturday, January 2, 1971, was a cool, sunny Southern California day, the kind of brisk winter day for which the Los Angeles area is famous. Richard Nixon was nearing the end of his second full year in office as the nation's president. The Vietnam War was still raging with nearly 350,000 US troops deployed. Just the day before, a new federal law had banned all cigarette advertising on television.

The front page of the January 2 *Los Angeles Times* carried little national news, mostly highlighting the New Year's Day events focused on the Pasadena-based Tournament of Roses parade (in which the Rev. Billy Graham had served as grand marshal) and the story of how the underdog Stanford Cardinal football team had stunned the undefeated Ohio State Buckeyes, 27 to 17. The Cardinal had ridden the arm of Jim Plunkett, the 1970 Heisman Trophy quarterback, back to the Rose Bowl after a nineteen-year absence.

That Saturday, some twenty miles west of Pasadena in the San Fernando Valley just north of Hollywood, Jack W. Hayford Jr. was preparing to preach.

The then thirty-six-year-old pastor of a small Pentecostal[1] congregation in a Los Angeles suburb spent much of the day readying his sermons for the next day's morning and evening services at the Church on the Way, the First Foursquare Church of Van Nuys. When he finished his preparation, about 4:30 p.m., he stepped out of his office and, anticipating a chilly night, walked over to set the thermostat to seventy-two degrees. As he turned to lock up and go home, he was "bewildered" by what he saw in the little sanctuary he had just walked through.

> The room was filled with a silvery mist. The late afternoon
> sun slanted through the stained-glass windows, adding to
> the beauty of the sight before me; but there was no natural
> explanation for what I was seeing. The mist had not been
> there a moment before. My mind probed for an answer:
> "This isn't dust … smog … is it?"[2]

Even as he thought this, Hayford knew better, since it was an absolutely clear day with no smog at all. Besides, the mist he was seeing had a "glowing quality" even where no sunlight was shining into the room. Hayford sensed this was some kind of manifestation of God's glory, but he was hesitant to say so. Feeling the need to test it out, he stepped into a nearby prayer room and found no mist. Before reentering the sanctuary, Hayford rubbed his eyes and stepped back in, only to find that the mist was still there.

> I felt a particular sense of wonder—why this display?
> Strangely enough, I was also concerned about who could
> confirm that I wasn't just seeing things. Then the Lord
> spoke: *It is what you think it is.* The words struck me as
> moving and humorous at the same moment. The almighty
> God of the universe saw me worrying about a confirming
> witness and condescended to be that witness Himself. It

was as though God were saying, "I see it too, Jack." That was the humorous part. What moved me deeply were the words that followed: *"I have given My glory to dwell in this place."* I stood watching silently; and moments later the scene returned to the ordinariness of mere sunlight in the room.[3]

Following this experience, Hayford prayed a simple "Thank You, Lord" and went home to have dinner with his family—nothing more. Yet the next day the small church, normally attended by no more than 100 worshippers, had over 160 in attendance, with no reason to explain the surge—"except that the day before God had said He was giving a gift."[4]

It would be months before Hayford would share the story with his leadership team and, concerned it might be misunderstood and bring ridicule, over a year before telling the whole congregation.[5] Yet from that Sunday forward, the little church would experience continuous growth for the next twenty years. Hayford would always believe that there was no real explanation for the church's growth except that God's "glory gift was the key to this release."[6]

This "glory story" came to define the remarkable journey of Jack Hayford's thirty-year tenure as the senior pastor of the Church on the Way.[7] It is also our entrée into the "God drenched, Spirit saturated" world in which Jack Hayford lives.

From Jack's early childhood, he learned from his parents, especially his mother, Dolores, that God spoke to people and was intricately involved in the everyday affairs of life. So it was no surprise to Hayford that God would so tangibly manifest His presence in the "silvery mist" or that God would speak directly to him as he had that day in 1971. His mother had often explained supernatural experiences to her son in ways that made her accounts seem perfectly normal to him; "sane, sensible, and scriptural" is how he would later describe similar experiences.

More than anything, the story of God's glory in the Van Nuys sanctuary looked like the stories he read every day in his Bible. In other words, seeing God's glory was simply the world as the Bible described it, a world in which the visible and invisible dimensions of reality meld together seamlessly. The biblical narratives revealed to Jack a reality that never separated the secular and the sacred, showing God's active engagement within His creation, saving, empowering, healing, leading, and delivering everyone who called upon the name of the Lord (see Romans 10:13).

"PASTOR JACK"

Jack Williams Hayford Jr. has lived an extraordinary life. For all his acclaim, he has always preferred to be known as "Pastor Jack." In the nearly fifty years since January 2, 1971, Jack Hayford has become nationally and internationally known.

Most people came to know him in his role pastoring the Church on the Way. When he assumed the Van Nuys pastorate in 1969, it was a fading congregation of just eighteen members. Under his leadership over the ensuing decades, the church grew to a weekly attendance of over 10,000. It became one of America's flagship churches, an "Antioch" ministry center with numerous ministries extended, missionaries sent, and new churches planted.

Burbank—the "media capital of the world"—was nearby, and so Jack became pastor to many well-known celebrities in the music, film, and television industries. In the early years of the church's growth, young hippies from the Jesus People movement, which was burgeoning in Southern California, worshipped alongside wealthy professionals, media personalities, and everyone in between.

Many of those attending the Church on the Way were not even aware that it was part of a historic Pentecostal denomination, the Foursquare Church, started in the 1920s by the controversial evangelist Aimee Semple

McPherson. Most knew it only as the Church on the Way, not by its legal name, the First Foursquare Church of Van Nuys.

As the church grew, so Jack's ministry grew. During the Christian "cassette tape explosion" of the 1970s and 1980s, hundreds of thousands of Hayford's sermons were distributed around the world. In 1977, he wrote his first nationally published book, and he then went on to write more than fifty books, along with numerous articles featured in periodicals and journals. He also served as the executive editor of the popular *Spirit-Filled Life Bible*. In addition, for a quarter century, Hayford drew a vast audience through his radio and television broadcasts.

Uniquely significant and multiplying his influence was the role Jack grew into as a pastor of pastors. The Church on the Way served as the platform for expanding opportunities teaching and mentoring other leaders. Not long after the manifestation of God's glory, pastors began to inquire and visit the Van Nuys congregation, wanting to learn what occasioned its growth and vitality. By the early 1980s, Jack was regularly speaking to as many as 20,000 pastors each year at conferences and leadership events, and this continued well into the new millennium.[8]

In 1996, while Jack was flying back to California from Atlanta after speaking to some 40,000 pastors at the Promise Keepers Clergy Conference at the Georgia Dome, God spoke to him, saying, "Found a seminary." Hayford obeyed, and a year later in 1997, The King's College and Seminary—now The King's University—offered its first undergraduate classes on the Van Nuys church campus to train future leaders for pastoral and church leadership.

The Jack Hayford School of Pastoral Nurture also started in 1997 at the university, hosting several "consultations" each year, attended by around forty senior pastors, who spent a week being mentored by Hayford. In these consultations, Hayford candidly spoke about how he lived out his private life and public ministry. Over the fifteen years that these consultations were offered by the university, several thousand pastors attended from many different Christian denominations.

Jack Hayford is a man of many gifts. He is a poet, a musician, and a songwriter of considerable talent, having written over 600 hymns and songs, of which nearly 200 are published. His worship chorus "Majesty" became one of the most popular and widely utilized worship choruses in recent history. His teaching and leadership were significant in providing a biblical/theological basis for contemporary, expressive Christian worship, and he became a mentor to popular worship leaders and executives in the worship music publishing industry.

STATESMAN FOR THE HOLY SPIRIT

Perhaps more than any other factor contributing to Hayford's wide appeal has been his articulate and statesmanlike approach to ministry, coupled with his self-effacing manner and conversational preaching style. His high view of Scripture and his fidelity to biblical truth brought regard and respect for his preaching and teaching. While never apologizing for his Pentecostal beliefs, his public ministry has defied Pentecostal stereotypes.

All of this has made Hayford one of the most widely respected Pentecostal leaders in the world. He regularly received invitations to speak at non-Pentecostal conferences in denominations ranging from Baptists to the Seventh-day Adventists. He served for years on the executive committee of the National Association of Evangelicals (NAE). In 1989, he was asked to give a plenary session address to the Lausanne II Congress on World Evangelization in Manila, the only Pentecostal given that privilege. His role as moderator for the 1997 Promise Keepers event on the National Mall in Washington, DC, which some have said was attended by 1.3 million men, was another example of his pan-Christian influence.[9]

In 2005, the popular evangelical periodical *Christianity Today* perhaps best illustrated Hayford's broad recognition by featuring on its cover a photo of Hayford and a banner headline calling him the "Pentecostal Gold Standard."[10] By the 1990s, Jack had established meaningful friendships with many of the most respected evangelical leaders in America, including James Dobson, Rick Warren, John Maxwell, John Perkins, and Billy Graham, and he was serving on the boards of a number of national evangelical organizations.

Given his forthrightness in affirming that God regularly speaks to him, the wide respect Hayford has received outside of Pentecostal/Charismatic circles may seem surprising, especially considering that his preaching and writing make frequent references to God's voice in his life and to stories about God communicating to him in dreams and visions.

One reason there is so little negative reaction toward Hayford may be attributed to the matter-of-fact way in which he communicates these experiences and how "normal" he makes them sound—much like his mother had done for him when he was a boy. Jack knew that claiming God spoke directly to him could rattle some evangelicals, and he always sought to explain what he meant. When he said "God spoke to me," he was referring

> to something even more specific than general revelations or private impressions. I reserve those words intentionally for the rare, special occasions when, in my spirit, I have had the Lord speak directly to me. I do not mean, "I felt impressed," or, "I sensed somehow." Instead, I mean that at a given moment, almost always when I least expect it, the Lord spoke *words* to me. Those words have been so distinct that I feel virtually able to say, "And I quote." Had anyone else been present, I doubt that they would have heard an audible sound, for such words—however specifically spoken—are still heard internally, in our "spiritual

ears," so to speak. Nevertheless, we may say, "I heard the
Lord speak."[11]

Jack usually followed an explanation like this with a strong affirmation
that the "Holy Scriptures, His Eternal Word" must be the final authority
in judging whether God has in fact spoken personally.[12] He also readily
acknowledged his own fallibility and the need for "rules to be observed in
determining if what I hear is from God," referencing not only Scripture but
the counsel of close associates.[13] Importantly, he made clear that there was
nothing "special" about him but that God wanted to speak in similar ways
to all His children.

His confidence that God speaks to everyone was due, as already noted,
to his belief that he was simply describing what biblical writers described
and experienced.[14] In Jack's mind, God spoke then, and there is no reason
to suppose that God does not continue to do so now.

In addition, when Hayford speaks of the voice of God in his life, he
is articulating something he believes Christians everywhere experience but
often do not feel free to acknowledge for fear of appearing too mystical or
otherworldly. For Jack, God speaks to believers, and sharing his own stories
empowers others to recognize and trust God's voice in their own lives.[15]

Not only does Jack labor to carefully explain what he means by God
"speaking" to him, but he also explains other elements of a Spirit-empowered
life at the heart of Pentecostalism. His biblically founded and persuasive
descriptions of Pentecostal practice are part of why he is so admired beyond
Pentecostal and Charismatic circles.

In a 1991 *Los Angeles Times* feature article, Vinson Synan, a historian
of modern Pentecostalism, called Hayford "the most accepted Pentecostal
speaker in the evangelical world." The article went on to say that Jack
"adheres to traditional Pentecostal beliefs but enjoys wide respect for not
making a splashy show of them" and—in the words of one admirer—"not
acting as if he has all the answers."[16]

The late Lloyd John Ogilvie, former chaplain to the United States Senate, called Jack "an outstanding intellectual" and "a deeply rooted scholar of the biblical tradition."[17] In 2005, Steven Strang, founder and CEO of Charisma Media, called Jack a "statesman without peer; his integrity and theological depth are so well known that he can draw together all kinds of factions."[18]

The regard that Pentecostal and Charismatic leaders had for Jack meant his voice was highly valued in their arena as someone who could mediate problems and controversies, and a number of notable renewal leaders invited his personal counsel into their lives, seeing him as a spiritual father.

Hayford graciously but forthrightly spoke out about his concerns that Pentecostals weren't holding accountable leaders who had failed morally and also were not providing pathways for their recovery and restoration. He was a prophetic voice in calling for Pentecostals and evangelicals to take seriously their failure to support the African American community during the Civil Rights Movement and the need to actively work for racial reconciliation. He was a strong voice in support of national Israel and the Jewish people and was an advocate for the Messianic Jewish movement.

Jack's courage to speak to issues facing the larger church led some to see him as a modern-day apostle—something Hayford would never publicly claim for himself. Robert Morris, pastor of one of America's largest congregations, Gateway Church, said that he believed Jack was "the Apostle Paul of our generation."

Although he served for five years (2004–2009) as the president of his Pentecostal denomination, the Foursquare Church, Hayford is hardly a pedigreed Pentecostal. His childhood church experience was a mosaic of several Christian denominations, including the Foursquare Church (his parents had received Christ at a Foursquare church). His interdenominational church experience as a child and teenager contributed to his identification with his parents' Pentecostal roots and his connection to evangelicalism. He knew both worlds well and was aware of their similarities and their differences.

This awareness helped Jack be a bridge-builder between Pentecostals and evangelicals, never viewing evangelicals as adversaries. His ability to make sense of Pentecostal practices like expressive worship and speaking in tongues was motivated by his conviction that he was simply appealing to New Testament experience and not by a strident desire to defend Pentecostalism as a movement. In fact, Jack had his own concerns over aspects of Pentecostal belief and practice. This is an important part of our story.

A WELL-LIVED LIFE

Despite his keen intellect and many gifts, the Jack Hayford we meet in this book is surprisingly simple, even childlike, in his relationship with God. He sees his private prayer life as the essential foundation of his ministry, and he deeply yearns to know and please God and live in radical dependence. His journals are filled with prayers of confession, praise, and especially lament for his weaknesses and shortcomings. And yet almost always his journal entries end with grateful affirmation of God's faithfulness to His promises. He is a devoted disciple of Jesus.

Authentic discipleship, to be "Spirit-formed" as Hayford terms it, involves embracing basic disciplines and practices that nurture an intimate relationship with God. Referring to his private walk with Jesus, Jack has committed himself "to seek him daily (1) to *lead and direct* my path, (2) to *teach and correct* my thoughts and words, (3) to *keep and protect* my soul, and (4) to *shape and perfect* my life."[19]

Central to Jack's prayer life is a passionate quest to be "brutally" honest before God. This, more than anything, has made him the man that he is. As we will discover in chapter 2, Jack Hayford learned as a little boy that "integrity of heart" meant telling the truth "in front of Jesus" no matter how difficult or embarrassing it was. As a young man, he began nurturing an intimacy with God that included personal and corporate prayer, heart-felt worship, experiencing the "living word" of Scripture, and obedience to the slightest leadings and promptings of the Holy Spirit in his life. His private walk with God was and still is the foundation of his life.

Telling the truth "in front of Jesus" has helped Jack Hayford, now well past eighty, be a model of a man "finishing well." Despite having achieved remarkable success by almost any measure, he has done so without any hint of scandal. Some refer to Hayford as Pentecostalism's "Billy Graham," affirming the integrity of his life and ministry. A colleague of Hayford, reflecting on his peculiarly blessed life, said his success was more than anything a result of having a "clean soul."[20] Although this biography is not a hagiography, the story of a saint (Hayford would not want that title since he has been more than transparent over the years about his own humanness), it is a celebration of a life well lived.

The narrative that follows is laid out chronologically—with a few exceptions where I seek to explain Jack's wide popularity and influence. The early chapters explore Jack's childhood, college years, and early ministry, focusing on key events and experiences that Hayford saw as life-shaping and seminal to his maturation. The latter chapters cover his years pastoring the Church on the Way and his place as an educator, bridge-builder, statesman, and especially his place as a pastor to pastors. Throughout the story, biblical and theological themes that were central to Hayford's life are presented.

Jack's preaching and writing are filled with personal stories and anecdotes used as illustrations. There are literally hundreds of them.[21] His stories, many about his own sin struggles, helped people identify with him as someone "like us" rather than the great man on a pedestal. Jack never saw his transparent storytelling as a gimmick. Rather, it came from his desire to authentically model how walking with Jesus is a journey filled with ups and downs and twists and turns. His stories are also significant because he saw them as important and often life-defining.[22]

In drawing on these stories, my aim is to write an account of his life that would be recognizable to Jack Hayford as *his* story. I tell his accounts of how God spoke to him and the workings of God in his life in the same straightforward manner in which he communicated them, avoiding language like "according to Hayford," "Hayford believes," and other phrasing that might be perceived as judgment from the biographer. It will be up to the reader to decide the validity of Hayford's accounts and any interpretations of them.

I have been aided in writing Jack's biography by the full cooperation of Hayford himself. Since 2003, I have conducted over thirty personal and phone interviews with Jack totaling nearly sixty hours of conversation, most of which were recorded. Hayford also gave me access, without restriction, to all his personal records, including his sermon notes, correspondence, and, most importantly, his personal journals, which reach back to the 1960s.

He also gave his permission to associates and friends to speak to me on all matters "personal and confidential" regarding his life. Although Jack Hayford has no editorial voice in what I have written, his assistance helped me better appreciate the things that mattered most to his own understanding of his life and ministry.

With the aim of making Jack Hayford's story accessible to a wide audience, I have had to select the accounts of his life I deem most essential and significant to this biography. My apologies if I left out one of your favorite Hayford stories. This is, in the final analysis, my interpretation of his life.

Every life is complex and difficult to reduce to the written page. Every life involves many influences that flow together and are open to varied interpretations. What follows is a record of one life well lived and then presented through the labors of Hayford's first, and likely not the last, biographer. It is no more and no less. It is, however, a remarkable story.

Part One

THE EARLY YEARS

Chapter 1

A PROPER CHILD

THE VISION

Dolores Hayford knew something was wrong when the nurse shouted "Orderly!" With a tiny foot visible in the birth canal, Mrs. Hayford was rushed into the delivery room at the Los Angeles County Hospital. Barely eighteen years old and giving birth to her first child, she didn't realize how dangerous breech birth was, especially in 1934. Still, she was aware of the obvious concern of those attending her as the doctor decided to anesthetize her and try to push the foot back and see if the baby could be turned, which he was unable to do. It was early in the morning on June 25.

As she later recounted in her journal, once anesthetized, she "lost contact with the physical world" and "entered a place of great light."[1] Dolores found the vision very difficult to describe. She saw what she called a vortex-like "great spiral," spinning with "intense speed," which she and her husband had entered. The vortex was rushing them back to the creation of Adam and Eve, at which point the vortex reversed, bringing them back to the present. In both directions of the whirling vortex, she sensed they were passing other couples. The vision ended and the great light and spiral disappeared. Minutes later, at 3:26 a.m., Jack Williams Hayford Jr. was born.

It was not until she later reflected on the experience that she understood what the vision meant. She realized that the couples she and her husband had passed in the spiral were the parents of God's special, predestined messengers, and she and her husband were blessed to join these parents in bearing a chosen child of promise.[2] She would later say, borrowing the King James Version phrase referring to the infant Moses, that her son Jack was a "proper child,"[3] specially chosen and graced by God. She realized her son was called to be a servant of the Lord; he would be a peculiarly good boy growing up.[4]

Dolores Hayford never told the story of her vision publicly, and she told Jack only after he had entered the ministry.[5] On the rare occasions when she privately communicated the vision, it was without undue drama. She simply told the facts, always cautiously aware that it could easily be misunderstood or sensationalized. Nevertheless, the vision characterizes the enchanted world that she would introduce to her son as he grew up. For Dolores, the invisible dimensions the Bible described were inseparably linked to the visible realities of everyday life.

DADDY AND MAMMA

In the summer of 1934, America was experiencing the worst of the Great Depression. Southern California, with its more diverse economic base and supported by the Depression-resistant movie and defense industries, was faring a little better than other parts of the nation. As a result, thousands of migrants streamed west, only to discover, as Woody Guthrie sang, that California only looked like the garden of Eden. Steady jobs were hard to come by. "Hardship and suffering were not in short supply, especially in the early years of the decade."[6]

Jack Williams Hayford Sr. had avoided many of these struggles while serving as a United States Navy Seaman from 1929 to 1933.[7] He met his future wife, Dolores Farnsworth, in 1931 at a naval base open house in Long Beach, California. Hayford was one of the sailors leading groups through his ship, the USS *West Virginia*. Dolores, just fifteen, was with her family on one of the tours, and Hayford took a liking to her. Dolores was impressed by the way he treated her like a woman although she was so young. Hayford pointedly pursued her and, since she was so young, had to arrange dates without her parents' permission.

Over the next year, they carried on a surreptitious courtship and, without her parents' knowledge or consent, they were married on September 28, 1932.[8] She was just sixteen years old, and Jack Sr., who had lied about his age to get into the Navy, had turned nineteen only in August.[9] It was the beginning of a tumultuous relationship.

The couple rented a small house and would meet in the afternoons when Hayford got off work at the naval base about 4:00 p.m. Dolores, still living at home, would go back to her parents' house every night at dinnertime. The secret marriage went undiscovered by the Farnsworth family for six months.

The Long Beach earthquake on March 10, 1933, severely damaged the Farnsworth home, so they went to stay with an aunt as repairs were made to their house. While they were there, a high school acquaintance of Dolores', who lived next door to the aunt, saw her going in and out with her family. The girl knew that Dolores was married and told her mother, and this was quickly communicated to Dolores' parents. They could not believe the news.[10]

Dolores' father quickly found out where the little house was, went to the place, barged in, and found Jack and Dolores in bed together. It was an embarrassing moment. The intrusion enraged Jack Hayford Sr. and left him angry at Dolores' family for years. Later, when his children were born, he was never comfortable with the children seeing their maternal grandparents. After the marriage was discovered, Dolores quit high school and moved in permanently with her husband.[11] Obviously, the whole circumstance added strain to the unconventional marriage.

Struggle and stress were not new to Jack Hayford Sr. He had had a very difficult childhood. He was born in Montana on August 16, 1913, to Allyn and Margaret Hayford, and they lived there for at least six years.[12] The family then moved to Ajo, Arizona, a small but thriving copper-mining community in the southwestern part of the state.

Jack Hayford Sr.'s father was an alcoholic and he was very strict and demanding. When his thirteen-year-old son was caught with a group of other boys breaking into a local school, Allyn Hayford was outraged. Because one of the boys had taken a few coins from the librarian's drawer, Hayford's father felt that his son had shamed the family, and he promptly kicked him out of the home. He gave his son directions on how to catch freight trains and hobo his way from Arizona to Oakland, California, to live with his older brother, who was twenty-three at the time.[13] The incident forever scarred the young boy. Dolores would later say her husband was a "broken and abused vessel."[14]

Jack Hayford Sr. finally found a home when he joined the Navy at sixteen. He loved the discipline and regimen of the Navy, and it would forever shape his approach to life. He also loved the travel and adventure. He became the stereotypical strong, brawling, hard-drinking, womanizing sailor.[15] This too would leave its mark on his life. His hard living, however, was interrupted when he met Dolores, who was very different from the women he had met in other ports. She was sweet, kind, and naive, and he fell in love with her. He realized he had found someone special, and he made sure he treated her that way.

Dolores Farnsworth was born on April 20, 1916, in Fort Morgan, Colorado, where, except for a brief stay in Wyoming, she lived until she was five.[16] Her father found work driving a truck in Phoenix, Arizona, where the family then lived for nearly ten years. Her dad had been in and out of jail before the move but stayed out of trouble in Arizona, eventually doing quite well selling Chrysler automobiles.

When Dolores was fifteen, her family moved to Long Beach, where her father continued to work in the automobile business. Despite her father's troubles when she was very young, most of Dolores' childhood was stable and pleasant.[17] Her mother, Marguerite, was a bright and vibrant woman who brought a cultured sensitivity to her home.

However, the discovery of Dolores' marriage put an abrupt end to her home life.

MARRIED LIFE

Jack and Dolores struggled to make the marriage work. After leaving the Navy, Jack had to scramble to provide a survivable income. He worked various jobs for the next two years. They managed to make a living the way many did during the Depression, learning to make do and deal with what came their way. From 1933 to 1938, they lived in some seventeen different houses.[18] Jack Sr., growing up as he did and drawing on his Navy experience, learned to be especially resourceful for such a young man, fixing and repairing things and helping out others around him. It was an ability that would endear him to many throughout his life.

Dolores and Jack Hayford Sr.

Their young age, along with their financial challenges and the disapproval of the marriage by Dolores' parents, put severe stress on Jack and Dolores' relationship. Their contrasting childhood experiences had helped create two very different people who struggled to get along together. After four years in the Navy traveling the world, Jack saw things very differently than how the more sheltered Dolores saw them. Also, Jack's short temper did not help the two get along. All this contributed to four painful separations during their first four years of marriage.

It was in the middle of this time that Jack Jr. was born. As might be expected, his birth did not fix the marriage. The real help would come nearly sixteen months later, when Jack Sr. was working as a watchman at a mattress factory in Los Angeles.

Bill Hanson, another watchman at the factory, always wore a pin that said *Jesus Saves,* which Jack liked to make fun of. Hanson consistently stood his ground, realizing that Jack Sr. was not intending to be hostile. Over time the two became friends and, in late September 1935,[19] the Hayfords accepted Bill's invitation to attend the Long Beach Foursquare Church, a large Pentecostal congregation for the time, with several hundred in attendance.[20]

They went with Bill to an evening service. The church's pastor, Watson Teaford, preached and gave an altar call for people to open their hearts to Jesus Christ as Lord and Savior. Jack and Dolores responded and, as the old hymn "Whosoever Will May Come" was being sung, came to Christ.[21] Two weeks later, they dedicated to the Lord their sixteen-month-old son, Jack Jr., at the same church. Pastor Teaford held young Jack and prayed, "Lord, if it's Your purpose to call this child to ministry, we ask You to do that."[22]

Their son had already experienced a supernatural healing before the night they were converted. His breech birth had caused an injury to tendons in his neck, leaving a lump below and behind his ear that became more noticeable at six weeks. Dolores took him to see a physician, who began regular massage and compress treatments both at his office and at their home. Despite the treatments, she noticed that her son's chin and head were being pulled to one side and that the baby was avoiding turning his head in the other direction due to pain.[23]

In December, a cousin of the family, who had heard of a church that prayed for the sick, submitted a prayer request for Jack Jr.[24] The church was the very Long Beach Foursquare congregation in which the Hayfords would later become believers. Unbeknownst to Dolores, the church had prayed in midweek prayer service for the boy. That following Saturday, Dolores' mother came by to see the family and noticed that little Jack's neck looked better. By Monday, the lump was completely gone.

That same day, Dolores took Jack Jr. to the regularly scheduled therapy session with the doctor, who was Jewish. When the doctor saw the boy, he began to cry and told Dolores, "This is an act of God. You are right to say that God healed this child."[25] He made sure that Dolores knew that he had nothing to do with this healing. He had never fully charged them for his services, and now he told her why. All along, he believed the child's condition would only worsen as he got older and might leave him permanently disabled and, in the worst case, take his life. He'd not had the heart to tell the couple before.

Years later, Dolores Hayford reflected on the healing: "Oddly, none of us knew we were not [at the time] true believers in the sense of being born again. All the family freely spoke of the miracle although none of us were in church anywhere."[26] This dramatic healing no doubt helped prepare the Hayfords to be open to the gospel message preached at the Long Beach Foursquare Church ten months later.

Nearly a year after their October 1935 conversion, the Hayfords faced another health challenge with their young son, now nearly two and a half years old. Little Jack would often wake early in the morning, climb out of the crib he still slept in, and get in bed with his parents.

One particular Sunday morning, Dolores was awakened by the sound of her son falling, and she jumped out of bed to help him.[27] At first, she was not concerned, thinking he had tripped, but the little boy said his leg was "broke." Dolores assumed his leg was asleep and began rubbing it to restore circulation. When she stood him up, he fell again. By now, Jack Sr. had joined her. After again rubbing his leg vigorously, they stood the little boy up, only to have him fall once more. It became very clear that he seemed to have no control of one of his legs.

Since the 1934 Los Angeles polio epidemic was still in the minds of many Southern Californians, Dolores became very concerned and called her dad, who arranged to have a physician he knew meet the Hayfords at his office to examine Jack.[28] After the initial exam, the doctor told them that there was paralysis in the boy's leg and that they needed to go directly to the hospital.[29] They said they would do so but first wanted to go by the church so Jack Jr. could be prayed for. "This angered the doctor and embarrassed [Dolores'] father," who had met them at the doctor's office. The doctor refused to handle the case any further since they were going to be so "irresponsible."[30]

Reluctantly, Dad Farnsworth took the family to the Long Beach Foursquare Church, where Pastor Teaford and two elders came out to the car and prayed for the child. After praying, the pastor told them that after falling so many times already, the boy would be frightened if they tried to have him walk again so soon. He suggested they take him home, have him take a nap, and perhaps when he awakened, he would have forgotten the whole ordeal and might walk as usual.

As Dolores later wrote, "It happened just that way. Even though the testing at the office & the several attempts had all ended with his falling, he got out of bed seemingly unaware that anything had been wrong & never mentioned it to us at all."[31] Later, the little boy remembered the incident when they talked with him about it. It was another miracle story that left its imprint on Jack Hayford Jr.'s sense of God's call on his life.

Through the rest of 1936 and all of 1937, the Hayford family attended the Long Beach congregation, despite their frequent moves, all of which were in the Los Angeles/Long Beach area. Jack Hayford Sr. found ways to provide for his family in the midst of the Depression. It was week-to-week living since there was never any certainty whether or not he would have work the next week.[32] Nevertheless, as new Christians, they had learned to tithe 10 percent of their income to the church, and they were unquestionably committed to the practice. Each week, they set aside, in two cups, money for rent and money for their tithe.

They lived on whatever was left. Occasionally, that meant that nothing was left. They later regularly recounted the story to their son about how one week, with no food in the house and no money to buy any, they simply prayed, asking God to bless their obedience to give in such hard times. That same morning, they opened their front door and found a bag of groceries on their porch.[33] It was a faith-building experience that helped the couple endure the hard times they were facing.

When Jack was turning five, his parents wanted him to learn the blessings of giving for himself. Sitting the boy down at their dining table, his father gave Jack his first allowance—earned doing simple chores—putting ten cents in coin on the table: a nickel and five pennies. After instructing young Jack that the Bible taught that 10 percent of whatever we earn belongs to the Lord, he asked, "What part of this ten cents belongs to the Lord?" Jack took a penny and answered, "This is the Lord's." Each week, the boy gave his penny in Sunday school. Their son never forgot the lesson of giving.[34]

Young Jack with his mother, Dolores

MOVING ON

In late spring 1938, Dolores Hayford was well along in her pregnancy with their second child. Jack Hayford Sr. found a more permanent job working in the magazine and newspaper distribution business in San Luis Obispo, a small city just inland on the Central California Pacific Coast.[35] In June, the family moved and just days later, on June 20, the Hayfords' second child, Luanne Hayford, was born.

Things started out well that summer, with Jack Sr. driving a delivery truck. The Hayfords would live in San Luis Obispo almost a year. Son Jack was excited to have a baby sister, and he enjoyed playing in the field and the eucalyptus grove behind their house, a place where he remembers another close call.

A windstorm brought down a large eucalyptus tree that crashed into their house. It fortunately "landed at the one point where the structural capacity of the building could bear the shock and weight [that] kept the tree from smashing down exactly where [the boy] was sleeping."[36] Jack Hayford Jr. always saw this as another sign of God's providential grace.[37]

While living in San Luis Obispo, the family began attending a small Foursquare Gospel church that had just started there. Initially, things went well at the church, but it didn't last. Hayford, with his Navy background and independent upbringing, had openly smoked cigarettes since he was a young teenager. He became infuriated after overhearing two women at the church talk about his smoking in a manner he felt was pompous and self-righteous. As a result, he refused to go to church for the next ten years.[38]

Without church as a regular part of his life, Hayford fell back into some of his old ways and got involved with another woman. Dolores was "wounded to the core of [her] being" when she learned of the affair. She planned to end the marriage for good this time.[39] Dolores' father came up to San Luis Obispo and brought his daughter and grandchildren back to

Long Beach, where for several months they lived in a small cottage behind the main house.

Just months into the separation, Dolores' father took her back to San Luis Obispo to deal with matters of the divorce, and there she ran into her husband on the courthouse steps. He looked desolate. Jack Sr. had lost weight, quit his job, and returned to drinking. He wept and begged her to forgive his infidelity and give him another chance.

Dolores' father, who had been standing nearby the whole time, tried to hurry her inside the courtroom, which would have been a relief to her because she had no interest in trying again at the relationship. "But I heard another voice," she later recalled. God clearly spoke to her heart that if she left her husband for good he would "never make it."[40] To her father's disgust, she agreed to give the marriage one more chance. She wanted to obey God's voice, however difficult it might be.[41] It would take years for the wounds to heal inside her, but Dolores never regretted her decision.

The family was back together, but things were far from stable. Although the Great Depression was nearing its end, times were still hard and work not easy to find. People did what they had to in order to survive and it was no different for the Hayfords.

Early in 1939, Jack Sr. went alone to Montana, where he had lived as a young boy, and found a mining job. Later that year, he returned to Long Beach and took his family back to Anaconda, Montana, where they lived for over a year. For Hayford, it was a relief to get Dolores and the children away from the Farnsworths, a relationship that for him had become even more strained because of the circumstances surrounding their near divorce.

Young Jack started school in Montana, attending first grade in the 1940–41 school year. It was a good beginning for him as he adjusted well, made friends, and even became a leader in a small music ensemble.[42] In spring 1941, however, Hayford lost his job in Montana. Through his older brother, he had an opportunity to move back to California and work for Southern Pacific Railroad, a job that would give the family a more secure future. In June, they all moved to Oakland, where Hayford had to undergo a three-month training period without pay to get the job.[43]

Somehow, the Hayfords survived those three months and he got the job. Jack and Dolores Hayford would live in Oakland until his death in 1978. Jack Hayford Jr. attended Oakland schools until his high school graduation in 1951. Jack would always see Oakland as his hometown and the place where his family found stability. It was to be a happy time.

Chapter 2

IN FRONT
OF JESUS

GROWING UP

When the Hayfords arrived in Oakland in the summer of 1941, the city's population was just over 300,000. Oakland was a port city supported by major rail lines, making it a center of trade and commerce in Northern California. The Oakland Bay Bridge with its twin decks had just opened in 1936, connecting the city to San Francisco and the upper peninsula to the south. The economic boom that would mushroom during World War II was beginning, and the job Jack Sr. had as a switchman would prove very stable. Oakland was a nice place to live.

Son Jack started second grade at Washington School in Oakland in 1941. It was not easy to start over again as a new child in an unfamiliar setting, but he adjusted.[1] Young Jack was largely unaware of the winds of war that were blowing at the time. For a seven-year-old, Europe, Japan, and Hitler were distant sounds ... until Sunday, December 7.

Young Jack with his sister, Luanne

On that day, Jack Jr. and three-year-old Luanne were playing in the early afternoon at a nearby park. Jack was trying to coach his little sister down a large slide when he saw his father running toward them across the sprawling park lawn. Jack could tell even at a distance that something was wrong by a clear disturbance written across his father's face. His father picked up Luanne and took young Jack's hand, and as they walked, he began explaining the news of Pearl Harbor. Hayford later wrote: "Seven-year-olds generally do not analyze international political issues, but one thing is certain—they can feel the shock and the pain of war."[2]

The family followed the war's ups and downs, tracing the battle lines on newspaper maps.[3] Like all Americans during World War II, the Hayfords faced the hardships that came with the war. Jack Hayford Sr. became a block warden, organizing blackouts, which were a common event on the West Coast. They had to reckon with the near hysteria that followed the attack, which had occurred just 2,400 miles west of the California Bay Area. For months after the Pearl Harbor attack, there was a real concern over the possibility of air raids in California. Despite all this, they managed the times well and Jack Jr. had a fairly normal childhood during the war years.

One thing that was not normal was the family's pattern of church attendance. Hayford Sr. had not attended church since 1938 when he was offended in San Luis Obispo, and Dolores had decided early on that she would not go to church without her husband.

But this did not keep them from sending their children to Sunday school. Starting with their Montana stay, the children went off to whatever Bible-believing church was closest to their residence. It did not have to be a Pentecostal church. Over the next eleven years, Jack Hayford Jr. attended Friends, Methodist, Presbyterian, and Christian Missionary Alliance congregations, with two stays in Foursquare churches.[4]

The Hayford home was strict. It seems that Jack's father never left Navy life behind. "Daddy" saw his home as his ship, and of course, he was the captain. Domestic life fit into a particular model:[5] though Jack Sr. was never lazy, he did not do housework,[6] and Dolores was to be the homemaker, preparing meals and keeping house, a role she accepted without protest. Hayford Sr. was very particular about how he wanted things to be in their home. Everything had to be just so and "spit shine," or else.

The kids were expected to work, and chores were assigned even when they were very young (the Hayfords' third and last child, James, was born on October 8, 1944, when Jack was ten and Luanne was six).[7] Saturdays were work days, and there was no play until work was done. Chores could take several hours for the children to complete, and their work was subject to inspection when their father came home in the afternoon. Any sawdust left unswept on the floor of the workshop, any weeds still in the outside gardens, and any other less-than-perfect tasks were immediately corrected under their father's watchful eye.[8]

Once, when Jack was fourteen and feeling his independence a bit, he tried to get his dad to let him do some work at a later time. His father did not let Jack finish the sentence: "Do it now," he ordered. Feeling that his father was being terribly unfair and "seething with anger," Jack Jr. went downstairs to the workshop. He was not a kid who regularly swore, but he slammed his hand down on the workbench and said, "Damn him!"

Immediately "my heart was smitten … and I understood the power of speech and how evil it would be to damn your own father." Trembling, Jack "backed away from the bench and began to weep." He asked God to forgive him not only for giving place to anger but because he had dishonored his father.[9] However unfair he may have thought his father could be at times, he loved and respected him. He has always said that his father's demand for hard and thorough work, along with his white glove inspections, inspired in him a strong work ethic that served him throughout his life.[10]

Hayford was also a disciplinarian who expected immediate obedience from his children. There were no warnings. The children were told one time and one time only to do something or not to do it. Spankings were commonplace and sometimes attended by Jack Sr.'s anger. But usually the discipline, though strict, was fair.[11]

This was not always the case, however. Since Hayford was not living as a Christian from 1938 to 1948, there were times when he would lose control.[12] Once, when he was drunk, he struck and bloodied Jack's nose. His mother stepped between the two to shelter her son and told her husband to stop. It remains a vivid memory for Jack.[13] As he has reflected over the years, while there were those difficult times in his relationship with his father, he has always been emphatic that his father was "a great man."[14]

Mamma Hayford learned to live with her husband despite his shortcomings, which, besides his anger, included a few drunken binges during the ten years he was out of church. Jack Sr. was opinionated and could be quite stubborn. From a twenty-first-century perspective, it may seem that she tolerated too much. In the 1940s, however, divorce was frowned upon, and marriage was not seen as primarily about personal fulfillment. Adding to that was Dolores' sense of Christian commitment to her wedding vows.

Part of it, too, was that she was strong, and although she stayed home from church because to go would have also made her husband angry, she could still stand her ground when need be, as evidenced by the earlier separations.[15] Simply put, she loved Jack Sr. and she wanted her marriage to work.

She focused on the good that was in her husband and helped her children to see it as well by explaining to them why he did some of things he did. Dolores recognized that her husband had deep insecurities that had bruised his sense of worth, fueling his anger and sometimes erratic actions.[16]

Indeed, there were many good things about Jack Hayford Sr. He worked hard to provide a decent living for his family in difficult times and wanted his children to experience the stability and emotional security he never had in his childhood.[17]

He loved his children, and though he struggled sometimes in giving affirmation—affirmation was something he had never received growing up—he would do special things for them, building playhouses in the back-yard and the like.[18] During the war years, when bicycles were hard to come by because of the steel shortage, he managed to get a used bike for Jack that he painted and fixed up.[19] Another time, he worked three days of overtime for the railroad so he could buy Jack a leather jacket.[20]

Although he was not attending church, he still wanted his children in church, and he made sure the family gave thanks to God at mealtimes. For the entire ten years that he was not in church, he made sure that they always gave their tithe.[21] Hayford was also loved by the neighborhood, where he was regularly out fixing things for his neighbors.

Dolores and Jack Sr.

In 1948, Jack Hayford Sr. recommitted his life to Christ. That very day, he gathered his family in their Oakland home and told them that he was walking with Christ again. He purchased a big plaque from a local store that carried the Scripture, "As for me and my house, we will serve the Lord" (Joshua 24:15 ESV), and he placed it on the wall above the mantle as Dolores and the children watched.[22]

Hayford Sr. soon began attending a nearby Bible institute in Oakland and earned a two-year ministerial diploma. He had always revered the Bible, even in his years away from the Lord, and now he delighted in studying it. While doing so, he started preaching at the Oakland Peniel Rescue Mission every Saturday night. Dolores and the children would go with him and provide music for the service. Jack Sr. continued to preach at the mission for the next thirty years.

After Hayford's rededication, dinnertimes became much more special. Mealtimes had always been graced with conversation and fun in the Hayford home, and now the Bible became the primary discussion topic.

Jack and Dolores made learning the Bible fun with competitive memory games and playing twenty questions. They drew their children into each Bible story, and the children became very familiar with the biblical narratives.[23] The children memorized all the names of the books of the Bible and delighted in reciting them. It never stopped with just memorization or simply learning a Bible lesson, since the final dinnertime question was always: "What does this story mean to the Hayford family?"[24]

Even before the 1948 turnaround for Jack Sr., it would be a mistake to make too much of the negative aspects of the Hayford home. Jack Hayford remembers his childhood years in Oakland as a happy time without the religious legalism that could often attend Christian homes, particularly those with a Pentecostal heritage. After chores were done on Saturdays, the children were allowed to go off to the movie theater as long as they had attended Sunday school the week before.[25] Thanksgiving and Christmas were special times filled with good food and thoughtful gift-giving.

Birthdays were happy times, as well. Somehow God was a part of it all, in an everyday kind of a way.

Although his father deserves credit also, it was Jack's mother who was most responsible for creating a sensible, balanced, spiritual climate in the home. Dolores steadied the family.[26] She was an articulate and able communicator who carried on constant conversation with her children on just about everything. The Hayford children were always told the "why" of whatever they were asked to do, whether it was a spiritual issue or a matter of discipline.

Dolores talked openly of how God spoke to her and revealed His direction.[27] All this was communicated in a matter-of-fact manner that made it seem a normal part of the Christian life. She taught her children that walking with God made good sense and that holy living was not about unthinking religious duty.[28]

As Jack remembers, it was "Mamma's" natural spirituality that left a lasting impression on him. His mother prayed all the time, especially early in the morning. Growing up, he saw his mother as an intercessor "in the most delightful sense, in that she didn't 'seem' like one."[29]

Dolores Hayford never tried to appear spiritual, in that her humanness was always present in her unpretentious spirituality and yet was never an obstruction to it. Over the years, Jack saw his mother "a hundred times—wrapped in a blanket, sitting on a chair, rocking slowly, kneeling quietly, gazing out the window, bowed over the table—with dawn barely tinting the sky." But it never was for show.[30] As an adult, Jack Hayford continued the same practice, often praying early in the morning wrapped in a blanket.

Jack once said, "From my mother I learned to listen for the voice of the Lord."[31] Dolores believed that God rarely spoke "in a voice we can hear with our ears. But He speaks to us deep in conscience, where we hear differently and truly."[32] She would often ask Jack if the Lord had spoken to him or given him an impression about something. She would guide him toward a decision that way. And "if you ever told her anything the Lord told you, she would hold you to it." She would call you back to the "benchmark place of what you said."[33]

What really taught Jack was the way she modeled it. On a few occasions, Jack Sr. would call the family together and say to the children, "I want you to listen to what the Lord spoke to your mother."[34] One unforgettable time, fifteen-year-old Jack was sitting at the kitchen table, and Jack Sr. asked Dolores to share a dream God had given her, in which she had seen a burned-out hillside. The Lord told her that Christ was coming soon and that there was no time to "walk in barren places."[35] The family was gripped by the vision.

The most significant lesson Dolores taught her children, and something Jack Hayford Jr. has retold again and again, was the importance of telling the truth.

> Whenever Mama thought any of us might be tempted to be less than truthful because of the pressure of a situation where possible correction may follow an honest confession, she would take a precautionary step.
>
> Instead of simply asking, "Did you do (such and such) …?" she would precede the question with a statement. This statement had a sobering effect on me because it so vividly evidenced the reality of my accountability to be truthful in the eyes of God. Mama would say, "I'm going to ask you a difficult question, Jack. But before I do, I want to say, I'm asking you in front of Jesus."[36]

Jack never saw this as a threat or a religious ploy intended to scare him or his siblings. Instead, it helped him and his sister and brother take "the Lord seriously.… And when Mama would say, 'in front of Jesus,' a powerful image would come to my mind."[37]

> We all knew God is everywhere, all the time. But there was
> a unique sense of the immediacy of the Living Lord when
> those words were spoken. I could imagine Jesus seated on
> the throne immediately to my left as I stood face-to-face
> with my mother and prepared to hear whatever question
> she had.[38]

The impact of this lesson was inestimable on Jack Hayford's spiritual development, and it would stay with him for life. Although Dolores questioned Jack in this way only fifteen or twenty times during his years at home, nothing would become more central to his view of Christian spirituality than the need for complete honesty with God and others at all times. Jack realized what it was to live in the fear of the Lord, in the best sense.

Chapter 3

CALLED TO THE MINISTRY

"I'LL EVEN BE A PREACHER"

Dolores realized when Jack was very young that her firstborn son was an unusually good boy who was always eager to please and wanted to do his best at whatever he did.[1] She and her husband were also aware that son Jack had a calling from God, although they never directly discussed this with him and never sought to steer him in any particular vocational direction.[2] Somehow they found grace to leave the issue in God's hands. It proved to be a wise choice.

Jack says he was aware that he had a pronounced spiritual sensitivity and that, as young as five, he sensed his need of the Lord in his life. Around that same age, he came home after church one Sunday and told his parents he had received Jesus as his Savior. Hayford does not dismiss this experience entirely but places more significance on a later experience when he received Christ "with awareness and comprehension."[3] The journey to this full conversion started when Jack was eight.

In the summer of 1942, not long after his eighth birthday, he attended a vacation Bible school at a Methodist church in Oakland. One day, there was an appeal for the children to give their lives to Christ, but Jack consciously refused to respond, partly because he did not want other children to make fun of him. But there was more to his reluctance. Jack sensed that to go forward would mean he would be committing his life to ministry, which he did not want to do.[4] It was something he would soon have to reckon with.

Jack with his bicycle

Later that year, Jack's parents arranged his first job, selling *Collier's, Woman's Home Companion,* and *Ladies Home Journal* magazines door to door in his neighborhood. Every week, he sold twenty magazines. For a number of regular customers, Jack simply left the magazines on their front porch and he would go back later to collect the money.

Somehow, he got confused one day and ended up a magazine short. He knew he must have left one magazine on the wrong porch, but since the houses looked so much alike, he could not figure out where he had left it. Even though it amounted to only fifteen cents, no small change in 1942, he was distraught. He vividly recalls walking about two-thirds of the way down 59th Street, between Gross and Gilbert Streets. As he stood by a tree near the sidewalk, Jack started crying "out of fear because I'd lost a magazine."[5]

> I was praying and I said these words ... "Lord I ask you to help me find this magazine.... And if you'll help me find it, I would do anything, I would even be a preacher." More important than what I said was the internal sense of what I was saying. I knew the one to whom I spoke knew what I was thinking. As I said "I would even be a preacher," I was not inventing an idea to negotiate with God. I already knew that was what I was supposed to do.[6]

Hayford cannot remember if he ever found the missing magazine. But at age eight, he had expressed an openness to answer God's call, something he had internally been resisting and that he would still struggle with in the years ahead. At the very least, the incident prepared the way for him to commit his life to Christ.

That commitment finally occurred on February 25, 1945, when Jack was ten. He and Luanne were now attending a new Foursquare Gospel church in Oakland.[7] Jack went to church by himself that Sunday night and responded to the altar call given by Pastor Maurice Tolle.[8] Jack went home afterward "over-whelmed and joyous ... because I knew that Jesus had come into my life."[9]

With his commitment, young Jack actively sought to live as a Christian. Though he had acknowledged the call to be a preacher when he was eight, and though now he was committed to Christ, he remained hesitant to answer that call. He still had plenty of growing up to do.

Jack Hayford Jr.'s spiritual encounters never kept him from being a normal boy. He made friends easily and loved playing in the neighborhood. The times were very different, and his parents allowed him to roam around on his bike for hours to explore and play with friends. He liked school and always made good grades. He was athletic and enjoyed playing baseball and basketball and running track when he went to high school. He especially liked basketball, and being tall for his age, he was good at it.

He also discovered he had musical ability. His father loved music and made sure all the Hayford children learned an instrument, which he picked out for them. For Jack, he selected the marimba. Jack came home from school one day when he was eight and there was the marimba. His father said, "This is what you are going to learn to play." And he did.[10] To help him play the notes without looking, his father built a plywood apron that kept Jack from being able to see the keys when he hit them. He memorized the instrument and became a skilled marimba player.[11]

Jack learned to read music, and although he didn't possess perfect pitch, an ability to recognize musical notes without any reference tone, he was able to train his ear to identify various notes and chords especially well. He could also begin a song in a given key from memory. These were skills that proved invaluable later in life.[12]

When Jack was fourteen, he was inspired after watching a musical performance at his church that made him think of how "thrilling it would be to write something that long after you were gone people would still sing to praise God." He would write his first song when he was sixteen.[13]

Jack in his teens

By age fourteen, Jack was having regular morning devotions on school days. After dressing and doing his morning chores, he would kneel beside his bed. "I would simply pray for my own need, my parents, my brother and sister, my relatives, my school and personal pursuits." After praying, he would read his Bible and make notes on simple truths that impressed him.[14] Through the morning devotional time, "a relationship was cultivated which secured my life through years of growth, development and ministry to come."[15]

Also at fourteen, after hearing a speaker at a church meeting, he received his "life verse" from the Bible: "Brethren, I count not myself to have apprehended: but this one thing I do, forgetting those things which are behind, and reaching forth unto those things which are before, I press toward the mark for the prize of the high calling of God in Christ Jesus" (Philippians 3:13–14).[16] It defines the tireless energy and drive he had into his eighties.

Indeed, by the time Jack was in high school, he was a busy and energetic teenager. He played sports and participated in both school band and choir. All this was on top of his involvements at church, which were increasing the older he got. His younger brother remembers Jack being out of the house a lot: "He would get up early on Saturdays so he could get his chores done and be off to baseball practice in the morning."[17] After his magazine job, he had a paper route for several years, and in the ninth grade, he started working at a local pharmacy and began to think seriously of becoming a pharmacist.

Teachers were also taking notice of what an excellent student he was. Counselors and teachers at Oakland's Tech High School were encouraging Jack to consider attending pharmaceutical school, believing that he would easily be accepted at the nearby University of California in Berkeley, just miles from his home. More and more, this was what Jack was convinced he should do.

"Then one evening, *everything* changed."[18] He later described what happened:

> I suddenly found myself at an unexpected crossroads in
> my life—and things didn't look quite so pat and secure

anymore! It happened at a youth conference at (of all places) The *Berkeley* Presbyterian Church. When the speaker that night gave the appeal for those who would surrender everything about their lives to the Lord, I purposely stood and walked to the front of the auditorium. And just like that, my life plans changed forever.

Walking down the aisle at that meeting was no whim. My response to the Lord that night was an echo of an experience eight years earlier—a memory that came flooding back to me with piercing clarity at the youth rally.[19]

The call of God he had first agreed to when he lost the magazine, a call he had never pursued, was the call to which he now finally yielded. He would go into the ministry. Jack's parents were delighted with his decision. The teachers at his school, however, were not at all pleased, feeling that a ministry career would be a waste of his bright mind. Undeterred, he pursued his spiritual growth.

His needs were changing as he grew older, and he started attending a large Christian and Missionary Alliance (CMA) church in nearby San Leandro that had a vibrant youth ministry. Jack was impressed with the congregation's pastor, Earl Sexauer, and just as impressed with the evangelistic thrust of the church and its spiritual vitality. As a result, he made up his mind that after he finished high school, he would attend the CMA's Nyack Bible College in New York, there to prepare for ministry. But more turns were ahead.[20]

While Jack Sr. and Dolores had never forsaken their Classical Pentecostal roots, they were concerned about the lack of order and excessive emotionalism they saw in many of the Pentecostal churches they had attended since leaving the Long Beach area.[21] This, not just proximity, was part of the reason their children usually attended evangelical churches.

The Long Beach Foursquare Church where they were converted had been different. There they had always appreciated Pastor Teaford's sound

Bible teaching and the way the church made room for the power of the Holy Spirit in an ordered manner. Of course, because of the miracles they had witnessed in son Jack's early life, they deeply believed in divine healing, and when Oral Roberts brought his healing crusade to the California Bay Area in 1951, they eagerly attended.[22] They were so impressed with the meetings that they encouraged their busy teenage son to attend.[23]

Jack had never heard of Roberts before, but he went on his parents' recommendation. They also let Jack know that Roberts was a Pentecostal. He later explained that even though he and his parents had met Christ in Pentecostal churches, he shared his parents' concerns. "Some of my experiences in [them] had bred a certain hesitation, a noncritical, yet distinctly cautious feeling toward this tradition." But he quickly realized that Roberts was different.[24]

The first evening he attended, he was surprised to find real substance in Oral Roberts' preaching, something he thought was frequently lacking in many of the Pentecostal meetings he had attended. When he arrived for his second night at the crusade, he watched people streaming into the meeting and sensed that the evening "would bring a life-directing decision."[25] That second evening, Jack wasn't uncomfortable as he had been in similar settings before this. "Though hands were raised and voices were lifted in audible praise to God, there was a sense of holiness present, not merely exuberance."[26]

Oral Roberts' preaching was again "stirring, searching, and solidly scriptural," but what made the greatest impression on Jack were the results that followed the message. Roberts gave a simple invitation for people to come forward and acknowledge their need for Jesus as Savior, and many responded as Jack looked on. "But the miracles didn't stop there."[27] He watched as Roberts sat in a chair and passionately prayed for people in the prayer line one by one. Jack was impressed by how evident it was that people were being touched by God. "Equally impressive was the reverent, sensible, and non-intellectual-insulting fashion in which all of this was conducted."[28] Hayford says of that evening:

This was the same pattern I had seen characterize the
night before, so I know this wasn't a fluke of circumstance.
It was a genuine flow of the divine grace of God. I felt I
was witnessing something so close to what the Scriptures
presented of Jesus' ministry, as well as church life in the
book of Acts, that I was being edged toward a life changing decision.[29]

Before this, Jack had "wanted a ministry in the Spirit's power but was
reticent of what [he] perceived to be the stigma of Pentecostalism."[30] Just
months before, he had gone forward to be baptized with the Holy Spirit at
a meeting at the CMA church he was attending.[31] He thought his best path
for ministry preparation would be with CMA. But the Roberts crusade
experience changed his plans.

After watching Roberts' unashamed exercise of his Pentecostal faith in
a meeting that was "throbbing with the best of the Pentecostal tradition,"
Jack W. Hayford Jr. decided to pursue ministry as a Pentecostal. He knew
there were issues he would have to face for this to happen.

As the meeting was closing, Roberts invited anyone present who
wanted to be baptized with the Holy Spirit to go to the prayer tent after
the service concluded. Hayford had not yet spoken with tongues, a vital
component of the Pentecostal experience and "a subject that was somewhat
frightful to me."[32] Jack responded to Roberts' invitation and there in the
tent he prayed:

Lord, I come to You tonight to lay my life and my soul
open before You. I don't know all that my future holds
in Your will, but I do know I need to surrender my fears.
I know I need to pursue this kind of ministry—the kind
that meets people at every point of their need. You have
allowed me to see a ministry that shows Your heart for the

lost and the sick, and which doesn't apologize for giving
place for the power of the Holy Spirit. So now tonight, I
commit myself to that and trust You to fill me with Your
power to do Your will.[33]

In the corner of the tent where he was praying, he once again asked
to be filled with the Holy Spirit. This continued to make him feel uneasy
because of the potential of speaking in tongues, but he knew that to truly
pursue Pentecostal ministry, it was something he must be willing to do. He
did believe that speaking in tongues was scriptural, and he was encouraged
by the fact that he had once heard his CMA pastor speak with tongues, so
he took the step. He told the Lord he was willing to speak with tongues.
And though he did not experience tongues that night, he knew for sure
that he "was willing to let all [God's] fullness overspill all of [him] and to
welcome that in just the same way the early church had welcomed it."[34]

Jack's graduation picture

A few months later, Jack finished high school. He was able to skip a
semester and complete his senior year midterm and decided to attend the
Foursquare Church's primary ministry training institution: L.I.F.E. Bible
College in Southern California.[35] Some of the same teachers who thought
Jack was making a mistake by going into ministry were now bothered that

he was going to a little "nothing" Pentecostal college that wasn't accredited, and they tried to change his mind.[36]

His school counselor, Helen Voekel, a Lutheran, born-again believer, encouraged Jack nevertheless. "I understand what it means when you say God has called you," she told him. "Hang in there, son."

Jack did hang in there. It was January 1952, and seventeen-year-old Jack Williams Hayford Jr. was now a young man and ready to step out on his own. His parents had left their indelible mark on their son and he would be forever grateful to them. But he was leaving home, and New York was no longer his college destination. Jack Hayford was returning to the place of his birth, Los Angeles.

Chapter 4

THE COLLEGE YEARS

A "FOURSQUARE" EDUCATION

Union Station in Los Angeles remained a magnificent terminal in 1952, though train travel was fading in the wake of the post–World War II economic boom. Planes and automobiles were taking over, and no place would become more associated with cars than Los Angeles.

Jack Hayford arrived at Union Station with $100 in his pocket and plenty of anticipation to begin his ministry training at Life Bible College, which had been founded in 1923 by Aimee Semple McPherson.[1] Jack took a taxi for the two-mile journey to the college campus, which was adjacent to McPherson's historic church building, Angelus Temple, a facility that would seat over 5,000 persons.[2]

The taxi dropped Hayford off at the curb near the Temple, which stood across the street from Echo Park, not far from downtown Los Angeles. While Jack had never seen McPherson in person or attended services at

Angelus Temple, he had heard the stories about her and the remarkable meetings held there. It was the afternoon and classes had ended at noon. Jack decided to go into the massive domed sanctuary to take a look.

As he walked inside, he ran into an elderly woman. "Son, can I help you?" she asked. Jack told her he was a new student entering midterm and politely continued looking around.[3] Before he left the sanctuary, the woman approached Jack again and handed him a $20 bill. Embarrassed, he told her, "I really can't take this." The woman insisted, telling him, "The Lord told me to give this to you to encourage you."[4] Jack hadn't even been on campus half an hour and he saw it as clear confirmation that he had made the right decision in coming to the college. That evening he called his parents and told them what had happened and said, "This is where I'm supposed to be."[5]

Jack and marimba, college years

That confirmation was important. After the decision he had recently made at the Oral Roberts crusade to pursue Pentecostal ministry, his parents, with their Foursquare Church background, had recommended the college to their son in part because Watson Teaford, their former Long Beach Foursquare Church pastor, who had played such a significant role in their lives, was the dean of the college.[6] His father suggested that Jack try the school for one semester and see if he liked it.[7] Jack didn't need a semester; his mind was made up and he knew he would stay at the Pentecostal school.

THE FOURSQUARE GOSPEL

The International Church of the Foursquare Gospel, which was the denomination's legally incorporated name, was born out of the ministry of Aimee Semple McPherson, who barnstormed America in her "Gospel Car," holding evangelistic crusades during World War I.[8]

Aimee was born in Canada and raised in a Christian home. As a teenager, she surrendered her life to Jesus under the preaching of Pentecostal evangelist Robert Semple, who was conducting meetings in Ingersoll, Ontario, near where she lived. The two fell in love and were married in 1908. Aimee and Robert felt God called them as missionaries to China, so they moved to Hong Kong in 1910.

Eleven weeks after they arrived, Robert contracted malaria and died. Pregnant with her first child, Aimee stayed in Hong Kong until her daughter, Roberta, was born a month later. Then she returned to New York City to live with her mother.

Still distraught over Robert's death, Aimee met and quickly married Harold McPherson. At first, Aimee tried to live as a housewife, but she believed she was frustrating God's call on her life. She decided to start an itinerate evangelistic ministry in which Harold initially joined her. Wearied by travels, Harold withdrew and later divorced Aimee, who felt she had to obey God's call to ministry no matter the cost.

By 1919, her evangelistic campaigns and crusades, which increasingly emphasized prayer for divine healing, were attracting thousands, and "Sister Aimee" became a national sensation. Eventually, Aimee grew tired of life on the road and decided to settle in Los Angeles. With her growing popularity among Angelenos, she raised the funds to build Angelus Temple, which she dedicated on January 1, 1923.[9]

McPherson's illustrated sermons drew thousands to her meetings. Often, hundreds had to be turned away because the Temple was filled to overflowing. The church's commissary gave food and clothing to hundreds each week, and Aimee spoke forcefully against many societal ills.

Angelus Temple was a thriving ministry center in Los Angeles that began establishing branch churches almost as soon as it was built. These branch churches eventually became a new denomination. In December 1927, when the denomination was formally incorporated, there were over 100 branch churches. And just seven years later, in 1933, the Foursquare Church had over 250 churches in twenty-nine states.[10]

Aimee's theology was Pentecostal through and through.[11] She first fully articulated her so-called Foursquare Gospel at an Oakland, California, crusade in 1922, when she preached from the text in Ezekiel 1:4–10 that depicts the four beasts: a man, a lion, an ox, and an eagle.[12] Based on her interpretation of the passage, she proclaimed Jesus Christ as Savior, Baptizer with the Spirit, Healer, and Coming King.

This fourfold formula was the core of her Pentecostal faith.[13] For "Sister," Jesus Christ was the same yesterday, today, and forever (Hebrews 13:8). This "seemed to become a reality inside her Foursquare churches, where the blind saw, the lame walked," and sick children like Jack Hayford Jr. were healed because people prayed.[14]

Significantly, although she was a first-generation Pentecostal, by the early 1920s she sought a middle-of-the-road expression of her Foursquare Gospel that fused aspects of both the more mainstream branches of Protestantism and Pentecostalism.[15] While not playing down her Pentecostal beliefs, there was a distinctly interdenominational orientation to Sister Aimee's ministry at Angelus Temple. She was more moderate in the ways in which Pentecostal manifestations were expressed in her meetings. Aimee was unafraid to stop anything she thought was fanatical.

For a season, this won her recognition and a measure of acceptance beyond Pentecostal circles. Her five-week disappearance in 1926—she claimed she was kidnapped, while her detractors said she was having a lover's tryst—and the controversy that swirled around it afterward eroded her broader popularity among many traditional Christian churches. A third marriage in 1931, followed by a quick divorce, further soured her wider appeal.

In the 1930s, Aimee began reemphasizing her Pentecostal beliefs and, in a public identification with the movement's popular birthplace, the 1906 Azusa Street Revival in Los Angeles, she celebrated its thirtieth anniversary. Braving the possibility of fanaticism of "the Azusa Folks," Sister Aimee, joined by African American evangelist Emma Cotton, organized a series of meetings featuring "the old Pentecostal leaders who had experienced Holy Ghost baptism at the small ... mission a generation earlier."[16] Aimee Semple McPherson was once again very publicly a Pentecostal.

Throughout the 1930s, Sister Aimee continued her ministry amid many challenges and criticisms, leading the Foursquare Church into the 1940s. The demands of leadership had weakened her and she was in poor health when she traveled north to Oakland in 1944 for a series of meetings "to coincide with the opening of a new church" being established in the city.[17] On September 26, 1944, the morning after the first Oakland meeting, Rolf McPherson, Sister Aimee's son and second child, found his mother dead in her hotel room from an apparent accidental overdose of prescription medication.[18]

Despite the controversy that often surrounded her life, "McPherson had proved herself a most capable female leader in a world dominated by men." The social dimensions of Sister Aimee's ministry were unique among Pentecostals at the time and "continued in part the vision of her Los Angeles [forerunner], William J. Seymour. Aimee's Angelus Temple ministry embodied in substantial ways the ethos of Azusa Street with its emphasis on ministry to all the people, especially the marginalized."[19] With her death, the International Church of the Foursquare Gospel was faced with the task of carrying on the legacy of their gifted founder. Her drive and creative vision would be irreplaceable.

Rolf McPherson succeeded his mother and led the denomination for the next forty-four years until he stepped aside in 1988. Even without Sister Aimee, the Foursquare movement grew, and by 1949 there were 521 churches in thirty-five states.[20] In 1948, the International Church of the Foursquare Gospel was a founding member of the Pentecostal Fellowship of North America, an association aimed at fostering interchurch dialogue and cooperation among Pentecostals. Although Aimee had long sought a moderate position as a Pentecostal and aspired for interdenominational cooperation, the stance did not seem to help her when the National Association of Evangelicals (NAE) formed in 1943.[21] Even though founding denominations included other Pentecostal denominations, the NAE delayed their decision to admit the Foursquare Church so long that the denomination withdrew its application in frustration.[22] The Foursquare Church's reapplication in 1952 to join the association was finally accepted eight years after Sister Aimee's death. There were many changes in those eight years, but the denomination learned that it could survive the loss of its gifted founder.

By 1952, when Hayford arrived on the college campus next to the Temple, California and the rest of the nation were in the midst of a wave of church growth that was a part of the suburbanization of America following the economic upswing after the war. With the hardships of the Great Depression and World War II behind, denominations in the United States went along for the ride. Church buildings were erected in suburbs and people filled them; Pentecostals benefited as well, moving their congregations into better neighborhoods and gaining increasing respectability. Foursquare churches were not left out of this.[23]

There were some who felt that with the social lift and its resulting prosperity, Pentecostals were becoming too concerned about acceptance and were accommodating themselves to the culture and other mainline churches. In doing so there was "a muting of Pentecostal distinctives such as speaking in tongues, prophesying, and praying for the sick. Along with this came a sense of dryness and aridity in many Pentecostal congregations."[24] In addition, many second- and third-generation Pentecostals were simply longing to see a revival of miracles and healings. These concerns were part of the foment of the late 1940s and early 1950s that gave rise to the Latter Rain and Healing movements that further shook, and in some cases divided, the Pentecostal world. Seventeen-year-old Jack Hayford was largely unaware of these issues.[25] He was just glad to be in college and on his own.

SETTLING IN

Jack got a job right away and would work most of the time during his four college years to pay for his education.[26] He picked up where he'd left off in high school, working hard and making good grades. He got involved in school activities, enjoyed sports, and began playing in the school orchestra. He also kept growing in his understanding of his calling and of his Pentecostal faith.

That first spring, a missionary came to the campus to speak to the students in a chapel service. Since Jack's full surrender to ministry at age sixteen, he had feared that God might call him to be a missionary in some faraway place, something he had no interest in doing. Still, he knew that he must be completely yielded to the Lord, as he had promised in Berkeley two years earlier. In a 1993 interview, Hayford remembered that, after the message, the crowd was singing, "I'll go where you want me to go, dear Lord." And I went forward. I was sitting near the rear of the auditorium and I hadn't gone five rows forward in the aisle when the Lord spoke to me very clearly and said, "I haven't called you to be a missionary. I've called you to be a pastor. But you could never be the pastor I want you to be until you surrendered to being anything I wanted you to be."[27]

Soon after this, when he was playing in the school orchestra at the May 1952 commencement exercises, God spoke to him again. After the musical portion had concluded, Jack sat down at the left side of the sanctuary where there were not many people. A voice spoke to him: "You have not chosen Me, but I have chosen you, and ordained you that you should go and bring forth fruit" (see John 15:16). He knew God was telling him that his response to God's call was not his choice and that God's hand was on his life.[28]

That first semester at college, Jack became very serious about a girl he had met and begun dating. For a while, Jack wondered whether she might be the girl he would marry. But that all changed when she abruptly ended the relationship, saying "the Lord had spoken to her that [they] were not to go together." It happened near the end of his first semester, and Jack went into the summer heartbroken.[29]

MEETING ANNA

After working over the summer in Oakland, Jack returned to college for the fall semester 1952, on Labor Day weekend.[30] He and his roommate, now "sage and sophisticated sophomores," dropped their things off in the dorm and strolled the campus, getting reacquainted with friends and anticipating a new school year.[31] Jack and his friend went up into the balcony in the school auditorium, where a group of students were watching a choir rehearsal, and for a few minutes the group of eight or ten students talked and laughed together.

One of those students was Anna Smith. Anna had heard about Jack before he'd returned to campus.[32] She had traveled from her home in Nebraska to Los Angeles earlier that summer to find work to pay her way through school. She'd started living in the dorms with a few of the girls. Some had talked with her about a young sophomore, Jack Hayford, saying he was good-looking, athletic, a good student, and most importantly, dedicated to the Lord. When she was introduced to Jack in the balcony encounter, she remembers thinking, "So that's Jack Hayford."[33]

After saying good-bye to the group, Jack and his friend continued their stroll around the campus. Something had clicked for Jack after meeting Anna, and he turned to his friend and said, "[You know] that girl with the glasses and long hair? I'm going to take that one out."[34]

He soon took Anna out to a Hawaiian luau sponsored by the college ministry at Angelus Temple. Anna really impressed Jack, as he did her. For Jack, however, it was a lot more, and just six weeks after meeting her he knew she was the woman he wanted to marry.[35] Anna was not as quick to respond. When Jack finally found the courage to say, "I love you," Anna simply responded, "Thank you," and left him waiting for "grander affirmation, but it didn't come."[36]

Anna may have been slower to express her feelings, but it did not keep them from being together constantly. Besides attending the same college, they both went to church at Angelus Temple, where Jack played in the orchestra and Anna sang in the choir. It was easy for them to see each other every day.

The relationship was serious enough that during Christmas 1952 Jack took Anna home to meet his parents. While no firm commitment had been made in their relationship, Jack's mother knew better. Dolores had had a dream in which Jack brought home the girl he was going to marry. "She clearly saw the girl's face in the dream and wondered who it might be, since she looked slightly like a girl they knew in Oakland. When Anna stepped off the plane, she realized Anna was the girl she had seen in the dream." Dolores did not share this with her son until after he proposed, which did not take long.[37]

"On Valentine's Day 1953, Jack took Anna to Echo Park, where he had planned a romantic boat ride, intending to propose out on the lake. Unknown to Anna, he had already purchased a beautiful engagement ring." Anna said over the years that Jack could be very romantic. Apparently, he was still learning at age eighteen. Concerned not to lose the ring he was keeping in his pocket, he spontaneously proposed before they got into the boat. Although the proposal caught Anna by surprise, she still said yes. She knew Jack was the man God had chosen for her.[38]

Jack and Anna would be engaged for another eighteen months.

ANNA MARIE SMITH

Jack and Anna came from two different worlds. Anna Marie Smith was born in North Platte, Nebraska, on March 31, 1933, as the seventh of nine children born to Elmer and Emma Smith. She grew up in what she called a poor farming family. The house in which she was born had straw for a floor and no electricity or phone.[39] Her father's heart condition had left him unable to provide adequately for his family, and Anna's mother had to take on many different jobs over the years to help make ends meet.[40] The family was on welfare until Anna was seventeen, and she remembered her mother standing in line for government surplus food.[41]

Growing up, they lived on two acres of land, which, in Nebraska, was too small to be called a farm, but large enough to supply many of the family's needs.[42] Summer was a busy time tending the garden, weeding, watering, harvesting, and canning.[43] But it helped to keep them fed and to get them through the Nebraska winters. Anna learned to cook on a woodstove. All the children's clothes came from welfare.

Through it all, Anna grew up without feeling deprived. The family had a large flower garden and Anna was the one in the family who would pick fresh flowers to decorate the home. Her dad cut wood and made sure their home was always warm, and even though he could not work, he still found ways to do the extra things, like repairing the kids' shoes when they couldn't afford new ones.[44]

It was a loving home, and her mother always greeted Anna with a good-morning kiss when she came into the kitchen. More than anything, it was the family's belief in God that sustained them. Doctors expected her dad to die in middle age, but he lived to the age of ninety-two. Anna watched her parents pray daily in the midst of their hardships and over each of their nine children.[45]

Anna never hid the hard realities of her childhood and credits her parents for instilling in her a "solid, down-to-earth, middle America foundation." According to Anna, "Living is a lot easier when you're truthful about who you are and where you've come from instead of trying to put on a façade."[46] This honesty was one of the qualities that Jack found so attractive in her.

Anna at age 18

Anna's parents gave her a heritage of faith. From the age of two weeks, Anna was in church. She received Jesus into her life at eight years old, and when she was nine she was baptized with the Holy Spirit at a Foursquare church.[47] From that time on, she realized that the Lord was turning her heart toward the work of the ministry.[48] This sense of call brought her to Life Bible College.

GROWING TOGETHER

Waiting nearly two years to be married had its challenges for the young couple. Both Jack and Anna were virgins and there was never a question whether they intended to keep their relationship sexually pure until they were married, but "this was not without a struggle."[49]

Their commitment was in large measure a result of the fact that they'd both been brought up to honor what the Bible teaches. Jack's mother and father played a very important role in helping them keep that commitment. It was another instance when God spoke to Dolores.

During Jack and Anna's engagement, Dolores had a dream in which she felt that the two were on the brink of sexual failure. In her dream, it was not that the couple was somehow scheming to have intercourse but that their affection for each other was so strong that it could lead them to yield to temptation. After Dolores told her husband, he telephoned Jack immediately and told him to "get on a bus and come home now."

It scared Jack "to death."[50] Dolores' dream had come at a critical moment. Jack and Anna at the time were going too far in expressing their affection, and while they never came close to intercourse, on occasion they felt bad enough about their petting to apologize to each other and pray together. After praying, for two or three weeks their relationship would be fine, but it would happen again.[51]

After his father's telephone call, Jack returned to Oakland to meet with his parents in what he called a "panicking trip." He did not know what to expect, since his dad had not given any details. Dolores picked Jack up at the bus station and, after arriving at the house, he found himself sitting in front of his father.

"We both feel very concerned. Your mom is concerned. She's prayed for you and she's had a dream and we want to ask you point blank, 'What's happened between you and Anna?'"

"Well, what do you mean?" Jack asked.

"Okay, first, have you had intercourse?"

His folks were visibly relieved when he told them they had not. Jack did tell them about their petting and that neither he nor Anna felt it was right.[52]

From that moment on, for Jack and Anna, "there would be no more playing around."[53] They were forever grateful that the confrontation helped them come to their wedding day pure.

Jack and Anna's wedding day

They were married on Sunday, July 4, 1954, at 2:30 p.m. in the Crimson Chapel at the Oakland Neighborhood Church. After the wedding, they returned to Los Angeles to finish their ministry training.

Besides holding jobs to pay for college, Jack and Anna were both very busy during all their school years.[54] Jack lettered in three sports: basketball, baseball, and football (in which he was captain of the team).[55] After his first semester, he became dorm adviser working with other students, an assignment that sharpened his interpersonal relationship skills.[56] He had enjoyed journalism since high school, and he got involved in the school newspaper during his sophomore year, later serving as sports editor. The couple were just as busy after getting married.

They both continued their musical involvements in the orchestra and choir, and they participated in special "singspiration" events at the church. In addition, after they were married, they served as youth leaders heading the college department at Angelus Temple.[57] All this was in addition to keeping up with their college studies.[58]

Jack and Anna were involved in student leadership at Life Bible College from their sophomore years onward. Anna served one year as the class vice president and Jack served as student body president in 1955. In his last semester at the college, Jack served as president of the Letterman's Club.[59] Teachers and administrators at the school were starting to take note of Jack's gifts and abilities.

So were the leaders in the denomination. The couple's involvement at Angelus Temple, the Foursquare Church's flagship congregation, and its proximity to the denominational headquarters, then located in the same buildings, brought Jack considerable recognition. He was invited to give a presentation in an afternoon seminar session on youth resources at the Foursquare Church's annual convention in 1955, a rare honor for a student. While the spotlight was on Jack, whatever the future would hold, it would involve both Jack and Anna Hayford together in ministry, albeit in very different ways.

BREAKTHROUGH

Two other experiences were important to Jack's understanding of his Pentecostal experience during the college years. The first had to do with overcoming his reticence to strongly vocalize praise to God.

Having been raised for the most part in non-Pentecostal churches, he tended to be more subdued in worship expression than many of his peers. Jack "was now at a college where the atmosphere not only pressed [his] Christian commitment to the Word of God with serious academic requirements, but a climate of open, forthright praise and worship prevailed."[60] For a time, he justified his reserve as a matter of temperament, but he realized that this was not the real issue. The more honest he became with himself, the more he recognized he was wrestling with the Holy Spirit.[61] He wrote later:

> Little by little I began to see that the problem was twofold. First, *fear*: I was afraid of becoming something other than what I perceived myself as wanting to be. Second, *uncertainty*: I didn't know how to break the syndrome of my own reserve, feeling that the expressive-yet-orderly praise which surrounded and summoned me was somehow beyond my abilities.... That's when I made up my mind.
>
> Quite frankly, it was incredibly simple, although it required a solid decision and a mindset to confront myself. Alone. In my room. And it was there, after a few moments of a prayerful preamble, when I humbly told my Lord Jesus that I wanted to be freed from the foolishness of my own fears of forthright praising, that I buried my head in my pillow so as not to disturb the whole dorm, and I shouted as loudly as I could. "Hallelujah! Praise the Lord! Glory to the Name of Jesus!"[62]

Jack began to laugh and thank God for understanding his fears and freeing him from the "self-preserving concern" of how he appeared to others. He had risked doing something embarrassing, and it became an important entry point into bolder praise and worship that, according to Jack, "broadened my horizons without narrowing my mind."[63] Considering the prominent role he would have in the decades ahead in leading the broader Christian church into more expressive and passionate praise and worship, it was a breakthrough moment. Learning this lesson in praising God also opened the way for Hayford to speak with tongues.[64]

Jack believed he had been baptized with the Holy Spirit at the meeting in the CMA church in Oakland while he was in high school. Although he did not speak with tongues at the time, he did hear in his mind four syllables he had never learned.[65] They stayed in his mind, and over the next three years, he heard four more syllables, making a total of eight. He knew all along he had not "conjured up, overheard, or worked at mentally forming these words." But he had never vocalized the sounds he'd heard.[66]

Not long after Jack had the praise breakthrough in his dorm room, he was part of a youth rally at the nearby Norwalk Foursquare Church in May 1955. Jerry Jenson, later to become the editor of *Voice,* the principal magazine of the Full Gospel Businessmen's Fellowship International, was speaking. He brought a message from John 5:8, entitled "Take up your bed and walk!"

In Jenson's closing, he issued this challenge: "If you haven't received from God what His promises provide, why not?" Hearing Jenson's call to exercise faith to receive God's promises, Jack knew he had to act.[67] As he had learned from his earlier breakthrough in vocalizing praise, he knew that speaking in tongues would require a determined decision. Kneeling at the front of the church, he began to pray without "sentiment or emotion. It was almost embarrassingly matter of fact."

> "Lord, I've been hesitant to speak these words for all this time, even though I know and believe they have been prompted by Your Holy Spirit. But now I'm going to speak them. In doing so, I bring myself under the power of the Blood of Your Cross, to assure that nothing I do would in any way displease You or be self-deceptive. If I speak these words and nothing more occurs, I'll rest the

matter with You in faith. But if, as I believe will be the case—if I *do* continue to speak with tongues beyond these few syllables—I ask one thing: I ask that it continue a part of my daily life and not simply end with this single event.... In Jesus' name I speak these words...."

I began to speak with tongues.[68]

Jack "went into an extended season of prayer, exercising a new language enabled by the Holy Spirit." Praying, Jack expressed his praise to God for bringing him to this point of release. He had "finally broken into an arena of privilege so openly available to any Christian."[69]

When Jack got home that night, Anna rejoiced with him in his new experience, one she had received years earlier. The next morning, he rose from bed and went into the living room of the small apartment they were living in. In his usual place of prayer, he worshipped and prayed in tongues, something that would become a daily part of his life thereafter.[70]

Eight months later, Jack graduated from Life Bible College midterm. Anna had completed her three-year ministerial diploma at the end of the spring 1955 term.[71] He was honored as the class valedictorian in the January 26, 1956, commencement exercises for the twenty-five graduating students. He played a significant role in the service, leading a choir in the class song and speaking briefly to attendees, including Foursquare Church president Rolf McPherson and other denominational leaders.[72]

Jack Hayford was unquestionably on the Foursquare map, and opportunities lay ahead. He and Anna felt they were ready to begin their ministry. They had already committed to a plan for the next few months that would mean leaving California.

But Jack first had another lesson to learn from his mother.

Chapter 5

LAUNCHING OUT IN MINISTRY

NO "CORNER" ON TRUTH

Not long after the college commencement exercises, Jack and Anna went to Oakland to visit Jack's parents before embarking on their new ministry journey. On one of the days at home, Jack stood with his mother in the kitchen as she prepared lunch. Dolores began the conversation.

> "Well, son, now that your studies are completed, how are you feeling about your preparation for the Lord's work?" "I feel good, Mama," I replied. "It's a very exciting thing to be ready to go out now, to teach and to preach with confidence that I have a message that will completely meet the needs of human hearts and lives." "That's fine," she said, "I'm glad. But I want you to remember one thing. Nobody has a 'corner' on truth."[1]

Jack knew his mother meant "the word 'corner' in the classic stock-market usage; in other words, no group controls *all* the shares." His "response to her betrayed a place in [his] soul which had already begun to shrink" in the years at Life Bible College.

As his mother bent down to put something in the oven, Jack asked her: "You mean, of course, don't you Mama, 'nobody who lacks the full gospel message *we* preach'?" He never forgot what happened next. Dolores rose up slowly and, as she looked straight at her son "with grave intensity ... and a deep and penetrating gaze, her eyes spoke infinitely more than even her measured words could have: 'Jack ... I said *nobody*.'"[2]

Jack was momentarily shaken by the conviction with which his mother spoke to him. Knowing his mother's commitment to Christ and to the Scriptures, he realized "her reasoned response as born of experience which mandated more than mere parental respect." He and his mother discussed the matter more fully that day and Jack still questioned just what more of the gospel there could possibly be and where Foursquare might be wrong.

Dolores told him, "I didn't say that I think anything we believe is wrong, but that we don't necessarily understand everything there is."[3] "Mama was not argumentative, but she held her ground." Jack was respectful, and, while not completely convinced, "a crack had appeared in the dike."[4] In the years ahead, he would acknowledge and confront his own sectarianism in many ways. This was a vital lesson that prepared Jack for the new adventure he and Anna were about to begin.

FORT WAYNE, INDIANA

Months before finishing college, Hayford was in conversation with Dr. Vincent Bird, who at the time was district supervisor for the Great Lakes District of the Foursquare Church, providing oversight to churches in Iowa, Minnesota, Wisconsin, Illinois, Michigan, and Indiana. Jack sang in a quartet at the Bible college with Dr. Bird's son, who was a year ahead of him in school, and he'd gotten to know the Bird family during the annual denominational conventions frequently held at Angelus Temple.

In June 1955, Dr. Bird formally invited him to work in the Great Lakes District to promote summer youth camps and encourage youth ministry in local churches.[5] The Hayfords accepted Bird's invitation, and in early February 1956 they set out from Southern California for the Midwest in their blue '51 Chevy. They sang their way east as they traveled through the Mojave Desert as the "shadowy forms of giant Joshua trees whizzed by."[6]

Their first speaking assignment was in Iowa, and after years of study and in-service training, they were both excited to be on their way.[7] In his morning devotion just days before leaving California, Jack had read the words, "By faith Abraham obeyed when he was called to go out to a place that he was to receive as an inheritance. And he went out, not knowing where he was going" (Hebrews 11:8 ESV). Later that morning at breakfast, he shared with Anna: "We're not alone, Honey. In fact, we're in good company when it comes to heading out without a sure landing place!"[8]

It was true: they had no idea where they would finally end up. The only firm commitment they had was the temporary spring assignment touring the Great Lakes District churches and holding youth revival services on occasion. Despite car problems and the difficulties that came from constantly being on the road, their three months of itinerant ministry in the district were well received by the churches.[9]

But Jack wanted to pastor and had told this to Dr. Bird when he'd first accepted his invitation. Dr. Bird had told the couple, "Come on and let's get started together ... [u]ntil a permanent pastorate opens up." This was always their primary vision, to have their own pastorate, "however humble or obscure."[10] It would not take long, and without question it proved to be a humble start.

In the spring of 1956, a Foursquare pastor in Muncie, Indiana, started holding afternoon church services in Fort Wayne, eighty miles north of Muncie.[11] He contacted Dr. Bird to inform him that about thirty people were attending the meetings held at the Fort Wayne YMCA and that he would like to start a church. Bird asked Jack and Anna if they would be willing to pastor the small group and officially form a new Foursquare congregation in Fort Wayne. They heartily agreed. By May, only weeks short of his twenty-second birthday, Jack Hayford was pastoring for the first time.

Jack and Anna in Indiana

In Fort Wayne, he and Anna found the situation to be much different from what they had expected.[12] The couple discovered that the Muncie pastor had often brought as many as twenty people with him to the services. The actual congregation they inherited turned out to be only about eight people, all elderly, who attended the church after eating a meal the YMCA provided for seniors.

It was a discouraging start, and before Jack's second service as pastor of the little group meeting at the YMCA, he prayed that God would give him three signs. He asked for at least ten people to show up, that there would be ten dollars in the offering, and that there would be some type of encouragement. All three happened that day. The encouragement came in the form of supportive words from an older man who attended that day and, along with his wife, would become their most loyal supporters in the coming months. It helped him keep going.[13]

One of the challenges the Hayfords faced in Fort Wayne was the relative obscurity of the Foursquare Church outside the western region of the United States. They were constantly explaining what the church was all about, and mentioning Aimee Semple McPherson frequently made matters worse, since many had negative impressions of McPherson. Moreover, while many Pentecostal churches were growing in the mid-1950s, others were seeing the beginning of stagnation that would plague some Classical Pentecostal denominations through the 1960s.

Middle America was far more provincial in the 1950s, and although people were friendly, Jack and Anna were "Pentecostals from California."[14] They also were isolated from fellow laborers in their Foursquare circle, with the closest denominational church nearly eighty miles away and the Great Lakes District office 200 miles distant.

Hayford took on the challenges he was facing full force, determined to make the church a success.[15] In June, he found a building in the south part of Fort Wayne to house the tiny congregation, and he convinced Dr. Bird that the denomination should purchase it, which they later did.[16]

It was a small, 24'-by-36' building that had been a Lutheran branch Sunday school years before and, at that time, had been on the edge of the city. But by 1956, Fort Wayne had grown around the little building and it was in disrepair and stood out like a sore thumb. Jack and Anna cleaned it up, painted it, and did their best to make it presentable.[17] They ended up tearing out the basement furnace, coal bin, and restroom themselves.

In that and other ways, Jack and Anna were the typical church-start pastors. They themselves did everything that had to be done. Jack "taught youth and adult Sunday School and she [Anna] taught the children (even developing her own materials for age 2–12); she led songs, and he played the piano ... and while he preached the sermon she conducted

Children's Church."[18] Of course, they cleaned toilets and Jack did the yard work. He also canvased the neighborhoods door to door, but without much result.[19]

TO BE OR NOT TO BE A PENTECOSTAL

The time in Fort Wayne would be a milestone for Jack Hayford as a Pentecostal pastor. Ever since he had begun speaking in tongues in May 1955, he had continued the practice privately. But he was wavering in presenting himself and his Fort Wayne church as distinctly and publicly Pentecostal in practice.

He and Anna never questioned their own experience of Spirit baptism. In 1956, however, many evangelicals still looked down on Pentecostals. Consequently, Jack's conviction regarding the importance of the baptism with the Holy Spirit as something to be forthright about was waning because, he thought, "it was an obstruction to gaining a following." He recognized that "it's a lot easier to be like a Baptist Church."[20] As a result, the little church was Pentecostal in name but not much else.

This went on for over a year, and by October 1957 the church had grown to almost forty-five people, but the congregation was, in Jack's words, "bogged down." He was restless and knew something needed to change. According to Hayford: "As I would pray there would well up in me this heaviness that I didn't know at the time the Lord was beginning to do a breakthrough job in ministering the gifts of the Spirit.... I felt a complete failure."[21] It was not all bad, because the church had seen several conversions to Christ since the Hayfords had come, but Jack felt that the power of God was "anywhere but there."[22]

The breakthrough came weeks later on a Sunday night in the little sanctuary that would seat only fifty people and thus made the dozen or so present that evening seem like more. It was a very cold winter evening; Jack was pleased with the attendance and "had a good message prepared to feed the tiny flock."[23]

He began to preach but was dismayed as he watched his listeners either falling asleep or looking back at him with glazed eyes only thirty seconds into the message. Jack sensed "that something was happening here beyond natural explanation." Without any obvious displeasure or irritation with the people, he simply stopped the message and told his listeners, "Folks … I really think we need to stop and pray."[24]

Hayford recalled what followed: "If I had [had] any idea of what was about to happen I probably wouldn't have [had] the nerve to begin the prayer, because the opening months of this little congregation's experience had involved almost nothing of what might be called Pentecostal or Charismatic activity." But he continued. "Let's pray."

As he did, he saw a vision of "an indescribable blackness [that] began to churn like a cloudy veil." Although he did not recognize it at the moment, he was "receiving a 'word'—a prophetic picture-type message" for the people who were present that evening. It was something that had never happened to Jack before. He immediately understood that the awful blackness represented the suffocating "grotesqueness of sin" that blinded the "soul's vision of God."[25] This was a lot more important than whether or not people were listening to his preaching.

> I had only begun my prayer with the words, "Lord God, I pray that …," when the vision burst over my awareness like a sudden storm. As it did, I could only begin to tremble with a sense of the horror of sins' blinding capability. So I paused briefly, to gain my composure. And then continued with the words "… that You would help us see …" Then it happened. The word exploded from my lips: "Sin!" That single word rumbled up from out of my deepest being, breaking over my lips with force

that shocked me. I virtually bellowed it. Just once. But the effect was staggering to everyone present: "Sin!" I cried out, almost as if pained by the word itself.[26]

Since the whole incident was uncalculated, Jack was not sure what to do after shouting so explosively. One thing was obvious: no one was asleep any longer. Jack lifted his head, and "every head snapped upward." With a boldness and authority that was uncharacteristic, he "pointed straight at those in the pews and ordered, 'Bow your heads.'" Just as fast as the heads had popped up, down they went. It was a laughable sight in the midst of serious sobriety.

For Jack, "what made the moment most memorable wasn't the shock of any human behavior, it was the Holy Spirit's presence. It was the unforgettable onset of a genuine spiritual awakening for a season in that small congregation's life."[27] The fruit was evident immediately as the whole group passionately sought God, with the men kneeling at the altar and the women kneeling in the pews. "The room was vibrating with an aliveness unbegotten by man."[28]

That night, back in the little parsonage behind the church building, Jack and Anna talked. "Honey," Jack said to Anna, "I wonder what's going to happen now. The people have never seen anything like this. What will they think when they get home? Do you think they might decide it's only fanaticism—and never come again?"[29] Anna did not need to answer, and in the end it did not matter what the people thought.

Although the next day the phone "bounced off the hook" with people calling about how wonderful the meeting had been, the real issue was that Jack Hayford had turned a corner. God had surprised him and he had learned the power of the Holy Spirit's work in prophecy, when God speaks a word to His people.[30] Jack was now willing to be a Pentecostal not only privately, but in public ministry, as well, just as he had told the Lord he would at the 1952 Oral Roberts crusade when he was a senior in high school.

In a 1973 message, Jack spoke pointedly of what he had learned from the experience: "The human heart is hungry for the working of the Spirit of God and you don't have to apologize for the working of the Holy Spirit. You don't try and defend God."[31] As unashamed Pentecostals, the Hayfords began teaching their small flock the basic elements of walking in Spirit-filled life and ministry.[32]

ON THE STRETCH FOR GOD

Just before Jack and Anna had moved to Fort Wayne, he had learned a lesson that they would need to know if they were to survive the rigors of their first pastorate. It was a lesson that would forever shape his understanding of the centrality of prayer in the life of a leader.

It happened while they were still on the itinerant jaunt through the Great Lakes District churches and were in Michigan, conducting a series of meetings at a small church there. They were staying with the church's pastor, and one evening Jack noticed a little book on prayer in the pastor's study, *The Preacher and Prayer* by E. M. Bounds.[33] He remembered that Dr. Clarence Hall had discussed the book with him, and he picked up the little volume, eager to read it. Jack later said that the book affected his life "as no other." As he read the book later that evening, "one phrase throbbed within: 'We need to be on the stretch for God.'" The words spoke to Jack not

> of a "stretching" of human effort or creative enterprise in ministry, but of a stance of the soul, which refuses ever to take comfort in the shape of things as they are— within or without. Whether the issue in question be the condition of one's own spirit—healthy or otherwise—or the circumstances in the world around—stressed or peaceful—I was persuaded: a man on the stretch was God's avenue of action.[34]

It began a new and growing understanding about the importance of prayer as a means through which God accomplishes His purposes on the planet by calling His children to pray. He realized that prayer was world-changing, and Jack was determined more than ever to commit himself to prayer.

The next morning, still staying with that pastor, Jack got up before the sun rose, trying not to bother Anna. He was feeling "a deep hunger that no breakfast on earth could satisfy. It was an appetite created by the feast the night before."[35] He was up early with a new passion in his soul to pray. He had learned a lot about prayer watching his mother pray in the past, but this was another vital step. When one considers how vital prayer would become in Jack Hayford's life and ministry, it was indeed an important moment.

The new openness to the work of the Holy Spirit at the Fort Wayne Foursquare Church did not contribute to any significant church growth. In fact, for a season, the opposite was true. The following summer, they were losing members "hand over fist." Some left because they were relocating for better job opportunities elsewhere. Some did not want to "pay the price of being part of a fledgling congregation." Some left to go to other churches. And some left simply because other people were leaving.[36]

It was a very discouraging time for the Hayfords. On the second Sunday of August that summer, an oppressively humid day, Jack attempted to "sustain some degree of enthusiasm while preaching" to the six adults attending the service. When the service was over, Jack shook hands with the last to leave, and turned back to walk down the aisle of the empty sanctuary, having one idea in mind: he "was ready to get into the car and leave—that afternoon!"[37]

What made matters all the more difficult was that Anna, normally optimistic, was as depressed as Jack was. But it would get worse. That night, the Hayfords returned for Sunday evening service, and no one showed up. The only way Jack survived was to kneel and pray right there in the little church and struggle to find his identity in Christ, not in the success of his ministry.

As Jack prayed, God helped him "face up to the conviction that our being in that place was His idea." That night, his sense of promise concerning the Fort Wayne pastorate was rekindled.[38] As far as Jack knew, they were going to stay there for their whole lives.[39]

FINANCIAL HARDSHIPS

Throughout their time in Fort Wayne, money was scarce. They lived week to week, often barely scraping by, which was especially difficult as the family began to grow. Their first child, Rebecca, was born on April 21, 1957, less than one year after they had arrived. She was born on Easter morning at 3:00 a.m., and Jack preached his resurrection message while running on only two hours of sleep. Twenty-one months later, on January 31, 1959, their first son, Jack W. Hayford III, was born.

They did what they could to get by, including getting government surplus food on Tuesdays each week—with Jack standing in line with his suit and tie on, the typical pastoral garb for the era.[40] Jack sold reference Bibles door to door for a short time, and Anna worked in a department store accounting office.[41] Jack worked at creative ways to make spare change, including cleaning a dental office. Whenever possible, his parents helped out.

Through it all, God provided for Jack's family. Just before Rebecca's birth, Jack was so concerned about the looming hospital and physician costs that he seriously considered taking a permanent part-time job. But he felt instead that God was directing him to trust Him to work things out.[42] Just after his decision, a number of the churches in the Great Lakes District sent the Hayfords a sizable love offering to help cover the costs of the child's birth.[43] Hayford remembers "the marvel of miracles of God's provision that eventuated." They were able to pay off the doctor and the hospital completely and buy all the new baby equipment they needed.[44]

One Sunday morning in 1958, when the family was hoping to buy food from the day's offering, a winter storm made it impossible for anyone to get to church. Jack went to the Lord in prayer and worship and ended up writing a song expressing his hope in God through it all.

> My one necessity is Christ who died for me.
> Without Him I can't live. I need Him closely, nearby.
> His life is my supply. To Him my all I'll give.
> That I might know Him, to make my life complete.
> Each day at Jesus' feet, I find sufficiency.
> Dear Lord, I'm now confessing, for pow'r, for strength
> and blessing.
> You are my One necessity.[45]

The song turned his focus away from the immediate need and gave him hope and perspective to endure. Somehow, they survived once again and saw God's faithfulness.

Sometimes provision seemed truly supernatural. In January 1959, God provided in what Hayford describes as one of the greatest miracles to occur in their lives together. They were in desperate need of $75 (a large amount at the time) and had no idea where it would come from. It was well into January and any cash gifts from family or friends they could hope for had already been given at Christmas. "Every human resource was dried up, a baby daughter and another child on the way presented the specter of economic futility."[46] In the midst of their dilemma, they prayed together.

> So well can I remember that day, as we knelt by the kitchen
> table. I said, "Honey let me pray what I feel in my heart."
> She agreed with me as I said, "Lord, You are the One we
> trust, and we are thankful to be in so helpless a position.
> I want to ask this favor—this grace of You. Somewhere,

Jesus, You know someone who has $75 who could send it
to us. Would You speak to the person's heart to do that? We
will praise You whatever happens, but this is our request."[47]

Four days later, they received a check from a person they had never heard
of in their lives and whom none of their friends knew. It was for $75.[48]

Through all the stresses of their first pastorate, the Hayfords maintained
as normal a life as possible. They stayed up on current events, something
that was a part of Jack's home life in Oakland. Like many Americans, news
of the Cold War, Sputnik, and the space race was captivating to them.
Though their political views leaned toward the conservative side, they were
not very active politically, but they did stay informed.

Jack remembers well the September 1957 confrontation at Little Rock's
Central High when Arkansas governor Orval Faubus tried to stop the
desegregation of the school. While putting up bookshelves in the church
building basement, Jack listened to a radio commentary on the events and
recognized his own tendency to believe racial stereotypes. He has since said
that this was an important beginning of an awakening that prepared him
decades later to address racial reconciliation.[49]

Jack and Anna were not culturally isolated, which was another positive
influence that came from Hayford's parents. Jack's musical interests kept
him aware of many musical expressions, including the popular music of
the day. Whenever funds allowed it, which was not often, they attended
musical productions or movies that they felt were appropriate.

They learned to laugh at the financial challenges they faced. One
Saturday night, with not much left in the cupboards or the refrigerator,
Anna mixed up what was available in a dish she called "Hayfordian gou-
lash." Jack loved it, and it became a family tradition. Many Fort Wayne
Saturday evenings found them eating the goulash while watching *Perry
Mason* on the little TV they owned. They later called her creation "Perry
Mason Food."[50] Times like these kept them resilient.

GROWING AS A LEADER

Although the four years in Indiana never got easy, pastoring in Fort Wayne taught Jack to manage his expectations more realistically. He had come to his first church with drive and ambition to succeed, and he'd had reason to expect as much. His experience during high school and his time at Life Bible College had brought him considerable recognition and approbation. That was not his experience in Indiana.

The Fort Wayne years taught him "it was good to be nobody." Indeed, it was a humbling lesson.[51] The highest attendance ever on a Sunday was sixty-eight, and the monthly average was never more than forty-seven.[52] Most mornings, after the children left to go to children's church, Jack would preach to twenty people or fewer.

He learned that it did not matter how large the audience was. Jack made a commitment to prepare and preach his best no matter how many people attended the meetings. There were times when Sunday attendance was poor and he was tempted to hold a message he had worked hard on for another Sunday when the attendance was better. He felt this was wrong and always went ahead with the message. The people who were at the meeting were God's children, and they deserved his best. To give that to them, Jack "studied earnestly" for his sermons.

Like many pastors in the 1950s, he preached three times each week: Sunday morning, Sunday evening, and Wednesday night. Jack preached his messages from extensive and well-prepared notes and usually preached books of the Bible in an expository style week by week, going through at least two of the Gospels while in Fort Wayne.[53] Other times, he prepared topical or thematic messages.

While in Fort Wayne, Hayford began to articulate his "sane and sensible" Pentecostalism. In a message he taught both in 1956 and 1958, he addressed the question "What Is a Pentecostal Church?" contrasting the New Testament church with the contemporary Pentecostal church. He challenged his listeners to understand that being Pentecostal was more than a name; it required churches in which the Word is taught *and* practiced.[54]

Hayford's idea of practice was the need for obedient, united, loving, witnessing, and growing churches. He acknowledged the weaknesses many saw in modern Pentecostalism and admitted it often did not live up to its claims. He was particularly bothered by the factious tendencies of many Pentecostals. In a message using Acts 2 as his text, Hayford called for a restoration of the true Pentecostal experience found in the New Testament, with its balance of Word and Spirit.[55]

The message was an early Pentecostal apology by Hayford. Growing up, he had witnessed shallowness and disorder in many Pentecostal churches and, as a result, he had had no interest in being a Pentecostal minister. The Oral Roberts crusade had changed his plans but had not ended his struggle. His years at Life Bible College had helped greatly in giving him a biblical frame of reference for his Pentecostal faith.

Still, Jack realized that Pentecostalism, as it was commonly expressed in the 1950s, was a hard sell. Though Pentecostalism was maturing in some ways, many saw it as fanatical, and perhaps in some churches it was. Nevertheless, he knew his Pentecostal experience was real and life-changing and had life-begetting power in his ministry. This was the tension with which he struggled. At the very least, Jack Hayford learned in Fort Wayne that he was indeed a Pentecostal.[56] The task was to learn how to express it in his ministry as a young pastor and church leader. He kept at it.

A NEW ASSIGNMENT

In January 1960, the Hayfords were as committed to their little church as ever. That month, the congregation had a youth emphasis week for the seven teenagers in their youth group.[57] Jack was at the church praying for the week when the Lord gave him a vision of a map of America, filled with the faces of young people. He was unsure what the vision meant except that God must be calling him to pray for the youth of the United States.

The vision came to him on a Wednesday, so that night at the church's midweek meeting, he had the eight people in attendance pray for the nation's young people. As far as he knew, he had fulfilled the vision's purpose.[58]

Six weeks later, in early March, Dr. Bird called Jack. Bird had recently moved to Los Angeles to become the International Director of Youth and Education, a position of significant responsibility that had placed him on the board of the International Church of the Foursquare Gospel.[59] Dr. Bird, who had supervised Jack for most of the four years in Fort Wayne, asked Jack to pray and consider joining his team as the National Youth Representative, a role that would place Hayford as national youth ministries director for the denomination.[60]

It was about 10:00 p.m. and the call got Jack out of bed. After hanging up the phone, he went back to the bedroom. "You know who that was?" Jack asked Anna.

"It was Dr. Bird asking us to come to California" was her answer. Anna had not heard the whole conversation but knew it had been Dr. Bird on the phone.[61]

"What'll we do?"

"I don't know," Anna responded.

So they got up and went into the living room to pray. Jack relates what happened.

> No sooner—the instant I got on my knees—the picture
> starts playing of this map of the United States and the
> faces. And I knew that instant that the Lord had given me
> the vision so when this offer came, I would know that it
> was in His mind beforehand. So I just told Anna about
> it, and I said, "You know the Lord just told me we're
> supposed to do this." So I had the confidence that I was

accepting a role, not because it was a grand opportunity
for a relatively unknown pastor, but because the Lord had
ordained it.[62]

Jack promptly resigned from the church and prepared his family for
another trek across America.[63] It would be another two months before
they would leave for Los Angeles to assume the new assignment. The Fort
Wayne church plant had been a trying season, but as the family drove
out of town, Jack and Anna both cried; however costly it had been, they
had fallen in love with the people there.[64] Now after four years, Jack and
Anna Hayford were returning to Southern California. This time it would
be for good.

Chapter 6

SERVING THE DENOMINATION

IN CALIFORNIA

America was just five months into the decade that would become known as the turbulent Sixties. Jack and Anna Hayford and their two young children arrived in Los Angeles after a long automobile drive from Indiana. They were excited at the opportunity before them, and Jack was eager to get started in his new role as National Youth Representative for the Foursquare denomination.

With a trailer in tow, they were close to city hall near downtown when Jack heard God tell him, "You're going to do this for five years."[1] It left him more convinced than ever that God had commissioned him to serve the Pentecostal movement and that the move from their Fort Wayne pastorate had been the right thing to do.[2]

It was also an experience he would look back to when other job opportunities came his way between 1960 and 1965. Increasingly, Jack's decisions were being shaped by his sense that God was leading him, often in very specific ways. Dr. Bird, in his new role as the International Director of Youth and Education, was glad to have Hayford on his team. Jack would be responsible for the "Crusaders" youth ministry, in which he would write curriculum and produce materials for youth ministry as well as oversee the national camp ministries.

Jack, who had turned twenty-six that June, settled into his new assignment working under Dr. Bird, who was becoming his spiritual father. During his four years in Fort Wayne, Hayford had impressed Bird with his dedication and commitment.[3] It was in large measure due to the great potential that Bird saw in the young pastor that he had invited Hayford to Los Angeles.[4]

Jack's new role involved extensive travel, frequently with Dr. Bird, speaking at youth ministry and education conferences around the nation. The majority of these were Foursquare events designed to develop local church ministry. They also attended a number of conferences organized by other denominations and groups, at which Jack and Dr. Bird served as participants and observers.[5] The new position gave Jack high visibility in the Foursquare world. Over the next five years, he traveled to two-thirds of all the denomination's churches in the United States.

Jack and Anna moved back into the same apartment near Angelus Temple that they had occupied as students at Life Bible College. This time, they had two children with them. As was expected with Jack working for the movement's main offices, the Hayford family was again part of the congregation at Angelus Temple. Jack preached at the historic church early in September 1960, an honor that signaled his growing recognition in the denomination.[6]

With the concentration of Foursquare churches on the West Coast and many of them in Southern California, Jack was often asked to preach. When the venues were nearby, Anna and the children often accompanied him, but the birth of their third child, Mark, on August 18, 1961, kept Anna at home more frequently.

Jack drew on his writing talents and creative ideas to develop resource material for youth ministry.[7] He produced material for youth Sunday School programs and summer camp programs, as well as devotional material.[8] Hayford's careful articulation of Pentecostalism is evident in his work. In a small church doctrine study booklet created in 1963 for the Foursquare Crusaders summer camp ministry, he wrote on several basic doctrinal truths, including water baptism, the Trinity, Holy Communion, divine healing, and baptism with the Holy Spirit.[9]

In his booklet *Christian Doctrine: Comparisons and Contrasts*, he discussed how a student should answer the question: "Is your church one of those that believe in speaking with tongues?" Hayford told his readers that the question deserves "a sane, logical answer which not only *asserts* that you are a Pentecostal young person; but that also *makes clear* that you are *Foursquare*, and not to be identified with some of the foolish fanaticism running rampant in our time."[10] He further wrote:

> There are many good reasons to be thankful you are one of the group that believes in the Baptism with the Holy Spirit. To name a few: (1) LIFE Magazine [*sic*] has stated that we pentecostals are the fastest growing religious group in the world today; calls us "*a major force.*" (2) All mission boards recognize that pentecostal missionaries are outstripping all other missionary works in conversions; in many lands at the rate of *two to one!* (3) pentecostals have influenced a rising interest in the working of the Holy Spirit until there is a *revival moving* in many of the old line denominations.[11]

Considering that this was written early in 1963, at a time when only a few voices were speaking affirmatively of Pentecostalism and when the Charismatic Renewal was just beginning to gain national attention, it was a perceptive apology. His statements in *Christian Doctrine: Comparisons and Contrasts* should not be construed as a retreat from tongues speech and Spirit baptism.

All the years that Jack Hayford worked in the international church offices, he would have fully affirmed the denomination's creedal statement and was embracing core Pentecostal doctrine as fully as he knew how. Nevertheless, even at twenty-nine and in a national role representing a Classical Pentecostal denomination, he wanted to avoid a strident, pejorative stance. It was a harbinger of the Pentecostal statesman he would become.

Jack and Anna during his service as Foursquare's National Youth Director

In a 1993 interview, Dr. Bird commented that Hayford had been very productive during his five years as International Youth Director, a title given to him three years into his job.[12] Hayford's youth materials were not narrowly Pentecostal, and they came to the attention of a national evangelical Sunday school publisher, Gospel Light, who invited him to work for them and offered to distribute his materials nationally. He declined for a number of reasons, most importantly because God had told him he was to serve for five years in the Department of Youth and Christian Education office.

He also turned down an opportunity in 1963 to go to the Portland Foursquare Church, then the largest church in the denomination. He was asked to serve as an associate pastor for three years and would then become the senior pastor of the church.[13] It would have been an upward career move, but he was convinced that he was to stay in Los Angeles.[14]

A VOICE TO THE MOVEMENT

There was no questioning Jack's loyalty to the Foursquare movement. Nevertheless, he was not silent about problems the denomination was facing. From 1958 on, its pace of growth had slowed significantly. In the years from 1960 to 1970, the Foursquare Church in the United States grew by only five churches a year.[15] Some of the stagnation could be attributed to economic and cultural changes in the nation that were affecting all Christian churches during the 1960s. But some in Foursquare, including Jack Hayford, believed it was fundamentally a spiritual issue.

After assuming his role in Los Angeles, Hayford studied Foursquare history, learned its story well, and thus gained perspective on the denomination's current condition.[16] He also saw the inner workings of the central offices up close. Perhaps most importantly, his travels around the United States put him in touch with countless local church pastors and leaders who regularly shared with him their concerns about the movement's overall direction.

All this came to a head in early 1963.[17] After months during which he shared his feelings to only a few close associates, Hayford decided to take a risk and write to Dr. Rolf McPherson about his concerns.[18] In a diplomatic tone that would characterize much of his later ministry, Hayford, referring primarily to the movement's pastors, told McPherson of the low morale he was seeing in the field. Setting careful parameters and qualifiers for what he wrote, another characteristic of his emerging communications style, he told the Foursquare president that "there is not a prevailing feeling of great confidence in our denomination's progress."[19]

Hayford continued: "I have often tried to analyze just what it might be that seems to inhibit confidence, a sense of purpose and assurance of future achievement in our ranks. Please do not think me brash or undiplomatic when I state the conclusion to which I am forced everytime [*sic*]: there is something wrong with our leadership!"[20]

In Hayford's view, the problem involved the selection of leaders at head-quarters[21] who were not always spiritually ready for the responsibilities of leadership at higher levels or who had grown too comfortable in their roles after many years of service. He also observed that leaders were appointed to positions for which they were unqualified. He made some very specific recommendations that included term limits for corporate officers and other key positions in the movement, particularly district supervisors. Hayford quite simply felt that the current leadership was unresponsive to those they led.[22]

In a more detailed position paper written eleven months earlier, which he mentioned in his letter to McPherson, Hayford was emphatic and direct. This fourteen-page paper was a scathing critique of the International Church of the Foursquare Gospel executive leadership in the central offices, including Dr. McPherson. While the tone was conciliatory and expressed deep commitment to the organization, Jack did not pull any punches. He said "our headquarters" does the "poorest of [jobs] of public relations."[23]

He also thought there was a secrecy surrounding the finances of the movement, particularly around salaries, personal allowances, and reserve funds.[24] In addition, some national office workers received compensation "not commensurate with their abilities or their position." He cited several instances of a fear of spending money properly for essential purchases and improvements that would enhance the denomination's public image, including renovating Angelus Temple.[25]

All of these were fundamentally spiritual issues, he believed. Hayford appealed to the history of the movement and compared the present lack of growth to earlier days. Significantly, he argued not for a return to the "good old days" but actually for outreach strategies that were more progressive and realistic.[26] He also acknowledged improvements in Life Bible College's training program but bemoaned the lack of adequately prepared leaders.

Hayford was especially concerned regarding legalistic tendencies that he believed still predominated in many Foursquare churches. In his understanding, this was because many of the movement's pastors did not adequately understand the riches of the life available to us in Jesus Christ.[27]

Finally, Hayford presented his recommendations for all that he had critiqued, including a specific and detailed plan for restructuring the leadership selection and tenure process for senior denominational leadership positions.[28] In conclusion, he made it clear that he had written the paper first and foremost to spur discussion. It was a bold statement, by any measure.

Although the letter and paper had little lasting effect at the time, they made one thing certain: Jack Hayford was not just a hardworking team member; he was emerging as a strong and vocal leader. Working in the national offices, he was frustrated by the slowness with which change came to headquarters and by the tendency of its leaders to linger in the past. If anything, this fueled his passion to see young leaders emerge within Foursquare who could breathe new life into an institution he felt was lethargic. The continued frustration would take its toll and eventually be part of the reason for a later transition.

Jack was helped by key advocates, of whom none was more important than Dr. Bird. Bird served as the chairman for the 1965 Foursquare annual convention, which was being held in Moline, Illinois, for the first time. The Moline Foursquare Church was one of the three largest churches in the denomination outside of Angelus Temple.[29] Bird invited Jack to speak at one of the convention's plenary sessions.[30]

Jack's message, entitled "Above and Beyond," was a rousing call to return to the spiritual dynamism of the Day of Pentecost. Hayford declared that the pouring out of the Spirit that began in Acts 2 "has continued to flow forth from the upper room until today millions around the world can testify that the above and beyond kind of life is our potential. Why? Because Jesus has ascended to the right hand of the Father and is still pouring out the Holy Spirit upon us in this twentieth century."[31] The message continued his critique of Foursquare and Classical Pentecostalism. At Moline, he challenged the accommodation he was observing and asserted:

> In frightening contrast to the dynamic design of the Early Church stands the religiosity of our time. Traditionally we have pointed the finger of rebuke at the empty form held by old line denominations. But today [in reference to the emerging Charismatic movement that was renewing many historic denominations] it is disconcerting to have many of their members rise to point their fingers at us and say: "We're trying to become like you, and we can't understand why you're trying to become like us."[32]

Hayford expressed his deep concern that, at the beginning of the Foursquare's third generation, the movement was at a crossroads. Serving as youth director for the past five years, he was convinced there was a need to communicate "the throbbing, Pentecostal revival spirit to the generation that will soon be charged with carrying it on." He made it clear what he meant in a moment of personal testimony.

> Through the dynamic influence of Aimee Semple McPherson, a young man named Watson Teaford was won to Jesus Christ in the 1920s. In 1936, while he pastored the Foursquare Church in Long Beach, California, he led a young couple into an experience of saving grace. A few weeks later that couple brought their two-year-old son to the pastor for dedication to the Lord. I was that infant— fruit of the ministry of Aimee Semple McPherson ... but

I never saw her. Nonetheless, by the grace of God, I was fortunate to spend some [of] my teenage years in a church thriving with a revival spirit. Fifteen to twenty souls were saved every Sunday night; bodies were healed; demons were cast out; believers were endued with the Holy Ghost power. It wasn't unusual to see God move. It happened all the time! I have seen revival—but our young people today have not.[33]

Remarkably, although he never let his audience know it, the church where he had seen God move so mightily was not a Pentecostal church but the Oakland Neighborhood Church, the CMA congregation that he had attended during his last year and a half in high school. This demonstrates that, even in 1965, although thoroughly engaged as a Classical Pentecostal, Hayford was not parochial in defining Pentecostal expression. His passion was to see people experience God's dynamic presence and not just subscribe to a doctrinal formula.

What Hayford, now thirty years old, was calling for in his convention message was a recommitment to Spirit baptism. He said that the "answer to the current dilemma is in a Church which is driven forward on the wave of a tide of spiritual power.... God himself will raise up a great society of believers, who move forth in the power of God emboldened by the Holy Spirit and endued with the same quality enjoyed by the Early Church."[34] In a foreshadowing of the way in which he would later view glossolalia as much more than an evidential proof of Spirit baptism, he declared to the conferees:

Moreover, I believe we need tongues today. Not in any ridiculous spectacle or display, but as a channel of holy inspiration direct from heaven, to the individual or to the worshipping congregation. There is a spiritual battle going on and—thanks to God—He has provided a private line to headquarters so that believers may be refreshed from the warfare of daily combat with the powers of darkness. There is no way the enemy can intervene on this wavelength [glossolalia]; Satan cannot intrude upon my fellowship with the Savior here. I need that reprieve—that refreshing and blessing—in times like these, and the new tongue given with the fullness of the Holy Spirit is available to me ... and to all who will receive.[35]

In his message, Hayford went on to express another theme that would mark his ministry over the next thirty-plus years: his "sane, sensible, scriptural" Pentecostal belief and practice.[36] He asked, "Is it possible that we can experience a balanced ministry that combines Holy Spirit power and Christ-like character?"[37] Hayford believed it was possible, but Pentecostals had some work to do.

Many struggled at finding a balance, he said. Some Pentecostals relished "deeper teaching in the Word, but often at the expense of a surging movement of the Holy Spirit. Then, some ... prefer to glory in the intoxicating atmosphere of the Spirit's moving, but at the expense of genuine humility and holiness of heart."[38]

He summed it up this way: "How often I have prayed: 'God, give us a sane, solid and sensible Pentecostal revival. Sane, but not limited by man's intellectual pride; solid, but not immovable by the tide of the Spirit; sensible, but not to the quenching of the genuine moving of the Holy Spirit in its valid operation.'"[39] He closed his message like this:

Are there any of us reluctant to face up to the requirements of Pentecostal living and ministry? Let us repent. Dare we hedge on the requirements specified in the dynamic design the Early Church manifested? Never!

The Pentecostal message was never more relevant than it is today. The time is so short, the cry is so loud and the need is so vast that only eternal resources can suffice. Let us unite now as a body of believers who have joined hands to step above and beyond, into eternity; that we might bring forth with us into the realm of time eternal blessing to dying men—in *time*![40]

His message was followed by forty-five minutes of uninterrupted praise as the whole conference stood and worshipped God.[41] Hayford reflected on the experience in a 1993 interview. "People were crying out to God and seeking the Lord. It was a mighty thing. It was nothing anybody in the world could have predicted."[42] Two decades later, Vincent Bird still remembered the message. "Never did I hear a young man speak with such intensity and single-mindedness of purpose. There was no doubt he was going to see revival in his day."[43] This was a coming-of-age moment for Hayford as a significant leader within the movement.[44]

It was also a point of transition. For more than a year before the 1965 spring convention, Jack had reminded Dr. Bird that he believed his time as International Youth Director would end after five years. In November 1964, he wrote Bird and made it all the more clear.[45] He then made his resignation official in March 1965 and suggested that it be announced at the upcoming Moline convention.[46]

At first, he thought he might pastor again, something he wanted to do. This changed when he was offered a role at Life Bible College working with promotion and student relations. The role would involve teaching as well as considerable administrative responsibility.[47] It was a logical move given his five years of leading the denomination's national youth ministry.[48] Hayford actively lobbied for a title that would grant him proper authority to carry out his role.[49] After accepting the offer, he was given the title of Dean of Students, an entirely new designation for the college.

At that time, the college was struggling with declining enrollment. Considering how fruitful Hayford had been as International Youth Director, the invitation was a strategic move for the college administration. With Hayford's national exposure over the previous five years and especially with his travels related to youth, much of which had exposed him to teenagers around the nation, there was little question of his ability to attract students.

The timing of the announcement could not have been better. He was presented at the Moline convention as the college's new Dean of Students just three days after he had preached his stirring message "Above and Beyond." The announcement was received with "thunderous applause," not just because of Hayford's appointment but also because many conferees recognized that the college needed help.[50]

RECOGNITION AND STRUGGLE

During his years as National Youth Director, Jack was devoting himself to activities other than work. He continued to compose music and poetry because it was a way to express himself to God, and by 1962 he had composed close to 100 hymns, songs, and choruses.[51]

One of those songs would bring Jack wide recognition. In the fall of 1960, Jack and Anna had attended a conference of youth leaders in Estes Park, Colorado, and Jack had heard the hymn "To God Be the Glory" for the first time.[52] He was surprised that with all his church involvement he had never heard it before. The hymn "electrified" him and afterward he found himself wanting to write a song like it "that would have the quality of something that would last." After returning to California one week later, Jack was walking to his house from the office with "the mood of autumn … in the air."[53] It inspired him, and that evening he wrote the hymn "We Lift Our Voices Rejoicing."

A year and a half later, in spring 1962, when Jack's parents were visiting from Northern California, Dolores had in hand a copy of the Billy Graham

Evangelistic Association magazine, *Decision*, and she told her son about a hymn-writing contest announced in the magazine. On a trip to Oakland, Jack had played "We Lift Our Voices Rejoicing" for his parents, and Dolores had been impressed. She was certain that he would win this competition, which was sponsored by the National Church Music Fellowship, and she encouraged him to enter.[54] He submitted the hymn, but it would be over a year before he heard anything

Dolores proved to be a prophet. To Jack's shock, his hymn was chosen as the winner out of nearly 900 hymns.[55] He won the $100 prize given by the Graham association, but more importantly, he garnered much attention. *Decision* magazine published the hymn along with a two-column article and Jack's picture.[56] The publication gave permission for the hymn's use and it was published in several hymnals. It was a blessing in many ways, not the least of which was that the prize money helped out financially.

Despite the "impressive title" Jack had as National Youth Director, he was earning a meager salary. His family faced financial struggles as they had in Fort Wayne, but back then, they had done their best to view them as part of the price of ministry. Now, with three children, their budget was stretched beyond its limits and the Hayfords were forced to live completely without extravagance and had to be painfully practical in all spending.[57] The family might not have survived had it not been for the honorariums Jack received from preaching on weekends and other ministry events.

Unfortunately, this income was intermittent. After going two months without any speaking engagements in the summer of 1961, the family was in desperate need of funds. Throughout their previous financial struggles, Jack had continued to tithe and to give an extra 5 percent to missions, but in their present situation, he decided that something had to change. In September, he held back his missionary gift at the beginning of the month.

It did not seem to help at all. As expenses continued to pile up, Jack exploded in anger at God and, alone in his living room, feeling the weight

of the financial pressure, he screamed: "*God, it's not fair!*"[58] No sooner had
he shouted than he heard a "still, small voice" gently speak: "Neither is it fair
that you have withheld your offerings to Me." Jack broke down and cried.

> I wandered into the kitchen and leaned on the stove, telling
> God how sorry I was for my outburst, and how stupid I felt
> for having doubted Him. I recited some of the many times
> He had seen us through—fantastically, miraculously, faith-
> fully, lovingly—and I told Him I was glad for the words
> He spoke to me.... That same day I wrote a check for our
> missionary giving, and the next day the phone on my desk
> began to jingle with invitations to come and minister. Of
> course, the greatest joy was the privilege of bringing the
> Word of God whenever I spoke, but the divine providence
> of God supplying for our growing family through the
> honorariums was not insignificant.[59]

To Jack, this was an important lesson that giving was a lifestyle issue
and that God "would not allow me to shrink back" from a commitment
to give. Once again, he had encountered God's faithfulness. And he would
need every lesson he had learned to face a severe temptation that lay ahead.

During the 1960s, the central offices of the Foursquare Church in Los
Angeles employed a large workforce. In the everyday work environment,
different configurations of employees would be involved in carrying out
various denominational initiatives. At one point, Jack found himself feeling
an unusual affinity with a female colleague with whom he often worked on
projects and committee activities.[60]

At first, he thought this was simply a result of how "harmonious" the
woman was to work with and because the two shared values and commitments about ministry. Over several months, though, this affinity developed
into something more.[61]

Jack is emphatic that neither he nor the woman was acting seductively toward the other. Moreover, Jack was not unhappy in his marriage. While Jack and Anna had the regular squabbles common in all marriages, they were a happy couple. Nor was Anna doing anything that would make her husband more vulnerable to violating their marriage covenant.

Jack would later become convinced that the "near affair" was part of a demonic scheme to destroy his marriage and ministry. In short, he came to believe that he and the woman were being entrapped and that neither "realized the craftiness of the Adversary's designs nor the vulnerability of [their] humanness" to those designs.[62] The whole process of the enemy's seduction took place slowly and subtly.[63]

What made Jack unsuspecting of his own vulnerability at first was that nothing seemed sinister. He and the woman were together only during work hours and always in an open office with others nearby.[64] Still, as the weeks passed, he began to recognize that he especially enjoyed the admiration the woman showed him.

He was also impressed with how much the two thought alike—they would often laugh about this.[65] All this led to a mental preoccupation with the woman. While Jack was not having sexual fantasies about her, he did come to realize that she was increasingly on his mind.[66] He began to find himself strolling by her office frequently, and sometimes he suggested that she be added to particular committee meetings that did not require her presence.

"Though I didn't actually calculate it at the time, this afforded even more reason for ... conversations [with her] after meetings."[67] More alarming was that Jack started to give the woman personal compliments.[68] The relationship entered a dangerous phase when Jack and the woman began verbally to explore their feelings. He writes about what happened:

> So occasional hints seemed tolerable, hints like how we
> were both interested in the same things. Smiles were

exchanged over how unusual a mutuality we had on "so
many things" and, worse, over the idea that that mutuality
might possibly signal something of beauty or significance,
something that required definition and thereby discussion: "We think so much alike, and we certainly make
quite a team when they give us a job to do, don't we?" And
we began to sense that warm feeling that happens when
there comes such agreement.[69]

Their discussions about their unique "brother-and-sister relationship,"
as Hayford portrayed it, "was an attempt to spiritualize what was increasingly a deception that progressed with both of [them]."[70] While there was
no physical involvement whatsoever, the two were progressing dangerously
toward "going over the edge." In reflection, Jack has said that at this point
he had "succumbed to an undetected, adulterous mind-set."[71]

Jack was now mentally making comparisons that involved himself, Anna,
and the woman. They were not sexual or about physical appearance—he
believes that level of preoccupation would have forced him to see the reality
of the situation. Rather, he was comparing the differences between Anna
and himself "in ways of thinking, in attitudes and styles," and the similarities he shared with his coworker. He was "captivated" by how much the
other woman was like him. At the same time, he was failing to see how the
differences he shared with Anna in their marriage provided a complemen-
tary balance to his life.[72]

Consequently, conversation between Jack and the woman eventually
went beyond occasional hints to the point that "evil broke through." The
two began to discuss questions like "We really have an unusual relationship,
don't we?" and "What are we supposed to be to each other anyway?" Jack
later admitted that these really were not questions; instead "[t]hey were
explorations of a deepening quest to receive affirmation of something that
neither of us had the right to offer each other."[73]

The deception only became more confusing after this. Jack began to think that he loved two women. He went so far as to discuss this with the other woman. As he records in "The Anatomy of Adultery":

> "It's such a mystery that we feel such deep affection toward one another and that, even so, I don't love Anna any less." She would affirm her respect for Anna, and I have no doubt that she was sincere. We were two people trying to do right but actually doing terribly wrong, without real-izing how deep the bondage was becoming.[74]

Finally, at its worst, Jack began to wonder if his affinity and affection for the woman meant that Anna was going to die. He remembers that

> there were times when I was so deceived that I would wonder, *This is such a special relationship. Why would God put this relationship in my life unless He had some plan for it?* Though I am ashamed to say it, the response that would dance in and out of the background of my mind (I did not permit this thought to take shape fully in the front of my mind) was *It's not right to think this way, but I wonder if something's going to happen to Anna. Is there perhaps an accident that's about to take place? Maybe with this relation-ship God is preparing me for my future.*[75]

At this point, Hayford was feeling helpless and distressed beyond words.[76] He would come home in the evenings and lie on the floor with his face in the carpet praying for God's help. He knew most of his feelings were wrong, but he was conflicted.

For a time, he saw the struggle as a battle with the flesh.[77] He "wrestled long in prayer against the emotional tentacles seeking to tangle [his] soul … frequently with surges of spiritual language [glossolalia] gushing forth in intercession."[78] In the midst of utter turmoil, he pushed himself to praise God and sing in worship, seeking for a way forward. After weeks of struggle, Jack finally found a place of breakthrough and came face-to-face with the depth of deception. He describes it this way:

> When the Holy Spirit smote my heart and brought His revelation and conviction, I was shocked to realize so foul a spirit had succeeded in seducing me to wonder whether God was preparing me for the future by bringing this woman into my life. And, oh, how I wept! Obviously not because I would have sought or wished my wife's death, but because my soul had become so entranced by deception that my mind would even entertain the concept![79]

> When by His mercy and grace the Lord brought me to the place of confession, renunciation, repentance and deliverance, it was a painful, hard, emotional time for both Anna and me. I had vandalized my wife's emotions. She had not known what I had been thinking until it was over, but that did not mitigate the tremendous emotional trauma I caused her by making my precious wife feel rejected.[80]

It was indeed very painful for Anna and she was angry at first. To some extent, she reacted by keeping busy with her regular schedule, taking care of the three children and keeping the house. At one particularly low moment, she sought counsel from Dr. Bird, to whom Jack had also gone for help.[81] Although she was forgiving and gracious in her response to Jack's confession, it took "many, many months" to recover emotionally.

Although Jack had never let his relationship with the other woman become physical, he knew his actions had left Anna feeling rejected. Jack worked hard and, according to Anna, was "a great support" in the healing process. It was, however, over two years before trust was fully restored.

The episode was as defining a moment in his life as there would ever be. Most important, by God's delivering grace, his marriage was preserved. Also important was that he believed he had experienced deliverance from demonic attack.[82] The experience opened to him a seminal understanding of the realities of spiritual conflict that would mature in the coming years and later be a crucial foundation to his ministry at the Church on the Way. Further, speaking in tongues had played a critical part in his deliverance and became more central than ever to his prayer life. Glossolalia became far more than a badge to prove Spirit baptism.

In the year after his breakthrough, Jack grew in his understanding of the power of the name of Jesus in effecting not only forgiveness but also healing and deliverance for believers. He wrote the hymn "Exalt His Name Together," a song that found wide distribution, as an anthem proclaiming his growing conviction about "all that is given us in his name."[83] The third and fourth stanzas reflect the lessons he was learning:

> The sinful and suff'ring find peace in Jesus' name;
> For healing or forgiveness His pow'r remains the same.
> Whatever your need or burden, in faith look up on high,
> And praise the name of Jesus, deliverance is nigh.
>
> Amid the current conflict, whate'er your trial be,
> This confidence possess: Christ the Lord brings victory!
> Fall not beneath your burden, though tears your
>   pathway dim.
> But praise the name of Jesus, and be sustained by Him.[84]

The ordeal was something he had to come through for God to use his life later. After the breakthrough, Jack wrote in his journal that "the heavens were opened to me after passing the test."[85] He came through the "near fall" and went on to preach the message in Moline that secured his place as an emerging star in his Foursquare family. Certainly, a fresh passion was evident in his 1965 message at the Moline convention. The lesson learned, coming ever so close to losing everything and yet seeing God deliver him, had reinvigorated his vision for supernatural ministry.[86]

From 1960 to 1965, Jack had gained national exposure in winning the hymn contest. He had traveled the nation for Foursquare. And, especially after Moline, he had become highly regarded within his own movement. Now, with the five years behind him and having endured victoriously the severe trial that had threatened his ministry and marriage, Jack was moving on to a new season of service.

Chapter 7

NEW HORIZONS

DEAN OF STUDENTS

In September 1965, Jack began serving Life Bible College in the dual capacity of Dean of Students and Director of Promotion.[1] On the first day of classes for the new school year, Jack was very aware that his new role was significant, and he felt acutely the need for God's grace to successfully accomplish what was ahead. He wrote a simple prayer in his journal that morning. "My only qualification for the task is my contact with you!"[2] He was hopeful but challenged by his lack of experience in taking on a job so large.

Indeed, his position carried a weighty portfolio of responsibilities, and he knew the road ahead would be demanding of his time and energy.[3] His role would require him to travel to promote the college and increase enrollment, something that was sorely needed.

The year before Hayford was invited to go to the college, full-time equivalence enrollment had fallen to just over 350 students, half of what it had been when Jack had first attended the school in 1952. By the time he started his position, an appointment that had been cheered by the convention body in Moline, enrollment was already on the rise, at least in part as a result of news of his appointment.[4]

As he began his new job at the college, Jack wrote to Dr. Bird, who still was serving as the International Director of Youth and Education, to thank him for his support. He was appreciative of the five years he had worked so closely with Bird at the Foursquare central offices. He challenged the adage "familiarity breeds contempt," and said: "Rather familiarity has bred respect."[5] Jack went on to praise Dr. Bird for his leadership, wisdom, and genuine humility, among other attributes. What is revealing is his summation in the letter.

1. So, I shall only express in brief sentences my gratitude for a man ...

2. ... who was willing to offer a young man an unbridled opportunity to develop a program

3. ... who taught me some patience by his repeated display of that attribute

4. ... who bore in silence my oft repeated irritations with "the things that now are" (although I feel it would have been easier for him to agree or challenge the statements)

5. ... who understood the sometimes overambitious drive of a young man and didn't kill it, but rather tempered it with wisdom

6. ... who stood by a young man in a period of singular crisis when lesser men would have not been so gracious.[6]

Jack ended the letter by saying, "The greatest reward I can possibly hope for is that some day I shall be as great a help to another young minister as you have been to me." He signed the letter, "Your son in the faith, Jack Hayford."[7] Vincent Bird would continue to be a spiritual father to Hayford until his death in 1998.

With his transition to the college, Jack's new immediate supervisor was Dr. Clarence Hall, who had served as the college dean since Watson Teaford had left in 1953. Functionally, Dr. Hall had the highest-ranking position at the college. Dr. Rolf McPherson, by virtue of his overall presidency of the International Church of the Foursquare Gospel, had the formal title of president, but he had no actual duties at the college. Functionally, the school's president was Hall and Hayford was vice president. Jack also taught classes every semester.[8]

Jack was responsible for the college chapel services, something he enjoyed doing. He had been charged with revitalizing the spiritual life of the student body, which had fallen as enrollment fell. Although Jack was not a regular speaker, he led the services and treated it as a learning environment for both himself and, more importantly, the students. Since he was teaching a course called Song Direction, chapel became a time for him to practice insights regarding congregational worship.[9]

Jack worked as liaison between the college and the Foursquare Department of Youth and Education, which helped him maintain his contact with Dr. Bird. Besides his role in the central offices, Bird was also president of the Alumni Association for the college, which kept the two working together. The contact with Dr. Bird helped Jack in those times when he was not receiving the credit he felt he deserved for his service at Life Bible College.

From 1965 to 1970, the college rebounded and enrollment grew significantly.[10] Jack also played an important role in helping improve the physical plant of the school, which had been in disrepair when he'd arrived. For all his service as Dean of Students, he received "almost no credit," and Hayford had to check his motives through it all. He handled the unintentional slight by focusing on serving God first and foremost and not vying for recognition.[11]

During his years at Life Bible College, Hayford continued to voice his concerns for his denomination, just as he had done while serving as

International Youth Director. In October 1966, he again sent a letter to Rolf McPherson to inform him that he felt he had come to a "crossroads" in his service at the college.

Hayford first made clear his overall loyalty to the movement: God "'has closed me in' to this fellowship of Foursquaredom," he wrote. Hayford then shared his frustration with McPherson in trying to promote a college that was not accredited,[12] something that had been an issue well before he'd become Dean of Students. Now responsible for recruiting students, Hayford brought it back to the table, but he felt there was little response from the denomination's headquarters.

The accreditation process would require substantive changes to the college's existing structure of government, finance, and curriculum.[13] He believed that the college was lacking the "climate of growth and development" that was needed if the school was to grow in any substantial manner.[14] He also pointed out the need of greater autonomy for the college.[15]

The crossroads Hayford referred to in his letter was not a threat to quit so much as an expression of honest uncertainty. He was in a key role at Life Bible College and believed the school needed radical change to be more successful. The tone of the letter could have been easily misunderstood, so in his characteristic style of careful explanation he wrote:

> But the progressive development of circumstances, and the mood of the evolving situation has brought me to a place that requires I decide where I am going. Without elaborating on the various influences which press on me, suffice it to say that I feel no demanding urgency in this regard, but I have reached a crossroads where I must answer myself this question: will I change my attitude regarding the things I feel within myself about my work and my church, or will I continue being true to my heart as I have been in the past. What this amounts to is the

decision about this letter: will I remain silent and thus ensure my safety in the eyes of my superiors, or speak and risk their favor.... Obviously I have chosen to speak.[16]

As in his previous letter to McPherson, Hayford was respectful but unflinching in his critique of the movement's leadership. In discussing the need for qualified leadership, he called for leaders "who are abreast of the times, trained for the current spiritual warfare, and confident of their preparation."[17]

The idea of improving Life Bible College's success in preparing such leaders motivated the letter. He wanted to see leaders released into ministry who would help the denomination break out of its lethargy, and he believed that his suggestions toward this end were going unheeded. Nevertheless, Hayford ended his letter calling for "a largeness of spirit and with a bold faith in each other as well as in the Lord."[18]

His efforts eventually bore some fruit as preliminary explorations were made to accredit the school through the American Association of Bible Colleges. However, it would be over a decade before the school would receive accreditation.

Jack with his parents and siblings, mid-1960s

SEEING THE KINGDOM OF GOD

Hayford managed his frustrations through hard work and "heart keeping." The hard work was an inevitable fact of his daily life, arising from his many responsibilities, but this kept his mind focused. Heart keeping was something Jack had been growing in since, as a boy, his mother had challenged him to tell the truth "in front of Jesus." This was still the cornerstone to his spiritual life: to be completely honest with God. Frequently, this meant he had to bring his poor attitudes before God in confession and repentance. It helped him maintain proper attitudes even in the disappointment he was experiencing.[19]

He was also maturing in his understanding of Scripture and its implications. In the summer of 1966, Jack was preparing to teach, for the first time, the Synoptic Gospels in the fall semester. This forced him to spend significant time over the summer reading through the Gospels and consulting study resources.[20] He began preparing the class instruction plan and was outlining each Gospel.

A key moment of insight occurred while speaking at an August summer youth camp in Arkansas, where he was the main speaker. There in his little room, he wrestled with the interpretation of chapter 4 of the Gospel of Mark. Frustrated with his outline, he first thought of calling the section of parables and similes "a series of maxims," but he hesitated. He knelt down and prayed, "Lord, I don't get this, please help me understand."

Then he saw it.[21] It was a moment of revelation.[22] In 1982, he described what began to open to him. He wrote:

> In that task, I began to be convinced that much of Christ's Church had never been taught the conceptual keystone for its highest rising to ministry. As I see it, this lies in a clear understanding and sensible response to the heartbeat of Jesus' essential theme: *the gospel of the Kingdom of God....* I marveled that I had not seen it more clearly

before. The phrase *Kingdom of God* occurs more than 100
times in the Gospels (or its frequent synonym in Matthew,
Kingdom of heaven).… It was the heart of Jesus' message.
I was amazed, especially since it had never really been
defined for me. The Kingdom of God, for me as for most
people, was a vague generic [term] describing anything or
everything of spiritual substance.[23]

For Jack, the summer experience of 1966 began a prayerful, worship-
centered journey for the next ten years in discovering new horizons of
understanding as Bible texts took on new meaning he had never seen before.

He realized that, through Jesus' life and work, there had been a radical
inbreaking of God's kingdom authority on earth and that Jesus had further
commissioned His church to represent and bring that same authority to
bear in the human situation. The gospel declared that there was a new way
to live no longer tyrannized by sin and Satan and that faith and repentance
ushered in new life under the benevolent reign of God. He believed this was
the Good News the church was called to proclaim.

His new perspective on the kingdom of God slowly began to color
every aspect of Jack Hayford's life and ministry. Further, it put his earlier
deliverance from near adultery into clearer perspective. Jesus' words made
new sense: "But if it is by the Spirit of God that I cast out demons, then
the kingdom of God has come to you" (Matthew 12:28 NRSV). No longer
was God's kingdom an ethereal concept or a distant reality—it was at work
powerfully in his life right now.

Perhaps the most important result of this fresh understanding of the
kingdom of God was the dynamic new privilege and responsibility he began
to see in the church's call to engage in spiritual warfare with evil forces. His
developing theology of the kingdom of God was both a blessing and a problem. On the one hand, it made his Bible come alive in new ways. On the
other, it also put the shortcomings of his own movement in sharper contrast.

Those who know Jack Hayford the best describe him as fiercely loyal.[24] And that he was. Despite concerns about the college and the denomination, he kept working as hard as ever. He had what he describes as a "submitted spirit" and did his best within the prescribed parameters of his position, yet he stayed true to his convictions.[25]

Sometimes this meant conflict. For example, in his efforts to improve the quality of student life, he had to confront the highly conservative tendencies of the Pentecostal college that easily engendered legalism. His work benefited the students, but at times some saw Hayford as brash and arrogant, and perhaps he was. In his mind, he was just doing what was necessary to get the job done.[26]

As Dean of Students, Jack did a lot of counseling, and it was here that his own recent deliverance sparked a focus in understanding how to defeat the "works of darkness." His newfound perspectives on the kingdom of God made him aware of the authority given to believers and of the idea that spiritual conflict was something to be reckoned with. It made him have "a heart to see students set free" from points of demonic bondage in their lives.[27]

When missionaries on furlough from Colombia were at the college, they introduced him to a specific ministry of deliverance that confronted and expelled evil spirits in the lives of people. Some of the faculty at the school took exception to the idea, but Hayford knew that the missionaries were discussing something real.[28] With tacit approval from the college administration, Jack began helping students break free from demonic strongholds. He carried this out quietly, without the dramatic sensationalism or public fanfare that came to be associated with "deliverance ministries" in the Charismatic movement in the 1970s.[29]

His perspectives on church and ministry were being adjusted in other ways, as well. In 1967, one of the older students at the college came to Hayford, filled with excitement. Eager to enter his public ministry, he talked about being "an instrument 'in developing the capacity of *every* member of the Body for ministry.'" For Jack, it was another profound but troubling learning experience.

> I sensed his enthusiasm, but still listened unresponsively. The Spirit was telling me that the young man had struck a vein of truth, but for the life of me, I couldn't absorb it. As he left my office, I assured him of my encouragement as he moved on toward graduation. Yet somehow, deep inside, I knew something had been related to me that transcended my spiritual grasp.
>
> I finished with that encounter feeling that a key to how the Church was to fulfill its calling had been taught to me—and by a student of mine at that! But I did not really grasp it, not at all. Embarrassing.[30]

That would change a year later when he again encountered this concept. One of Hayford's regular teaching assignments at the college included the evangelism courses. Because of this, the Foursquare denomination's leadership asked him to represent them as an observer at an Assemblies of God conference on evangelism in August 1968. This conference, held in St. Louis, was another formative experience for Jack.[31]

One of the central themes of the conference was an emphasis on the fact that every member of Christ's church is a minister and that pastoral leadership assists and releases the people of God into service for Christ. Jack was finally getting it. He "saw that every member of the Body has the potential to be—and should be fed and led toward functioning as—a fully equipped agent of Jesus Christ, as His minister." It was good that he was not pastoring at the time, because the idea of ministry being given to the laity would have been too "threatening" if he had been.[32]

The picture was clearing up. This was not a threat to pastoral leadership, but a demanding, self-giving assignment. A person's years of study at college and seminary would not be wasted because of the sudden preempting of need for trained pastors or church leaders by a magically enlightened laity. The leaders were the key to the laity's release in ministry—in fact, absolutely necessary to it.[33]

This was a radical reordering of things for Jack. He had to consider seriously if he would be willing to lead in the manner he was learning about. He decided it was really the only option he had.

Just as revolutionary to his thinking were the two messages that began the conference on evangelism. "The first speaker startled [him] with a new idea: that evangelism begins with worship." Jack felt as if he had been "hit in the head with a five-pound sledge hammer."[34] After all, he thought, "Evangelism has to do with the great commission and you're talking about worship?" The speaker went on to discuss the simple outline of the priorities for ministry. They were first, ministry to the Lord in worship; second, ministry to the body [the church] in fellowship; and third, ministry to the world in evangelism.[35]

He listened in amazement. "And I was sitting there thinking, not critically in the sense of judgmentally, but thinking 'that puzzles me. This is a conference on evangelism and they just made it the third thing. You'd think they would make it number one if this is what the conference is about.'"[36] His confusion was understandable, since, for Jack, evangelism had "been rooted in method, training programs, witnessing campaigns, soul-winning approaches, altar worker guidelines, crusades and outreaches, etc. But worship?"[37] The notion that evangelism was a by-product of worship and fellowship was completely foreign to him.

G. Raymond Carlson, later to serve as the General Superintendent for the Assemblies of God, was the next speaker. His text was Acts 13, and his message explored the church in Antioch. There, in a gathering of leaders who were "worshiping the Lord and fasting, the Holy Spirit said, 'Set apart for me Barnabas and Saul for the work to which I have called them'" (Acts 13:2 NIV). According to Hayford, Carlson

> developed the message with two points of focus. First, the evangelism that was launched by that time of ministry to the Lord ... broke open the doorway of extending the Gospel to all the world, to the Gentile world, that as Paul and Barnabas set out, it broke open doorways that became the course of [Western Civilization].[38]

Next, Carlson focused on the church as a royal priesthood, emphasizing the importance of worship in the life of every believer. Jack recalls what happened next.

> I was seated there, way up in the balcony, it was literally like a veil came off my eyes. That the priority of worship unto evangelism, it became real. It became totally gripping. It was not a slogan, it was a revelation from out of the Word of God, of the Holy Spirit to my understanding.[39]

As Carlson spoke, other texts began to come together in Jack's mind. He thought of Acts 2 and the coming of the Holy Spirit and that all those filled were speaking of "the wonderful works of God" (Acts 2:11b). He remembered that in Exodus, just as vital to the story of the giving of the Law was the attention given to building the tabernacle, a place of worship. Particularly significant to him was that Israel did not leave Sinai before the tabernacle was dedicated and filled with God's glory.

Carlson had deeply impacted Jack Hayford. He remembers, "There it was: Worship paves the way to evangelism! Worship is the pathway to expanded boundaries! I could see it in the Word, though I had never seen it before, and it immediately began to change my life."[40]

WINDS OF CHANGE

Jack left the conference with an entirely new perspective on worship, but he was not sure what to do with it. Further, he now saw that pastoring was not about ministering to church members but teaching and discipling them to carry out the ministries to which God had called them.

Upon returning to Los Angeles, he attempted to apply some of what he had learned at Angelus Temple, but since he was not serving as the senior pastor, it was largely just a learning step.[41] He tried primarily to stay focused on his job at the college.

By the fall of 1968, Jack was feeling restless but wasn't sure just why. He had served the denomination now for eight years.[42] The Hayfords' fourth child, a little girl named Christa, was born April 11 of that year—a happy but unplanned surprise.[43] The family was still surviving on his small salary.

While serving Foursquare, he had clearly voiced his concerns about the stagnation within the movement, but little had changed. He knew he had made significant contributions both at the central offices as National Youth Director and at the college as Dean of Students. He was also well known within his denomination and had many options offered to him in his ministerial career, including the pastorate of one of the denomination's larger churches. Others had assumed that Hayford was being groomed to be Life Bible College's overall dean, a position that was equivalent to being a president at most colleges.[44] Still, while

Jack was not sure what his restlessness meant, he did know that he was hungering for renewal.

During this time, he followed the news of the Charismatic Renewal in the 1960s.[45] Some of its story was developing close to him. Not long after returning to Los Angeles in 1960, he and Anna were watching television news broadcasts about Episcopalian priest Dennis Bennett's glossolalic experience.[46] Jack was fascinated as Bennett spoke in tongues into the reporter's tape recorder. He also heard the stories of Melodyland Christian Center in Anaheim, pastored by Ralph Wilkerson, which was becoming a national Charismatic center. In addition, Kathryn Kuhlman's Southern California meetings at the Shrine Auditorium were a sensation.

For most of the decade, Hayford watched the events but really did not "have a category for them."[47] He remained curious about the renewal but did not embrace it completely because it had "little definition at the time."[48] Not all Pentecostals were happy about Catholics and mainline Protestants speaking in tongues. But Jack was.

The year 1968 came to define the tumult of the Sixties, and the Hayfords endured it like other Americans. Jack never publicly expressed his perspectives about the cultural changes that the nation was undergoing during the 1960s. He did, however, make several comments years later. His perspectives reflect the attitudes of many Christian conservatives who saw "a slow, steady evaporation of the American dream."

As a youth leader, he expressed concern about rock music and a loss of innocence as a "real spirit of perversion" was rising in the nation. Hayford believed that the most dramatic event in the spiritual arena of the 1960s was the phenomenon of the Beatles, whom he saw as more than just a music group. He saw them as "a wave of spiritual darkness and prophets who swept on the world."[49] He bemoaned the loss of respect for authority that he saw in many young people during this time.

On the other hand, Hayford was aware that America had experienced deeper trauma in the 1960s. Student unrest, the Vietnam War, the assassinations of John and Robert Kennedy and Martin Luther King Jr. had left many young Americans in dismay and confusion.[50]

The Civil Rights Movement was especially transformative, and he was concerned not just about the conservative and Pentecostal churches' lack of involvement regarding racism, but about their general unwillingness to take strong stands on ethical issues.[51] At the time, Pentecostals still tended toward cultural and political separatism.

A NEW ASSIGNMENT

As the 1960s' most dramatic year drew to a close, Jack Hayford was still in the midst of his restlessness and in a quandary regarding what to do about it.[52] On the first Friday of December 1968, God spoke to him once again. As he got up that morning for his devotions, the Lord said, "You're going to pastor a little church."[53]

At first, he did not think too much of this because two or three of the college faculty members had taken temporary assignments as pastors for churches in transition. Jack assumed it would be a temporary arrangement and decided that he should write a letter regarding his availability to Dr. Van Cleave, who was now the Foursquare District Supervisor for the Southern California District.

He had no sooner thought this when the Lord spoke again. "You don't write anybody. When I have the place, they'll talk to you. You don't talk to them."[54] With that, Hayford honestly wondered if anyone would even think to ask him to do a temporary assignment on top of everything else he was doing at the college, but he left it to the Lord nevertheless.[55]

To complicate things further, Jack learned in December that the Portland Foursquare Church, still one of the largest churches in the movement, was going through a pastoral transition.[56] He had long envisioned himself taking the helm of that church and had visited many times over the nine years in Los Angeles. It was very hard not to pursue an appointment to the Oregon church, but in January 1969 the Lord clearly confirmed to both Jack and Anna that they were not to go to Portland.[57] After all, Jack believed he had been directed to go to a small church.

Hayford family in late 1968

Just weeks later, in mid-February, Jack was sitting in his office at the Life Bible College with Dr. Van Cleave as they were waiting to meet with a young couple whose wedding they would be jointly officiating.[58] Van Cleave almost apologetically asked Jack, "I don't suppose you'd be interested in pastoring a little church on the side?" It would be only a few months, he said.[59]

Hayford laughed and looked at him with amazement. "Doc, I want you to remember that you said it, I didn't."

"Yes, I will."

Jack went on to relate to Van Cleave how the Lord had spoken to him in December.[60] The two discussed three small churches that were open. One of them was a church at which Jack had spoken regularly over recent years and it seemed like a good fit, but he felt that the Lord was telling him that this was not to be the one. Dr. Van Cleave talked about the First Foursquare Church of Van Nuys, a tiny, fading congregation almost entirely composed of seniors. At one time, Dr. Van Cleave had pastored the church himself. In Jack's words, "We just talked like maybe the Lord had his hand on that. And he did."[61]

Three weeks later, Dr. Van Cleave and his wife introduced the little congregation to their new pastor, Jack Hayford. Anna and the four Hayford children were there, along with sixteen of the church's eighteen members, a pretty good turnout for a Wednesday night. It was March 12, 1969, and, after nine years in other assignments, Jack was pastoring again. The congregation received the Hayfords with warmth.[62]

Jack stood before his new congregation and told them he would prefer to stand on the floor level with them rather than up on the platform. It had little to do with the number of people present. Speaking of the first night at the Van Nuys church, Jack wrote:

> No one seemed to mind, nor do I suppose anyone really grasped my point at the time, but I had a reason for my positioning below the elevated platform. I was determined that for however long I would serve these people, I would function from a new level of understanding about pastoral service; my position at their level was a kind of announcement.[63]

Although Jack didn't expect to be at the little church for long, he was determined to apply what he had been learning over the last few years. His preaching text that evening was:

> Not that we are sufficient of ourselves to think any thing as of ourselves; but our sufficiency is of God; who also hath made us able ministers of the new testament; not of the letter, but of the spirit: for the letter killeth, but the spirit giveth life. (2 Corinthians 3:5–6)

He told the little church that he read the passage "because it sets forth a principle that shall govern my thoughts and our life together for however long the Lord Jesus wills me to be your pastor."[64] Drawing on his growing understanding of the kingdom of God and his experience in St. Louis only eight months before, he told the church that Jesus wants every believer "to be an expression of His life wherever we find ourselves." He went on:

> "I see us as becoming a truly 'ministry-minded' church," I explained. "The Lord Jesus Christ is our center. The Word of God is our base. The Holy Spirit, filling us to extend the servant life of Jesus outward—that's our objective...."
> Then I added, "This will not be a pastor-centered ministry but a people-centered ministry, all of us serving in Jesus' name."[65]

With those words, Jack launched himself forward into a new season of ministry back in the local church as a pastor, the place he most loved.[66] It was a new day for Hayford, though on that March evening, he had no idea of all that lay ahead for him as pastor of the Van Nuys Foursquare Church.

Within months, he would decide it was time to step down as Dean of Students at the college. He felt that his hard work and faithfulness to Foursquare would soon lead to an opportunity to go to a significant pastorate elsewhere. It was no slight toward the few people who remained at the Van Nuys church, for he intended to serve them faithfully while there. God would speak again before the year was over to give him his permanent assignment.

Part Two

EXPLODING
MINISTRY

Chapter 8

"YOU ARE HOME NOW"

THE FIRST FOURSQUARE CHURCH OF VAN NUYS

Jack was thirty-four and in his prime. He came to the Van Nuys congregation grateful to have a "laboratory" to begin working out what he had learned in recent years about the kingdom of God, worship, spiritual warfare, and the ministry of every believer. He also came with a fundamental commitment that the congregation would invite "God's power and presence to move among those worshipping Him."[1]

His role as pastor of the little church gave him a new freedom to lead that was a welcome change from the frustrations over the slow pace of change in his years at the denomination's headquarters and college. He relished the creative space he now had. Nevertheless, he was careful and "wary of a reckless bent toward the anti-institutional" or of the hyper-independence among some in the Charismatic movement.[2]

Jack was still loyal to the Foursquare Church but was primarily on a quest for "a fresh walk in the Spirit" that allowed for "the Holy Spirit's work in [the] assembly according to the Father's will and way."[3] In short, Hayford and the little church were embarking on a journey of discovering "New Testament Church-life principles," as he termed it.[4] He wanted to learn these principles, avoiding the excesses of some Pentecostals while also avoiding religious or denominational prejudices.

This quest meant that much had to be unlearned from the past.[5] Though the Foursquare heritage was rich in many ways, to his perception the process of institutionalization had turned some practices into mere rituals that had lost their meaning. Hayford knew that the Bible speaks positively and negatively about tradition. Consequently, he had no interest in casting off all church traditions, but he was equally convinced that "where human or church traditions choke simplicity," they must be examined in the light of the Word and with much prayer.[6] He was experiencing a new freedom to embrace whatever helped to achieve renewal.

Hayford's interdenominational childhood was helpful here because he had gained respect for the "broad and blessed traditions across the face of North American Christianity." In his new role as pastor, coupled with his Pentecostal and evangelical history, Jack began to more closely examine the Charismatic movement, which was now growing rapidly in the United States.[7]

He remembers: "With this combination of historic Protestant and Pentecostal church experience, we became attuned to the sound of new showers of blessing that the Holy Spirit rained upon God's people everywhere."[8] In other words, Hayford decided that he was not going to be limited by his Classical Pentecostal background in his explorations of New Testament church life. Still, Jack's eagerness for change was complicated by the uncertainty over just how long he would be at the little church as well as the challenge coming from the congregation's history.

First Foursquare Church in Van Nuys, 1969

The First Foursquare Church of Van Nuys had been born out of a cottage prayer meeting in 1926 that was followed by several weeks of meetings conducted by students from Life Bible College. The students had held a campaign of old-time revival tent meetings on Friar Street in Van Nuys. Throughout the revival, the tent had been "filled to capacity every night. Many souls were saved and filled with the Holy Spirit."[9]

The tent meetings birthed the Van Nuys congregation, and a woman named Helen Isager Myers served as its first pastor.[10] A church building was constructed in 1927, and Aimee Semple McPherson was present at its dedication.[11] Twenty-four years later, in 1951, a larger facility was built on Sherman Way in Van Nuys.[12] At that time, the congregation numbered 200.[13] For most of the church's history, however, the average attendance was fewer than 100.[14]

During the congregation's first thirty-three years, it had eleven pastors, which did not help the church find much stability.[15] The pastor who had preceded Jack Hayford's appointment in Van Nuys had served there for ten years, but health problems had hindered his effectiveness and the church had dwindled in attendance over several years.[16] By the time Hayford came to the nearly forty-three-year-old church, its attendance averaged twenty-five.[17] The eighteen members who were still at the church, although they were older, proved eager to be trained. But, like their new pastor, they would need to be patient.

Given these challenges, Hayford knew he needed help, so he invited two young men with whom he was working at Life Bible College to come with him to Van Nuys. Fellow faculty member Chuck Shoemake and Paul Charter, a student, became Jack's closest coworkers at the church during the early years of his pastorate. Both men and their wives were at the church on March 16, 1969, the first Sunday Jack led the services. Soon, the three men were meeting on Wednesday afternoons to pray and talk together as they learned how to pastor the church in a new way. Gradually, a few other students from the college started attending the church.[18]

Jack was serious about cultivating the ministries of the people he was going to pastor, and he realized the implications of doing so. On a warm Saturday, not long after coming to the church, Jack sat down with Anna on the back patio of the house for a drink of iced tea after mowing the lawn. Sitting there, Jack told his wife, "You know, honey, if I really do what I think we're supposed to do here, we could be out of work in two or three years. Because if we cultivate the ministry of the people we won't be necessary."[19] In hindsight, it may seem naive, but he was serious.

The Hayfords decided to press ahead anyway, whatever the cost. In his work at the college, Jack had gained a growing passion regarding the importance of discipleship, and now he was going to apply this full force to the pastorate.[20] If it meant becoming unnecessary, then that was the price of obeying scriptural mandates.

"THIS IS YOUR VALLEY"

A few weeks into their interim pastorate, Jack was driving on Interstate 405 when God spoke to him. It was a crystal-clear afternoon as he was driving northbound. With nothing particular on his mind, his eyes "scanned the 'bowl' formed by surrounding mountains hemming this portion of Los

Angeles" called the San Fernando Valley. As he remembers it, the Holy Spirit whispered, "This is your valley."

"The impression was clear and the meaning was obvious, though I could fathom no way to apply it. 'Your valley' meant 'The place of your assignment, and the intended location of God for your ministry.'"[21] Although the Van Nuys church was located in the heart of the Valley, as far as he knew, the appointment at the church was temporary. At this point, Jack was not sure what to do with what God had said.

Located fifteen miles northwest of downtown Los Angeles, the San Fernando Valley in 1969 was one of the bustling suburbs of Los Angeles.[22] Its more than 260 square miles, filled with housing tracts and apartments, had exploded in development after World War II.[23] The Valley population had grown by over one million people in the first two decades after the war. It had required scarcely twenty years to convert the miles of lush farmland into urban sprawl.[24]

Founded in 1911, Van Nuys sat at the geographic center of the San Fernando Valley, and the Sherman Way location of the First Foursquare Church of Van Nuys was near the center of Van Nuys. When Hayford began pastoring the church, the population growth in the San Fernando Valley was slowing but still on the rise. In 1969, the Valley was roughly 85 percent Caucasian, 12 percent Latino, 2 percent African American, and 1 percent Asian. This began changing, and by the mid-1970s there was a significant increase in the Latino population, particularly in the Van Nuys area.[25]

While the Valley had its own diverse workforce, it was populated by large numbers of commuters who traveled out of the Valley to work, utilizing the Southern California freeway system. Many Valley residents worked in the entertainment industry, with North Hollywood, Studio City, and Burbank on its southeastern side.

Like San Francisco to the north, Southern California was symbolized in popular media as a center for the Sixties Cultural Revolution. Its music, television, and film industries had championed the social change that had made the 1960s infamous to religious conservatives.[26]

By 1969, however, much of the euphoric optimism of 1967's "summer of love" two years earlier had worn off. The brutal Tate and LaBianca murders in August 1969 by the Manson family shook Southern California and the nation. The December 6 Altamont Speedway Concert in Northern California, where a man was stabbed to death while the Rolling Stones played onstage, shattered what little "hippie" idealism was left. America was in the midst of a swing back to the political right that had helped Richard Nixon win the White House a year earlier.

GOD SPEAKS AGAIN

After nine months at the church, attendance in December was averaging sixty-five in the Sunday morning worship service. The year had gone reasonably well, except that Jack was overloaded with work and struggling to keep up with it all.[27] He was still serving as Dean of Students at Life Bible College as well as pastoring the church. The church responsibilities fueled by his passion for renewal were turning out to be much more than just preaching on the weekend. He and Anna were investing substantial time in the people.

In coming to the church, Jack was intent on bringing the congregation back to some degree of strength and was working hard at it. Still, he had always thought he would eventually be moving on to a "better" opportunity.[28] That idea changed on Friday, December 5, 1969.

On that day, Jack met with Dr. McPherson and Dr. Hall at the Foursquare movement's central offices next to Angelus Temple. Quite unexpectedly, and while talking about other matters, he heard the Lord say to him, "You are to stay at the church."[29]

Jack immediately understood that God was calling him to be the Van Nuys congregation's permanent pastor. It was the beginning of a difficult and life-changing journey, and the next few weeks were a particular struggle.

The thought of staying at the little church made Jack aware of what it could possibly mean for his future. "I really thought God was going to ruin my life." He wrote that he was being "consigned to anonymity"[30] and that "now, after thirteen years of public ministry, I was looking forward to what appeared a bleak future in an obscure pastorate lost in Los Angeles' urban sprawl."[31] Jack nevertheless yielded to what he was convinced was God's call and, after Christmas, moved his family closer to the Van Nuys church.[32]

His obedience didn't, however, keep him from fretting over the decision. In the second week of January 1970, he flew up to Oakland to visit his parents.[33] Jack's father was sick and wanted to see him. He arrived on a Friday and stayed the night at his parents' home.[34] The next morning, he was up early praying in the living room of the house, when he had a vision in which he saw a trophy with the word *Position* written on it.[35] It was "as if a video played" and the "Lord showed" him that position was something he had always been blessed with.[36]

Several incidents flashed before his mind from his past. He saw himself as a leader in many childhood situations, whether at play or at school.[37] He saw his valedictorian speech at the college and the favor and recognition he received in almost anything he had done since then. "And for the first time [he] realized that position was important to [h]im." As the vision continued, the trophy came closer and closer to him. God had given the trophy to him and now said, "Will you give it back to me?"[38]

He knew the vision had to do with God's call to stay at the church. He struggled for a few minutes but finally yielded the trophy to God. It was a dramatic decision. As far as he knew, it meant he would remain an unknown Los Angeles pastor for the rest of his life. As he saw it, with his surrender, any "star label" associated with Jack Hayford in Foursquare was no more.[39] "It was a conscious decision and call to surrender being 'anybody' ever again."[40]

When his plane landed on the return to the Burbank airport, he heard the Lord say, "This is where your life centers now. You are home now."[41]

Surprisingly, in a way he was relieved. The vision in Oakland enabled him to see just how "dominated" he was with living up to other people's expectations of him.[42] Jack knew he had been ambitious but also realized that most of the positions he had held had come to him more than he had sought them. Because of this, he always felt the pressure to please those who had given him opportunities to serve. Now that he had said yes in surrendering "position" to God and to staying on as pastor of the Van Nuys church, that pressure was gone.

He informed the college that he would be stepping down as Dean of Students in the summer of 1970 but offered to continue teaching for a season. With that done, there was no one in Foursquare he had to try to please. Hayford summed up how he expected the rest of his career to go: "I'd have a happy ministry, but I would never have any particular point of significance in anyone's perception."[43] When considering the previous ten years of travel and notoriety within his denomination, it would be a change. Getting there had been difficult, but with the decision now made, "I didn't feel hurt, I didn't feel bad about it. It was surrendered, I was at peace."[44]

But it was not as he thought. Just ten days after Jack's Oakland surrender, at the end of January, God spoke once again while Jack was on the freeway.[45] The words came out of the blue: "You mustn't think too small."[46] The voice spoke again, "You mustn't think too small, or you will get in my way."[47] It was as if the conversation was now continuing regarding his recent decision to pastor the Van Nuys church.[48]

He wondered what this could mean. As he drove, there was "a sudden sense of [God's] Presence."[49] One more time, he heard the voice: "You mustn't think too small, or you will get in my way; for I have set myself to do a great work."[50] "And I thought, 'You mustn't think too small?'" Jack realized that God was addressing his sense of resignation to anonymity and the notion of the Van Nuys church being small.

He began to cry and heard the Lord speak one more time: "When have you ever done anything I haven't blessed?" Now sobbing "profusely," Jack saw a vision "that lasted an instant of buildings and development," which he knew had to do with the future of the church. What he saw wasn't small.[51]

THE PRIORITY OF WORSHIP

In the months that followed, there was modest numerical growth. The year 1970 was, however, a year of significant spiritual growth for the congregation. Hayford's teachings during the last nine months of 1969 were a beginning step that he was now building upon, particularly on the theme of worship.[52]

Because of his musical background, song-leading had always been an important part of his participation in public worship services. After his 1968 experience at the Assemblies of God evangelism conference, at which worship had been presented as the church's first priority, he was figuring out how to apply the concepts in the local church.[53]

This became a prayer point for his Wednesday prayer meetings with Shoemake and Charter. They would get together at 2:00 p.m. and continue for two or more hours in prayerful discussion, though Jack recalls that there was usually more prayer than discussion. Sometimes, the three men would lie on the floor in the church sanctuary seeking God for different prayer needs. Frequently, they would bring up a subject like worship and talk about it, stop to pray for insight, then talk again.[54]

They consciously began to ask why certain practices were a part of church life and why others were not. Hayford and the two men "felt God wanted to do something fresh in the old church—something that would require [them] to be sensitive … and travel in ways" that would break new ground.[55]

This was a key part of the unlearning process. Hayford, Shoemake, and Charter would laugh and cry in their Wednesday gatherings as they discovered their own "holy humanness and human holiness," which came from their increasingly honest and transparent conversations. Jack Hayford, always the leader, was nevertheless learning the power of shared ministry. Hayford recalled, "Together we learned a thousand lessons—lessons in

heart renewal through repentance; in humbling of self through open confession; and in Holy Spirit–begotten discovery through the Word."[56]

Increasingly, Jack was realizing the goal of worship. It had nothing to
do with getting people worked up emotionally, nor was it simply a tune-up
for the Sunday morning sermon.[57] It was far more. "In both the Old and
New Testaments, God's revealed will in calling His people together was
that they might experience His presence and power—not a spectacle or
sensation, but in a discovery of His will through encounter and impact." In
his growing understanding of worship, Jack believed that the Bible taught
"God's desire that people worship Him, for *worship is the means by which a
place is prepared for God to meet with and move among His people.*"[58]

This was a major adjustment for Jack and for many of the Pentecostals
he encountered. An experience of God's presence may have been a part of
early Pentecostal worship, but Jack saw little real expectation of it any longer.

As he began to teach his new perspectives on worship to the church,
he realized that the congregation had little theological foundation for what
they did in the services. They could not tell, when asked, why they praised
God vocally, why they sang, why they lifted their hands, why they clapped,
or, for that matter, why they did any of the expressive practices common to
Pentecostal worship at the time.[59] Still carrying the imprint of his mother's
insistence on explaining the reason for everything, Jack embarked on teaching the "why" and "how" of worshipping God.[60] Teaching on worship was
a central emphasis for Hayford from this point on.

It went beyond teaching only. They began to change the worship
services. Instead of their usual pattern of singing songs one by one, inter-
spersed with conversation and introductions, the congregation began
singing songs one after the other without interruption. More contemporary
worship choruses, many coming from the Charismatic Renewal and the
emerging music associated with Calvary Chapel and Maranatha Music, as
well as choruses Jack wrote, were introduced and supplemented by older
hymns.[61] Hayford started to call the whole congregation a choir gathered

to sing to God.[62] He declared worship as the church's first priority and the fountainhead from which all ministry flows.

Hayford was developing a theology of worship that would inform much of his writing in the coming years.[63] In the first years at the church, he discovered worship as the pathway for people, saved and the unsaved alike, to find their true "destiny in life, their fullest personal worth, and their deepest human fulfillment."[64] Although Jack had experienced the power of worship for years in a personal dimension, he had not fully made the connection to the importance of the church's corporate worship expression. This required confronting the traditions of his past way of thinking.

> I had been ignorant of worship as a means by which God's presence could be realized consistently. Consequently, I had grown up to depend on preaching alone as the instrument bringing people to repentance. Suddenly I was finding the teamwork between the Holy Spirit and the Word—the Holy Spirit softening the hearts as we worshipped and the Word enlightening people's eyes in that new atmosphere of love.[65]

This understanding significantly adjusted how Jack approached public ministry.[66] Instead of haranguing people about sin and repentance the way so many preachers did, he trusted the Holy Spirit to do the work of conviction for both the believer and the unbeliever in the services. He emphasized the grace of God found in Christ and steadfastly resisted using guilt as a means to motivate repentance and sanctification. He left that to the presence of God. It affected his invitations for the unsaved to receive Christ.

> Biblical repentance does not require submission to a predigested, dictated, dehumanizing recitation that blasts the sinner for his sinfulness, but it does require a

full-hearted turning from one's own way to Jesus Christ—
to acknowledge ourselves as lost and Him as the only
savior, to acknowledge ourselves as dead in sin and Him
as Resurrected Lord.[67]

The approach worked, and in this environment, people came to Christ. In the thirty years Hayford pastored the Van Nuys church, 50,000 people received Christ in the worship services.[68]

In the early days, teaching the church to worship had its challenges. The older people at the church were not resistant to expressive worship—some of them had a history of fifty years in Pentecostal churches—but some had let their praise become shallow and programmed. From his early weeks at the church, Jack had sensed something resisting the congregation's worship that was more than a reluctance of the congregation.

Furthermore and quite apart from the people themselves,
the building's sanctuary possessed a strange and oppressive
atmosphere. It wasn't a matter of aesthetics, since the simple
building, modeled after a World War II Army post chapel,
was rustic and rather inviting. Yet one felt a clamminess
at times, a coldness not unlike the quenching effect when
a certain person brings gloom or heaviness to a group. "A
wet blanket," we say. It almost seemed as though a person-
ality resided in that room—someone intent on hindering a
free, wholehearted worship within those walls.[69]

Others had remarked about it too, so he felt it was not something he was simply imagining. However, Jack did not want to engender a "negative or superstitious way of thought" by drawing public attention to it. In fact, it might have remained unaddressed had it not been for the Holy Spirit's "signal."[70]

One afternoon while in the sanctuary, Jack saw something high in the corner of the ceiling's rafters. At first, he found himself "reticent to acknowledge 'seeing' things," but *there was something there*." The "small, dark, cloudlike object" was quickly gone. In that instant, the Holy Spirit confirmed to him that what he saw was a demonic spirit sent to oppress God's work in the church and that he was not to fear it. The Spirit also directed Jack to resist it with "steadfast praise."[71]

He devised a plan. Several times a week, he "made a point of walking through the sanctuary when no one else was there." As he did, he would shout the praises of God loudly and clap his hands, declaring glory and honor to Jesus Christ. He "rejoiced in the Spirit with singing, with a sense of commitment to praise God in defiance" of the oppressive spirit.[72] Shoemake and Charter joined him in resisting the demonic presence.[73]

Nothing noticeable happened for a number of months. Then, on October 29, 1970,[74] the church was gathered for Sunday morning worship. There were about sixty people in the meeting, and someone brought a word of exhortation that the congregation should praise the Lord.[75] Jack expected that people would respond in strong praise, yet nothing happened.

The young man leading the service did not know how to handle the situation. Jack was at first reluctant to confront the situation out of concern that it would not "look good" to the few visitors present. Nevertheless, he knew he had to respond. He stepped off the platform where he had been playing the organ and addressed the congregation:

> "First, I want to say to any who are visiting that I hope you will not be uncomfortable by reason of what I am going to say. Please understand my desire to make you feel welcome, but at the same time I must, as pastor of this flock, speak a few words of rebuke."
>
> Then I changed my tone, not to accuse but to express my pain: "Church, do you realize what we have just done?

God, by His Holy Spirit, has just called us in a beautiful and gracious way to praise Him for His great love and goodness to us, and we have responded with silence. I know neither you nor I want to disobey the Word or the Spirit. So we are going to stop everything and give ourselves to worship and praise, until together we sense that we have adequately responded to God's call to worship."[76]

And so the congregation stood and praised God as Jack led them in several songs. It was a strong declaration of glory to God. Loud praises filled the sanctuary and they worshipped for several minutes. As they did, "the room seemed to brighten." Later in the service, as the congregation sang again, Jack turned to Chuck Shoemake and exclaimed, "A tremendous spirit of joy and liberty is here." Shoemake agreed.

Jack dismissed the matter from his mind, but not for long. The following Tuesday, while he was driving home from the college, the Lord spoke to him: "*The reason for the liberty you experienced Sunday is that the hold of that spirit that has oppressed the church has been broken.*"[77] It was true, and from that time on the church experienced unhindered times of worship. Jack decided to be vitally involved in leading worship from then on.

The story illustrates how Jack seamlessly saw the visible and invisible worlds. He discussed the incident in his book *Glory on Your House*. Years later, in reflecting on the cleansing of the leprous house in Leviticus 14:53, he drew a parallel to the "cleansing" of the sanctuary in Van Nuys. "I think God was speaking this passage directly to the fact that the spiritual and the physical are not so much two different realms as two integrated realities. We all live in direct touch with both. The problem is, the majority of us learn to live life only with reference to the physical realm."

Jack continued: "The spiritually corrupt may take on a spiritual dimension that can dwell in our homes, our cars, our offices, our work, our school lockers—anyplace over which we have been given dominion."[78] Hayford realized that the church had been dealing with a "spiritual leprosy manifesting itself through a spirit of heaviness."[79] They had experienced spiritual combat in which what one did in the physical, visible dimension had direct impact in the invisible dimension.

Around the same time, Jack had begun a practice that continued for the rest of his pastorate, praying through the sanctuary on Saturday nights. Jack would lay hands on each chair, praying for God's loving presence to touch every person who would gather on Sundays for worship. One Saturday, Jack was joined by three of his leaders to pray through the little sanctuary. As they prayed, Jack "felt strongly prompted to have each person stand at a corner of the sanctuary. So, we scattered to the four corners of the room. I said, 'Let's extend our hands to the middle of the room as if we are lifting up a canopy of praise to the Lord like a tabernacle.'"[80]

As the four began to praise the Lord, there came a deep "sense of the presence of the Lord." Paul Charter, one of the four gathered that evening and pastoring the youth at the time, spoke up. "The Lord just impressed on me very strongly the reason that this seems so right. Each of us is standing at a corner of the sanctuary, and we are aligned with four angelic beings who are always there. We are kind of harmonizing with the heavenlies right now."

Just a few days later at a men's morning prayer gathering, the Lord spoke to Jack about Charter's words. "The four angels that Paul ... mentioned the other night are the four living creatures of the book of Revelation, chapter 4." It seemed so peculiar and outlandish that Jack nearly laughed out loud. He thought to himself, "The four living creatures of the book of Revelation.... The ones crying, 'Holy, holy, holy is the Lord of hosts' ... [here] in Van Nuys! I thought, mockingly.... 'There have been entire cult systems started with less material than this!!'" Jack didn't know how to respond. But ten days later as Jack walked through the church's parking lot, he had a "mental picture so vivid" and suddenly realized what God was teaching him.

> What he saw was an alignment between the throne of God
> described by John, and the church he pastored on Sherman
> Way in Van Nuys. One seemed to blend into the other: vast
> multitudes of praising creatures in John's vision overlapping
> with the praising people of the Church on the Way. As
> Hayford saw it, the entire San Fernando Valley ... became
> an amphitheater of praise surrounding God's throne.

Reality, as Hayford came to grasp it, is that God works simultane-
ously in the visible and the invisible, in the physical and the spiritual.
The worshipping church stands at the heart of His reign. Thus the church
Hayford pastored (and any church, potentially) was more than a gathering
of people dedicated to a far-off spiritual kingdom and to somewhat abstract
principles. The church at worship became an expression of the power of
the kingdom of God with the literal presence of God in the middle of its
sanctuary.[81]

When Hayford saw the visitation of God's glory just two months later
on January 2, 1971, the story that opens this biography, he was certain that
the "cleansed house" that occurred that October morning was an essential requisite preparing the sanctuary for God's glory.[82] Worship made it
possible.

Hayford was now clearly seeing the relationship between worship and
the kingdom of God. As he studied the Lord's Prayer, he became convinced
that worship was related to "the entry of God's rule."[83] Opening with
praise, "Hallowed be thy name," the prayer's first petition was a call to worship that was then followed by an invitation "for the entry of God's ruling
presence." According to Hayford, "Jesus is saying, 'When you pray, begin
with worship.'"[84] The congregation and Jack were growing in worship, and
things were changing as a result.

Chapter 9

THE CHURCH ON THE WAY

A NEW NAME

Just weeks before the worship breakthrough, Jack was sitting in his study at home when

> the Lord gave me what has become our slogan name for the Van Nuys Foursquare Church: "The Church on the Way."[1] The phrase *On The Way* focused on the fact we are all moving forward in ministry—that is, a congregation available to be Jesus' life wherever we go and in whatever way He directs.[2]

The name also referenced the location of the church building, which was on Sherman Way. Most importantly, it affirmed that Jesus is *the* Way.

Jack introduced the name to the congregation on the second Sunday of September in the morning worship service. It was a name that reflected the growing sense of ministry-mindedness that he was teaching the congregation and not intended to be clever. To Hayford, "only people willing to grow can correctly say, 'I am part of 'The Church on the Way.'"[3] However slowly things were progressing, the congregation was realizing their pastor was serious about building a people-centered ministry where people were "on the way" with Jesus.

On the same Sunday on which he introduced the new slogan name to the church, he also inaugurated a practice that continued through all his years as pastor. He had the congregation break into small groups to pray for one another.[4]

Jack was convinced that something had to be done that gave the gathered church a practical opportunity to minister to one another. The congregation could not be allowed to be mere spectators; rather, they needed to participate in ministry when the church gathered. The "prayer circles" were a starting place for people to practice listening to others and "find how to pray in His will and His Way." It was a stretch for everyone, especially visitors to the church. Yet Jack never pulled back. Prayer for one another at the Church on the Way became known as "Ministrytime."[5]

The focus on prayer in the Sunday worship service was not surprising—it reflected Jack's broader commitment to prayer. In addition to his Wednesday prayer meeting with Paul Charter and Chuck Shoemake, Jack made the church's Wednesday night service a true prayer meeting with significant time given to prayer. It was part of his conviction that the Holy Spirit was calling the congregation to become "a people of prayer power." He treated the Wednesday night meeting as another "laboratory to research the Church's power potential."[6]

So that prayers would not be vague or too general, he taught the people to pray specifically for concerns. Although fewer members attended Wednesday nights, they were being discipled in how to understand and practice prayer in expanding ways. A "new mood began to govern" their praying, and Jack became convinced that the Wednesday prayer gathering was the church's most important meeting.[7]

Jack was growing in his own commitment to prayer, as well. Prioritizing prayer was not easy, given the time demands of pastoring and teaching at the college. He was regularly journaling his awareness of the need to pray more consistently, but he also acknowledged that he often failed at doing so.[8]

The prayer times with Paul and Chuck were becoming even more important. The three were learning to pray with greater recognition of their dependence on God in how to lead the church. Not knowing how to go forward, they asked God what to do. They were applying concepts regarding spiritual warfare when they prayed and were "struggling to hold things together in prayer."[9]

Paul, Chuck, and their wives were also standing with Jack in ministry. They became the Church on the Way's first staff members. Paul Charter and his wife, Jerri, became the youth pastors, leading youth meetings and establishing a coffeehouse outreach to hippies and teens. Chuck Shoemake helped pastorally as a counselor, and his wife, Ruby, led ministry for children.[10] But the focus was not on church programs as much as it was seeking God's agenda for the church.

As 1970 drew to a close, Jack had pastored the Church on the Way nearly twenty months. There had been growth, with around 100 people attending Sunday worship service. But after seeing the "silvery mist" of God's glory that first Saturday of 1971, things changed.[11] God had told Jack that "I have given my glory to dwell in this place."[12] The very next day, on Sunday, January 3, the attendance jumped from 100 to 160 and would keep growing through the year, with over 300 attending the December 1971 worship services.[13] By the end of 1972, it was nearing 1,000.

The church's growth continued for over twenty years. Hayford has repeatedly said that the growth had to do with the gift of God's presence and not with promotion or church growth strategies. Instead, they sought to follow God's direction. Hayford insists:

> Everything we do that might be called a "program" is simply a response to what God has done and is doing. We do

our best to keep pace with *His* work—not try to get Him to endorse ours.

Thus, without any notable plan, other than seeking to be faithful to those principles the Holy Spirit has made alive in our hearts, "The Church on the Way" has grown; but His glory gift was the key to this release.[14]

In it all, Jack was enjoying his freedom as a local church pastor. He was still a loyal Foursquare pastor, but in terms of actual practice, he was happily experiencing broader boundaries now that he was no longer serving in any denominational leadership role.[15] He later admitted that, when he came to Van Nuys, he essentially "abandoned the church methodology [he] had used for the previous thirteen years."[16]

In reviewing his four-year Fort Wayne pastorate and the time serving the denomination, he felt he had seen "a certain amount of fruit," but mostly what he had experienced was "spiritually oriented human enterprise." Now back to the pastorate, he was glad to be doing things differently if, admittedly, far from perfectly. Instead of "performing," something he was well acquainted with from the past, he was now seeing the fruit of a simpler way of doing things.

Hayford knew it could easily sound like a boast, yet he genuinely believed that the Church on the Way was allowing the Holy Spirit to be the "director of its life and program."[17] In some ways, he was identifying more with the Charismatic movement than with his Classical Pentecostal family.

PLACED IN THE FOURSQUARE MOVEMENT

In the middle of this growing independence, Jack again encountered God's intervention. Late in February 1971, almost two months after seeing God's glory, Jack was up late praying, just past 1:00 a.m. "I sat in our living room rocking chair, my robe wrapped around myself against the late-night chill."[18] As Jack sat waiting on the Lord in prayer, the Lord asked him a question. *"You don't believe you're in My will, do you?"*

Jack sat there puzzled, because he did believe he was in God's will. So "I kept my mouth shut and my mind open."

The Lord spoke again. *"Do you believe you are to be pastoring?"*

Sitting in the chair, Jack "nodded affirmatively as though [the Lord] were seated across from my chair."

"Do you believe you are to pastor in Van Nuys?" Again, the answer was obvious but there was more. *"Do you believe you are to pastor the Van Nuys Foursquare Church?"*

Hayford remembers: "Of course, I did. What kind of quiz was this?"

Then came the punch line—the "knockout blow leaving me flattened—in complete, but enlightened disarray." This time, it wasn't a question but a statement: *"You believe that being in the Foursquare denomination is your own choice."*

Jack was left reeling. "A dozen streams of thought converged at once." He spent a few minutes trying to think it all through. He knew that what the Lord had said to him was true, though he had not perceived it until that moment. Jack realized he did think being in Foursquare was his decision. He also knew that he had chafed at certain points along the way, yet he was not particularly displeased being in Foursquare.

In looking back, he realized that he had indeed put the emphasis on his own decision to be a part of the movement. After all, he had chosen to go to Life Bible College nearly twenty years before, and he could see that "the natural flow of events seemed to draw [him] into that fellowship." He knew God had been involved, but he thought denominational affiliation was more about personal choice. Did God really care about "the whole ecclesiastical hodge-podge"?

It was clear now that God was telling him that, despite whatever he had previously thought, he did "not truly believe it was [God's] will …

to be in the Foursquare Church." More importantly, with that came the direct impression from God's heart: "It was His will for me to be in the Foursquare Church!"

> I suddenly saw the picture—*How stupid of me!* How ludicrous to suppose that I could claim to be in God's will while pastoring the Van Nuys *Foursquare* Church if the "Foursquare" part of the equation was immaterial to Him! They were two parts of an inseparable proposition—the church, the denomination and God's will for me were one and the same.[19]

Jack also recognized that God loved the whole church, including denominations. However, he was quick to qualify that God didn't affirm the sometimes-sectarian tendencies associated with the idea of denominational*ism.*

> Such "ism" may be embraced by independents or denominations and called "a kindred spirit." But the painful truth is that often the spirit of supposed unity is actually a sectarian party spirit, and a false order of joy derived through self-congratulation over one's own doctrinal purity, personal piety, ecclesiastical accomplishment or public recognition....
>
> Yet God does love denominations, because God loves people. The true essence of a denomination is that it is a distinct family of our Father, "of whom the whole family in heaven and earth is named" (Ephesians 3:15, KJV). Just as Israel had tribes with family groups within those tribes, yet they were all one people, so the Church is not outside of the divine will where denominations exist.[20]

This second insight was critical for Hayford at this juncture in his journey, since he was being influenced by the Charismatic movement, which by 1971 was becoming more than just a renewal movement in the historic churches. Vast numbers of Charismatics were radically independent, floating around without denominational affiliation. Many independent ministries and churches were springing up.

Hayford has admitted that, given some of his conflicts with Foursquare in the past, his commitment to the denomination was wavering after coming to the Van Nuys church. At some point, he had to decide whether to remain in the Foursquare movement or go it alone.[21] This confrontation with God about his relationship to the denomination was the decisive point.[22]

It helped him to see not only that being at Foursquare was God's choice for him but also that it did not require him to be narrowly partisan. Jack drew on his mother's lesson from years before that no group "has a corner on truth." With an ecumenical sensitivity, he wrote in regard to God's revelation late that night:

> What transgresses God's will is absence of love, and the pride that supposes any of us has a corner on truth. We need to see that our denomination of apple trees is only part of the ranch, and that trees of oranges, apricots, peaches and even *lemons* might be as fruitful in His eyes as our own self-approved corner of the field.
>
> Furthermore, it jarred me to see that God might have some isolated trees outside the orchards, as a professional land-scaper might have for ornamentation. In other words, what appeared to me to be "independent" churches may have a place in His plan, too.[23]

There was one more insight that night that was very specific and required immediate action. Jack recognized that, if God had sovereignly placed him in Foursquare, then he needed to "function in a spirit of submission" to the denomination.[24] This had to do with participation in the Foursquare movement's mode of operation. Jack did not believe that God intended to say that everything about the movement needed to be endorsed. But he did know that God had made it clear that Foursquare was his family and he needed to honor its policies.

This would require an adjustment for the Church on the Way. The Foursquare Church asks all of its member churches to send an "extension tithe," 10 percent of a local church's general tithes and offerings, to support the denomination's operational costs and to fund home missions. Although the Foursquare corporate bylaws state this tithe as a requirement, it was not enforced, and participation was largely voluntary.

When God spoke to Jack about his relationship to Foursquare, the Church on the Way was giving the denomination $100 per month, calling it a "token tithe."[25] Their actual monthly income was close to $2,500. Jack knew the token tithe was "ridiculous" and that it needed to change.

> As a result of this late-night encounter with the Lord, I asked the men of our church council [the church's advisory governing body] to meet with me. I told them I believed we should bring our church's extension tithe to a consistent tenth, and I explained why. Relating God's dealing with me on this matter.... When I explained how deeply it appeared to me that God was summoning us to manifest our submission to those authorities that [God] had placed over us in family association, the brothers consented heartily. We paid our tithe, retroactive to the preceding month, and from that date we have given it as a faithful minimum.[26]

At the time, they had little idea how significant that decision would prove. In the next three decades, the Church on the Way gave the Foursquare

Church tens of millions of dollars, becoming the denomination's single largest contributor. For a number of years the Van Nuys congregation contributed one out of every thirty dollars the denomination received in tithes from churches in the United States. With such substantial giving, Hayford and the Van Nuys congregation gained an increasing voice in the movement.[27]

Hayford's revelation that night in February 1971 was crucial in another way. As the congregation began growing rapidly during the 1970s, and given Hayford's rising profile outside of his denominational circle, particularly among Charismatics, there were those within the movement who had questions.[28] Some may have wondered about his loyalty to Foursquare.[29] But this was never a question in Hayford's mind, not after he'd heard God speak regarding his placement in the movement. If anything, this certainty of placement gave him confidence to explore afar in his transdenominational activities in the years ahead.

CHURCH GROWTH

The Church on the Way was growing in many ways.[30] In January 1972 they passed the 400 mark in attendance and had run out of room.[31] For a while in the spring of 1972, they thought about moving the Sunday worship service to Van Nuys High School but decided instead to go to two Sunday morning worship services that June.[32]

Dealing with growth was more than a matter of finding space; Hayford wanted new members to understand his approach to church life. In addition to the information conveyed during the regular teaching and preaching times and classes offered, Jack also used the Sunday bulletin strategically to help manage the influx of new people.[33]

From today's perspective, it may seem odd that church bulletins became an important communication tool. Starting in 1972, the bulletins regularly carried one to three paragraphs of copy expressing the Church on the Way's philosophy of ministry to introduce people to the church's values. Though they were not signed at the beginning, Jack wrote them.

There was strong emphasis on being "a New Testament Church," which was a frequent heading. Under it, five commitments were listed: "Adherence to the Word of God," "Exaltation of the Lord Jesus Christ," "The Ministry of the Holy Spirit," "Interdenominational Fellowship," and "The Ministry of the Believer."[34] Each one of these was further elaborated.

Jack's aim for a balanced ministry is evident in his frequent references to being a church that, in its ministries, particularly as it touches supernatural activities, does so in a "sane, sensitive, sensible, and scriptural" manner. Other bulletin articles welcomed people to the church's "experiment in New Testament Christianity" and the congregation's quest to "find the fulfillment in life which the first century believers experienced."[35]

Besides calling for a restoration of New Testament experience, the bulletin identified the church with the Charismatic Renewal.[36] For example, a February 1973 note mentioned the church as a part of the "fresh breeze blowing today" as God was renewing the church.[37] Another article spoke of the "mighty surging of the Holy Spirit through the Church around the World" and the church's readiness to "move in this contemporary revival God is pouring out."[38]

Usually, no reference was directly made to Foursquare in these small articles, but that connection was never hidden. All through Hayford's tenure at the church, every bulletin carried a title or banner with the name First Foursquare Church of Van Nuys, even after the slogan name was given. A recurring article that ran every few weeks mentioned the congregation's association with the International Church of the Foursquare Gospel. Far more prominent, however, was the name "The Church on the Way," which was what everyone regularly called the church.

Throughout 1972 and into 1973, the small bulletin articles increased in length. Jack started signing them in April 1973.[39] These left-hand pages were a means for Hayford to communicate to the church and were an important part of how he pastored the church, particularly once it became large.[40] He used the articles to rally the congregation, and he frequently shared personal stories. In church gatherings, he made regular reference to what he had written and asked every ongoing participant of the church to make sure they read the left-hand page each week.

In January 1975, Hayford titled his weekly column "By the Way," and it was an important feature of his leadership for twenty-four years.[41] The "By the Way" columns highlighted Hayford's writing talents, and years later they were utilized in devotional books Hayford wrote. For Jack, the bulletin articles were an important discipleship tool, as well.[42]

MERGING STREAMS

The congregation's growth did not come primarily from within Classical Pentecostalism. Beginning in 1971, most of the growth was coming from two streams: people impacted by the Charismatic movement and young people associated with the Jesus People movement.[43]

The first growth spurt that had occurred back in January 1970, after Hayford had heard God say, "I have set Myself to do a great work," had come almost entirely from a group of over forty Charismatic Christians who had been forced out of a nearby Baptist congregation. After the "glory" incident a year later, the same trend continued, as Charismatics from many different places found their way to the church.

Among them was a Hollywood and music celebrity named Pat Boone.[44] Boone was the first of a number of well-known people from the entertainment industry who would come to associate with the Church on the Way.[45] Boone and his wife, Shirley, came to the church because Shirley's sisters were among the group that had been forced out of the Baptist church after being baptized with the Spirit and speaking in tongues. They told Pat and Shirley about Hayford and the congregation, and they felt they would fit in.

Pat and Shirley knew firsthand the pain and trauma of being unwelcome in a church. After they had been filled with the Holy Spirit, their Church of Christ congregation "disfellowshipped" them.[46] Soon, the Boones were holding Bible studies in their Hollywood home, and these were attended by personalities in the entertainment world, including Glenn Ford, Doris Day, Priscilla Presley, and Zsa Zsa Gabor.[47] The Boones and their four daughters found a spiritual home in Van Nuys, where Pat would later serve as an elder and become a close friend to Jack.

The "Jesus People" were part of the generational revival that began in the late 1960s as hippies became Christians en masse. One of the early centers of the Jesus People movement was Southern California. Chuck Smith, a Life Bible College graduate and onetime Foursquare pastor, became the patriarch of the Jesus People movement, with his nondenominational church, Calvary Chapel in Costa Mesa.[48] But the Jesus People were by no means limited to Calvary Chapel and the churches that they established. They were all over Southern California, and many found a home at the Church on the Way.[49]

When the church began to mushroom after 1972, many people who attended the Church on the Way were not Charismatic or Pentecostal and were baptized in the Holy Spirit only after becoming a part of the congregation.[50] Most significant were the large number of those who were not yet Christians when they first attended services at the church and were later converted. Actor Dean Jones and his wife, Lori, were a part this group. They made a public confession of Christ in February 1974 after Hayford had extended an invitation in a service.[51]

With all the growth the church was experiencing, Jack was convinced that the church needed to steward the blessing God had given them. He believed the growth was related to his and his core leaders' willingness to follow the prophetic direction God was giving them.[52]

He felt as well that the blessing of God was conditioned on the congregation "walking humbly before Him, and [honoring] Him with worship and praise."[53] This drove him to continually remind the congregation that renewal could never be taken for granted.[54] They must fight to maintain a childlike dependence on the Lord.

Jack also had to face his own insecurities about the church's growth. While he was not focused solely on numbers, he did think they were an important indicator about whether or not God was working in their midst. He dealt with his anxiety about the issue largely through personal prayer and worship in his own times of devotion.

This meant pouring out his heart to God as honestly as he knew how. Six months into the growth surge of 1971, he was sitting at his piano singing and found himself wondering "what it would be like if the all [the] blessing stopped. What if people go off on vacation and, with the summer coming, the grace upon the church faded?" It was an awful thought, and he was afraid.

> And I sat there that day and I said, "Lord I really need to
> confess to you that I'm scared that the thing we've tasted
> won't keep happening." And the Lord didn't answer me.
> But I can remember there coming to my mind, the words
> of Moses when he said, "Lord if your presence doesn't go
> with us, then we don't want to go any further." As I sat
> there at the piano that day, I took a paper and pencil and
> began to write down …
>
> > If Thy Presence go not with me,
> > Let me not go on from here.[55]

Jack had previously faced times of depression, financial need, want, and deprivation, and through it all he had believed there had never been a time when God had not blessed him. Now he was facing another trial, and it felt big at that moment.[56] Sitting at the piano that day, he thought about those difficult times in the past and knew he could still trust God in this situation.[57] Jack worshipped and prayed his way through the fears of that 1971 summer, and the church kept growing.[58]

Hayford later told the congregation this story. It was this transparency in his teaching/preaching ministry that was part of the reason the church was growing the way it was. Hayford's willingness to share his struggles and sins (the near-adultery story in chapter 6, for example) endeared him to people. His truth-telling helped people identify with him in the common struggles of life.[59] This was something he was learning in the early years at the Church on the Way.[60]

It was also an outflow of the "holy humanness" he was enjoying in his Wednesday prayer times with Charter and Shoemake. It was not some ploy to get people to like him—the self-effacing style was built on solid theological ground. Jack was certain of "the solidarity of the believer's position before the Father through Jesus' justifying work on the cross."[61] This certainty of the Father's love in Christ gave him courage to be honest about his life.

> Once I believed seriously in God's patience toward me, as a child seeking honestly to grow up in His will, I was emboldened to share with those I led some of my stumblings and failures as I followed Jesus. Episodes in my life began to become part of the learning process for the congregation. My teaching continued to be rooted in God's Word, but now could illustrate its lessons with the cases of my slowness to learn, inability to understand, stupid sinning and impatient presumptions.[62]

His approach bred similar openness among the people as well, and they learned to share honestly their failures. Over the years, Jack received hundreds of letters from people thanking him for his openness, saying that it had helped them realize that their struggles and failings were no different from his. The congregation was discovering the secret of true *koinonia*: transparent fellowship in the Holy Spirit.[63]

Chapter 10

ESTABLISHING FOUNDATIONS

A DIFFERENT KIND OF PENTECOSTAL

A major factor contributing to the congregation's diverse growth was the thoughtful manner in which Jack expressed his Pentecostal beliefs. With the growing acceptance of expressions of Pentecostal practice today, it is important to remember that in the 1970s many Christians still believed Pentecostals were doctrinally shallow and often fanatical.

Although this caricature had some basis in fact, it was never true of the majority of Pentecostals. What was true from their early twentieth-century beginnings is that Pentecostals believed the experience of being baptized with the Holy Spirit was at the heart of Christian life. Doctrine mattered, but theological formulations should not take priority over or diminish the importance of Christian experience. Modern Pentecostalism is a theologically diverse missionary movement and a "Spirit-centered, miracle-affirming, praise-oriented version" of contemporary Christianity.[1]

Many evangelicals were troubled by what they saw as an overemphasis on the experiential side of Pentecostalism. Compounding the problem was the perception that the Pentecostal emphasis on being filled with the Holy Spirit made those who didn't have that experience feel like they were "second-class" Christians.

The advent of the Charismatic movement had led to occasional church conflicts and splits over how one should understand what it means to be "filled with the Holy Spirit," an often synonymous term for baptism with the Holy Spirit. Pentecostals and Charismatics could be particularly zealous and consequently strident in their advocacy for a "Spirit-filled" life. In the early 1970s, the idea of the continuing presence of supernatural spiritual gifts, especially speaking with tongues, still stirred heated controversy among Christians.

From his early days at the Church on the Way, Jack was very aware of these issues and, as we have seen, he shared his own concerns. He believed that the perceived excesses in Pentecostalism were keeping believers from experiencing all that God had for their lives, and he set himself to not back away from Pentecostal belief and practice but to clearly root beliefs and practices in Scripture. Jack carefully explained Pentecostal practices in ways that helped people more readily accept not only their validity but to be open to them in their own experience.

Jack was unapologetic about the importance of Charismatic activity in the congregation. In a fashion that reflected Aimee Semple McPherson's more moderate "middle of the road" approach to Pentecostal practice, Jack welcomed and encouraged the exercise of the spiritual gifts such as prophecy and tongues and interpretation in the worship services at the church, but he was intent on not allowing disorder. He told the church that a key to "retaining the purest form of the Spirit's working is *solid teaching*, helping the revived believer to understand what is happening around them, to them, and as it expands through them."[2]

In other words, Hayford provided clear instruction on *how* the congregation was to function in spiritual gifts. This instruction often came ad hoc during the worship times at the church—the portion of the service when Charismatic gifts most frequently manifested—and also in his regular teaching/preaching times in the services.[3] He was very careful to explain any manifestation of spiritual gifts when it happened, usually talking from biblical passages where the *charismata* were mentioned.[4]

Jack was also willing to confront anything he felt was disorderly. He would stop or correct a prophecy or message in tongues if it was given too loudly or if he or one of the church's leaders thought the content was unbiblical or given in a judgmental or condemning manner.[5] This approach gave the congregation a sense of safety and protection from the fanaticism that many associated with Pentecostals and Charismatics. In 1972, he wrote to the church in the Sunday bulletin that the "*manifestation of the Holy Spirit through the gifts is governed by specific guidelines which maintain order and beauty (I Cor. 14:33, 40).*"[6]

Jack was adjusting how he understood and taught about speaking with tongues during the early years at the Church on the Way. His approach reflected his growing concern that many people resisted speaking with tongues because Classical Pentecostals had made it the marker or proof of Spirit baptism.

That believers needed to be baptized with the Holy Spirit was a given for Jack. The issue was how tongues related to the experience (there is little doubt that his relationships with Charismatics, many of whom interpreted Spirit baptism within their historic theological traditions, were having some influence on how he regarded the experience). In later years, he acknowledged that it became increasingly difficult for him to insist that one had to speak in tongues to validate Spirit baptism.

Significantly, since coming to Van Nuys, Jack was exercising tongues in his own private prayer times more than ever. The challenge before him was to help the church see speaking with tongues not so much as evidence of Spirit baptism but rather as a prayer language. Although Jack believed that tongues should be expected when one is baptized in the Spirit, he was bothered by the "pushiness" that characterized how some Pentecostals insisted that tongues were the initial, physical evidence of Spirit baptism, so much so that they would deny that a person was really baptized in the Spirit if he or she had not spoken with tongues.[7]

He was also concerned that an overreaction to this approach could lead to a lack of sufficient emphasis on the importance of speaking with tongues for prayer and praise. Still, he was increasingly unwilling to make the case that speaking with tongues was "the sign" of Spirit baptism. In a December 1973 message, he told the church:

> I declared something just about five weeks ago in a message ... that I never thought I would hear myself say if you asked me five years ago.... It is not a lack of conviction— not a lack of commitment, but a perspective on what I believe we need to see.... *And I've come to the place today where I am not ready to say, "to be baptized with the Holy Spirit, you'll have to speak with tongues."*[8]

Hayford was not saying that speaking in tongues was secondary or optional. This was made clear as he continued. Arguing from Saint Paul's statement in 1 Corinthians 14:5a, that "I would like every one of you to speak in tongues (NIV)," Hayford asserted that this verse revealed the "mind of the Spirit that all speak with tongues."[9]

He went on to say that he believed that everyone who was baptized in the Spirit would eventually speak with tongues or at least potentially could speak with tongues. But he made the very important qualification that they would not necessarily speak with tongues *concurrently* with their experience of Spirit baptism.[10] Instead, speaking in tongues could be experienced later if a person was open to all that came with Spirit-fullness. His own experience as a young man was an example of this.

In the same message, Jack argued for the value of tongues for prayer and used the term that became for him a synonym for speaking with tongues: "spiritual language."[11] Jack believed the reason the Holy Spirit had inspired Luke to place such primacy on tongues at Pentecost and throughout the book of Acts had to do with the importance of glossolalia for prayer, intercession, spiritual warfare, and worship.[12]

In the coming years, Hayford would adjust this schema and articulate his argument more carefully, but the core of his approach to speaking in tongues was in place in 1973.[13] Throughout his ministry at the Church on the Way, he continued to stress the necessity of Spirit baptism and never argued against initial evidence, but he reframed the argument in order to make the gift more desirable to his diverse audience in Van Nuys.[14]

His changing understanding to tongues as *the* evidence of Spirit baptism undoubtedly contributed to some of the questions that had arisen in Foursquare regarding his ministry at the Church on the Way and whether he was "fully" Pentecostal.[15]

PRAYER AND THE KINGDOM

In the fall of 1973, the Watergate scandal increasingly dominated the news as Richard Nixon's involvement with the 1972 burglary was the subject of a very public investigation. Six months earlier, President Nixon and his wife had attended the wedding of Mrs. Nixon's nephew, twenty-one-year-old Richard Ryan, which was held at the Church on the Way, with Hayford officiating.[16]

While Hayford never engaged in any significant political advocacy or personally endorsed candidates during his Van Nuys pastorate, he did write Nixon subsequent to the March 31 wedding, and after thanking him for the honor of his presence at the ceremony, he assured the president "that our congregation bears you and the leaders of our government up in constant prayer."[17] Nixon sent back a signed, personal note thanking Hayford for the prayer, acknowledging "the very great test" his presidency was enduring.[18]

Hayford's assurance of ongoing prayer was not an empty statement. Ever since the Wednesday night prayer meeting had been established after Jack came to the church, there had been a growing emphasis on intercession and prayer for national leaders. This was continuing in the fall of 1973. In the Wednesday, December 5, prayer meeting, a strong word of prophecy was given:

> The Lord is calling this congregation to a ministry of intercession for your land. You are to commit yourself to this ministry as though there were no other church praying for the nation. I do not say there are no others, but I command you to commit yourself as though there were no others. I am calling you to rise in faith, believing My Word: I will heal this land, but you must pray.[19]

Prophecies were not an unusual manifestation of the Charismatic gifts at the church, but this one was different and seemed to carry greater authority, and it was very specific about the assignment. Jack felt a "compulsion to exhort at length—spontaneously and extemporaneously—on the subject opened by the Holy Spirit's prompting." He also wanted to make sure the people understood that the charge "to pray as though there were no other church praying" was not some kind of elitist call. The point was that they needed to pray with passion because America was facing a great challenge at the time.[20]

Jack led the congregation in obedient response. In January 1974, they changed the Wednesday night prayer meeting start time to 7:14 p.m. to signify their commitment to the principles of 2 Chronicles 7:14 that instructed Israel to humble itself and pray for the healing of their land.[21] A significant portion of the meeting was devoted to praying for the United States.

Another response to the prophecy was that Jack embarked on several weeks of intense Bible study on the subject of intercession. This resulted in a prayer series that started in the spring. Over the next year, the teachings developed into a major prayer thrust for the congregation.[22] Increasingly, they saw themselves as a church charged to pray with great commitment.

This focus in prayer was tied to Jack's emphasis on the kingdom of God, which was increasingly becoming his theological matrix. He believed that prayer and worship made way for and invited the rule of God on earth.

The teaching emphasis in 1974 and 1975 eventually became Hayford's first nationally published book, *Prayer Is Invading the Impossible*, published in 1977. The book presented his theology of prayer, specifically his view of intercession, and the church's corresponding responsibility. In it, Hayford summarized the message of the Bible in eight statements and demonstrated how thoroughly the kingdom of God influenced his views on prayer and ecclesiology.[23] Hayford believed that the key to understanding prayer is to see its relationship to Christ's mission and the overall theme of the kingdom of God in Scripture. He wrote:

1. God created man to enjoy earth and inhabit it as a king does his domain, unhindered by any power that would diminish the quality of life God had given.

2. Man's rule of earth—God-given and God-ordained—was lost through disobedience. The control of the planet was forfeited to Satan, whose goal is to deprive man of God's intended purpose and destroy all hope of recovery.

3. God established Israel to teach man His desire for man's recovered rulership. By renewed obedience to God, joyous and peaceful living may be realized—personally and nationally.

4. Against a backdrop of man's failure to learn this lesson, God entered the human scene. "The Word became flesh." The life, which was the light of man, shone into the darkness. The Word spoke.

5. He spoke consistently of a kingdom. "The kingdom of God is immediately at hand," Jesus proclaimed. He spoke authoritatively of the fact that the earth's original ruler—God—was available. If man would receive his King, he could enjoy a renewed dominion of peace and joy here and now.

6. For His claim to be God's Messiah, here to restore God's rule, He was crucified. But by a power unknown to man, the blood of the Cross became the means of breaking Satan's hold on the power of death. Jesus rose again and commissioned His forces (He called them "a Church") to bring His world of God's restoring rulership to bear upon the world of Satan's destroying rulership.

7. The ultimate message of the Bible is that Christ will return to drive out the last vestiges of Satan's operations on earth. But,

8. In the meantime, His Church has been commissioned to walk the pathway to restored rulership. Jesus has committed the "keys of the kingdom" to those who know and obey Him. These keys are fitted to:

   a. Stop hell's worst and insist on heaven's best.

   b. Unlock mankind's captives and shatter Satan's chains.[24]

Hayford saw prayer (including spiritual language), fasting, and worship as among the essential "kingdom keys" that open doors, allowing God's rule to crowd back darkness and break in upon humanity. If the church did not pray, then God would not act. He believed that God's redemptive purposes were realized in partnership with humankind.

He was advocating an "already but not yet" eschatological stance. There was a real "presence of the future" for the church to be experienced immediately, but the church must also await the full consummation of the kingdom at Christ's return. Hayford's perspectives made prayer a dynamic necessity personally and corporately.[25]

Jack at his typewriter

The prayer revival from 1973 to 1975 at the Church on the Way proved decisive for the congregation's future. Congregational fasts and special calls to prayer became commonplace.[26] Year after year, Jack would return to prayer themes in his teaching ministry at the church. Prayer became just as central to the life of the church as worship was.

Another important development of the prayer emphasis was the musical production *If My People*. Written by church members and musicians Jim and Carol Owens, *If My People* was a direct result of the church's emphasis on praying for a deeply troubled nation. The Owenses were inspired to write the musical after hearing Jack preach "Our Responsibility for America's Survival."[27] The musical, based on 2 Chronicles 7:14, was introduced in Los Angeles in September 1975 with 30,000 attending over three nights.[28] Pat Boone and actor Dean Jones were narrators. Over the next year, the

Church on the Way invested nearly $400,000 into the production that toured eighty-one cities across the nation.

If My People became a rallying point that served to unite believers around the nation to pray for America. Hayford has always believed that the Church on the Way's prayers and its investment in the musical helped heal the nation after the Watergate debacle.[29]

AS THE SPIRIT DIRECTS

By early 1974, attendance at the Church on the Way had exploded from 160 to over 1,000 in just two years, a rate of growth nearly unheard of at the time. Hayford was becoming well known outside the Foursquare movement and even better known within.[30] His travel schedule again ballooned with invitations to speak around California and the nation.[31]

With responsibilities of an expanding local church ministry, Hayford was scrambling to keep up. He was aided, both pastorally and administratively, by a strong support staff at the church. He was able—something he saw as a gift of divine grace—to find capable and willing coworkers, some of whom would work at the church for decades, to sustain the momentum of the growth.[32]

Hayford found himself traveling with some regularity to Reno, Nevada. A group of successful Charismatic businessmen had invited him to speak in Reno and began lobbying Hayford to start a church in the city, something he seriously considered.[33] While he knew the Lord had called him to Van Nuys, he wondered if the Church on the Way was to be more of a base for his expanding ministry, leaving one of the other pastors as the day-to-day leader, although Jack would remain the primary weekend speaker in Van Nuys.[34]

Part of this had to do with a prophecy the church had received in January 1972, in which the Lord had told them, "I will make you as the church at Antioch." They saw this as a call to be a ministry and sending center for the expansion of the kingdom of God.[35] In addition, Jack was trying to decide what to do with a word God had "whispered" to him in June 1972: "You're an apostle."[36] Did being an apostle mean he would be moving from place to place, with his primary base in Van Nuys?

It all came to a head in the fall of 1974. Jack was exhausted, and although he was now fairly certain that he would not move to Reno, he was still unsure about what to do with his widening personal ministry.[37] Well past midnight after returning from a ministry trip in October, Jack was praying in his living room chair at their Van Nuys house. Depleted and distraught, he knew things were not right in how he was scheduling his life, but he did not know what to do. He prayed, "I don't understand anything. I feel like a flop."[38] He recounts:

> As I sat in that chair, I knew there had to be an answer that I couldn't find on my own. I sensed a stirring in my spirit. The recollection of that moment is as clear as any memory of my life. I remember looking in the soft lamplight across the living room at the open doorway that led into the hall.
>
> Exhausted, choked up, and at my wit's end, I said right out loud, *"Jesus, I wish You'd walk through that door right now and tell me what I'm supposed to do!"*
>
> The funny thing is, I meant it. It was a real prayer. That's how desperate I was. I can't remember uttering anything like that before or since, but at the moment it was the cry of my heart....
>
> As it turned out, He didn't step through the doorway that night. I can't say I really *expected* Him to, because that's not the way the Lord usually answers such prayers. I didn't feel disappointed, let down, or neglected. I just felt the same as I had before I spoke the prayer. Heavy. Worried. Bone tired. Desperately desiring His intervention in my life.[39]

He went back to bed, and as he did, Anna woke up and softly said, "Jack, you're pushing yourself too hard."[40]

He went to work the next day as usual. But what happened that October day was highly unusual. After he arrived at the office, he found a note on his desk from one of the associate pastors at the church, Darryl Roberts.[41] While Roberts' letter to Jack was loving, it was pointed and specific, telling Jack that he thought he was "not walking in full obedience" to the Lord. The gist of the letter was that Jack needed to cut his travels back drastically.[42] A little later, Jack's secretary asked him if she could have a word with him and said almost the same thing Roberts had written. But there was more.

At an appointment later that afternoon, a fellow Foursquare pastor told Jack, "You are traveling too much."[43] This was still not the end of it. At 11:00 p.m. that evening, his father called from Oakland.[44] He told his son, "This is really different for me. As long as I have been filled with the Spirit and walked with Jesus, I've never had a word from the Lord to give anybody. But He's given me a word for you tonight. I want to deliver it right now." In the prophetic first person common in a Pentecostal understanding of prophecy, he told Jack:

> My son, I have taken you not from following the mules but I have taken you from the sheepcote. I have chosen you because of sincerity & love & obedience. Yes I have told you not once, not twice, but [three] times I would make you be heard. I have said I will do a great work in the valley in which you now live. I have chosen you for this work & now appoint you as my apostle to this valley. Be strong and of good courage. Be faithful to do the work of an apostle in the place I, even I, have put you.[45]

Jack was in shock. Jesus may not have personally walked through the door the previous night, but the answer to his desperate prayer could not have been clearer. In the coming months, Jack canceled a number of ministry trips and refocused his energies on the local church. He would stay in Van Nuys, pastoring the Church on the Way, and any future ministry would always be an outflow of his foremost call to the San Fernando Valley. He was there to stay.

By the end of 1974, the emphases that would characterize Jack Hayford's future ministry were in place. They would only be refined and clarified over the next twenty-five years of his pastorate. That is not to say there were no other significant events or teaching themes, as will be evident. But what was ahead was built on the foundation of the first five years of Hayford's tenure as the pastor of the Church on the Way, when he and a group of leaders sought God's will and learned to practice principles of prayer and worship.

Chapter 11

BUILDING BIG PEOPLE

AUTHENTICITY

The themes of worship, prayer, and the kingdom of God, so essential to the future of the Church on the Way, had much to do with who Jack Hayford was as a person and as a pastor. The man the people met in the pulpit was no different from the private Jack.

Despite all the stories he told about how God spoke to him or of his supernatural experiences, Jack never sensationalized them. His manner was decidedly "*un*mystical."[1] His teaching style was casual and conversational, and people felt he was talking to them personally. He also openly challenged any tendency toward trying to "be spiritual." In doing so, he wasn't addressing hypocrisy. Rather, he was

> referring to the labored efforts of some sincere people
> who mean to serve Jesus with all their hearts, and they do

too. But they feel obligated to communicate some special
aura of "godliness." The attempt at it comes through some
affected tone of voice, a glazed look to their eyes, a certain
posture of the head that appears to be trying to balance a
halo, a … well, just an altogether unnatural bearing that
tends to become at least humorous, and at worst, spooky.[2]

Anna Hayford was in some ways even more authentic than Jack. She
never hid her modest upbringing and was content being "a simple farm girl"
from Nebraska. Although her role was never as public as Jack's—something
both agreed gave her freedom to focus on their children and home life—for
years she regularly led a hymn in at least one service each weekend. Jack also
made sure she was very much his ministry partner. As He had with Jack,
God had spoken to Anna not long after coming to the church and told her
He just wanted her to "love the people." She was good at it.

Anna was honest to a fault and she readily acknowledged the adjustments she had to make socially in mixing with the high-profile celebrities and
professionals at the church. "I have had to work harder than most at feeling
comfortable with people who come from different socio-economic levels
than I've come from. If I think too much about some of the social situations
we find ourselves in, it can be mentally overpowering. I have found that when
we get down to the basics, we are all very much alike, no matter who we are."
That was the Anna the congregation came to know and love.[3]

This absence of any "airs" of pious spirituality in Jack's and Anna's lives
fit well in Southern California in the 1970s. Disaffected young people,
especially those associated with the Jesus People movement, valued authenticity as did many people in mainline churches who had been turned
off by religion but were newly touched by the Holy Spirit through the
Charismatic movement.

Those coming to the church from the entertainment industry knew
more than most that "all that glitters isn't gold." They appreciated the

authenticity they sensed. People were hungry for something that was "real," and Pastor Jack and the Church on the Way provided a home for these seekers. It was an environment where they could grow without the religious excesses some associated with Pentecostalism or the ecclesiasticism of more formal church traditions.

Jack preaches at the Church on the Way

The openness and honesty in Jack's preaching added to this attractive authenticity. His approach was an intentional contrast to his previous practice before coming to the church. Jack's preparation for ministry was in an era when ministers were taught to avoid injecting themselves into their sermons. He knew that

> exponents of classical preaching either discourage or altogether speak against any use of personal episodes in the preacher's sermon. Some consider this to be "calling attention to yourself, rather than to the Word of God," and attempt to ennoble this denial of self-disclosure as though it were a form of righteousness. This not only removes the accessibility of our using the most practical illustrations we have—where we have had to come to grips with seeing

God's Word incarnated in our own lives as pastors, but it
flies in the face of Scripture.

The entire mood of God's Word is candid, forthright, transparent and self-disclosing. Uncompromising
honesty revealing human failure not only abounds in
Old Testament narratives, but also considers the frankness with which Jesus' own struggles are recorded in
the Gospels ("Father, if possible take this cup"; "My
God ... why have you forsaken me?"). Notwithstanding
the spiritual dynamic and intellectual brilliance we see
in Paul's persona, who can deny that we are most com-
forted to hear his pained heart cry when feeling rejected
or alone?[4]

Hayford felt that, if the Scriptures were unflinching in addressing
human sin and struggle, how could he do otherwise? He also filled his
sermons with his dry sense of humor, laughing at himself and his foibles.
A close associate remarked that Jack was "more likely to share his own
failures, struggles, and shortcomings—not his triumphs."[5] His was an
"earthy" spirituality that was a purposeful counter to pretentious behavior of those wanting to seem very spiritual, something he had observed
over his years in ministry and that troubled him. For Jack, Jesus was the
supreme example.

There is, in whatever one studies of Jesus, everything of
humanity and nothing of superficiality; everything of
godliness and nothing of religiosity. Jesus ministered the
joy, life, health and glory of His Kingdom in the most
practical, tasteful ways. There is nothing of the flawed
habit of hollow holiness or pasted-on piety that characterizes much of the Christianity the world encounters.[6]

For all the humor and honesty that laced Jack's preaching, he was always passionate, and there were times when he confronted the congregation head-on. He wasn't afraid to bring correction or to call the people to deeper commitment. He could also raise his voice and boom like a good Pentecostal preacher when he felt it necessary.

Jack and Anna kneeling while leading worship

What was clear to everyone in the congregation was that his messages were biblically sound and demonstrated a theological depth not usually associated with the stereotypical Pentecostal preaching. It was also clear that his messages were the product of both prayer and preparation. Most importantly, his illustrations and stories made it clear he was seeking to live what he taught.

He was learning how to disciple in a whole new way that put more emphasis on the example leaders set for the people. He believed his own transformation was essential to seeing the transformation of the people whom God had entrusted to him pastorally. Jack realized that his authority was not derived from his position as pastor but was "rooted in the Word and communicated in the power of the Holy Spirit."[7] What he taught others to do needed to be happening in his own life. As important as his teaching ministry was to developing disciples, simply giving people more information was not enough. What was needed was incarnation.

"INCARNATING" GOD'S WORD

In December 1973, and again with greater detail in 1975, Jack preached from the Annunciation passage in Luke's Gospel (1:26–38), in which the angel Gabriel announces to Mary that she would conceive and give birth to the Savior of the world.[8]

Jack saw the passage as more than just a historical account. He taught that it was an analogy of how God's promises in Scripture must transform believers' lives. Just as Mary conceived by the Holy Spirit the physical Christ in her womb, so God wants to form the likeness of His Son in the hearts of believers through the living presence of the Holy Spirit. The Apostle Paul made a similar analogy when he told the Galatians he labored in prayer for them that Christ might be "formed in you" (Galatians 4:19).[9]

Mary received from the angel a promise that she would give birth to God's purposes and that the world would be changed because of what God did in and through her. The parallel for Jack was that God was calling those who believe into genuine transformation and to "receive the promise of [God's] Word within them and carry it until it gives birth to his purposes and changes the world around them."[10]

The key issue for Hayford was faith; Mary was asked by God to believe in the impossible: that a virgin could conceive. God was physically incarnating the Word in Mary. Hayford argued that Christians must believe that God's promises will just as surely live in them spiritually.[11]

> The God who chose a virgin girl as the avenue through
> whom He would miraculously give mankind His greatest
> gift is still working that "Mary" kind of miracle today.

That is to say: What the Almighty did then in the physical/ biological realm—supernaturally begetting life, promise and hope where none existed—He is fully ready and able to do now in virtually any realm.

He does this same kind of thing today—in marriages, in businesses, in hearts, minds and souls. Where life or love, hope or strength, promise or patience have disappeared—or never been present at all—He comes to offer the Mary miracle. It's a timeless kind of wonder that is still being worked by our changeless heavenly Father.[12]

He did not downplay the "astounding physical reality of the supernatural conception Mary experienced," but he suggested that "the Mary miracle holds the promised potential of heaven's entry into all our life circumstances."[13] Jack was arguing that biblical truth must be incarnated—internalized and integrated—in one's behavior and lifestyle, in contrast to the mere intellectual comprehension of biblical truth. The Holy Spirit comes to make the Scriptures live in the believer. This was what Hayford always aimed for in what he called "incarnational preaching."

The Mary Miracle messages became some of the most widely distributed of Hayford's recorded teachings, and they illustrated a theme he would continue to preach widely afterward. The teaching was an expression of Jack's quest to see the Bible as more than a repository of facts and propositions about God, but also as a living instrument of the Holy Spirit that mediates God's presence as the text continues to speak today. It was foundational to the idea of "building big people."

DURABLE DISCIPLESHIP

"God hasn't called us to build big churches, but to build big people."[14] Jack borrowed those words from fellow Foursquare pastor and colleague

Jerry Cook, and it aptly described the discipleship emphasis that aimed to develop the ministry of every believer at the Church on the Way. If they achieved that goal, growth would take care of itself.

Jack felt charged not simply to feed the congregation through good Bible teaching as its pastor but also to lead those he pastored into spiritual maturity, which meant staying in touch with God's prophetic direction for the church.[15] His "feeding and leading" role created significant demands on his time and energy.[16]

The daily operations of the church were increasingly handled by the staff and volunteer leaders, something Jack had always worked toward. Nevertheless, he was the one leading the church. As before, much of the ministry development was a result of his sense of being directed by God.

Early in 1972, as the church was beginning to grow faster, Hayford was on a ministry trip to Illinois. It was bitterly cold but he was on a walk and "entirely unprepared for what would become one of the most important assignments" he would ever receive.[17] It had to do with training leaders.

"An encounter with the Holy Spirit ... burned these words on my heart": *Begin to meet with the men, and I will raise up elders and servants to accomplish My purpose* [at the church].[18] He returned to California and through a personal letter "issued an invitation to men of the congregation" asking them to begin meeting with him.

Thirty-five men responded and attended the first meeting with Jack. These meetings were of highest priority for him because they were a conduit to develop and release leaders for the church from that time on.[19] The monthly Men's Growth Seminars, as they were later called, remained front and center in Jack's ministry, and he trained thousands of men in the years that followed.

Training men was just another part of a model that was developing as a result of the priorities Hayford had learned at the 1968 Assemblies of God evangelism congress. This model had been central to his first years at the church: ministry to the Lord, ministry to one another, and ministry to the

world. Instead of the more traditional approach, in which the church building was the primary "place" for evangelism, in which people were invited
to "attend" meetings, at the Church on the Way, evangelism centered on

> the *formation of the individual believer* as the church serves
> "making disciples" as its reason for being. Those growing
> disciples, cultivated as sensitive, ministering members of
> Christ's body, become effective at touching others in the
> context of their daily life at home or in the marketplace—
> demonstrating the life, love and power of Jesus. They gain a
> platform for their witness by their character and skill where
> they live and work, and learn to move into contact situa-
> tions with unbelievers in ways that introduce the power,
> love and truth of Christ. Discipled unto confidence and
> equipped with spiritual power, the "body" evangelizes—
> doing "the work of the ministry" (Ephesians 4:11–16).[20]

Jack was convinced that this was the most effective way to penetrate
a culture that was increasingly disinterested in attending church. It was
also "an approach that will survive time and circumstance" because it was
a "biblical, non-culturally dependent model," rather than a time-bound
"program" of evangelism. This model was simple obedience to Jesus' Great
Commission (Matthew 28:18–20).[21]

Discipleship was at the heart of being a pastor who equipped believers
for ministry, and Jack knew he was called to the demanding task of shaping
a congregation of "durable" disciples.[22] He strategically used his teaching
opportunities to accomplish this task, outlining a three-year plan of the key
concepts that he needed to teach regularly and systematically if people were
to mature in Christ.[23]

The 1970s were a time when most churches still had services on Sunday
morning, Sunday night, and Wednesday evenings. The Church on the Way

was no different, and Jack called the congregation to commit to attend all three services as much as possible. It was not unusual for Jack to teach ninety-minute messages in each of the Sunday and Wednesday evening services.

Decades later, discipleship was still central to his understanding of pastoral leadership. He wrote in 2007 that "without discipleship, we are at risk of garnering believers in Jesus while not growing stable, committed, empowered agents of Christ. Jesus spoke of people who 'for Joy' lay claim to faith, but do not endure. They wither when trials or pressure come (See Mark 4:7, 17)—and Christians are facing an increase of both in our world."[24]

GOD'S IMAGE BEARERS

Jack Hayford's commitment to discipling the congregation was inseparable from his understanding of the significance of people in God's creation. Every human being was created with God-given potential, in Jack's eyes, because God at the beginning "delegated the stewardship of earth's affairs" to humanity as His image bearers.

"Genesis 1:26–3:24 describes the entire sequence of events from God's decision to create humankind—to give them (the first pair) dominion over all God's creation and set them in a garden paradise, to the tragedy of their disobedience and fall from their original state and their eventual banishment from the garden."[25]

Convinced that human beings were uniquely created in the image of God, Jack believed that God's image was marred or defaced by the fall, but it had not been erased. He disliked the term *total depravity* in describing the human condition because it suggested that humanity was without any worth.[26] However lost and broken people were because of the consequences of sin, they were still capable of enormous creativity and virtue. Of course, salvation was available only through Jesus Christ as Lord and Savior.

Jack was committed to a generous view of the human condition because it was rooted in the creation story, which he felt made absolutely clear the high destiny God had in mind for every human being. This meant every person had inherent dignity and worth before God. But sin had entered the world, leaving humanity estranged from their Creator. Jack's goal was to "convince people of the greatness of God's heart for them and his purpose toward them."[27] Despite humanity's flight from God, their Creator was reaching to them through the gospel message.

This perspective shaped his ministry in and out of the pulpit. Although Jack rarely preached evangelistic sermons, in almost every service he invited those who were not yet believers to open their lives to Jesus. His invitations to receive Christ usually emphasized God's love and the hope for a better life.

Hayford never played down sin or its destructiveness, but neither did he focus on how bad people were as sinners. The gospel, *euangelion,* was truly "good news," and Jack declared it as a message of recovery and restoration for broken lives and the vanquishing of the power of Satan. Only through Christ could their deepest longings and highest dreams be realized.

In a message on the kingdom of God in September 1973, his understanding is clear regarding the good news of the inbreaking of God's reign in the Messiah. He declared in almost one breath

> that another rulership is entering the dominion of man …
> that where hell has been ruling, heaven is going to begin
> to take over … where you've been enslaved there's going to
> come liberation … where your inheritance and your God
> appointed destiny as a person of authority and purpose in
> the will of God has been smashed, where you have been
> beguiled by the serpent and where there's come weakness
> in your own flesh, there will come a freedom and there will
> come a flow for what the living God has ordained for you.
> Your lot, your appointed dimension of possession was not

to be overruled and smashed and besmirched by the powers of hell but the dimension of your life was to be one where you could walk in the love and light of God. You're made in the image of God and the Lord said that the serpent which has come to squeeze you and wrap around you and reshape you and conform you and mold you into his pattern of this world ... his back shall be broken, his head shall be smashed by the seed of the woman, even the virgin born Son of God, one born not of man but one born of God, so that the living God could come and rule again and establish new rulership and those born of Him, as many as receive Him, He gave power to become sons and daughters of God and they would move in His life-flow and become a people who wherever they went the serpent has to look out because they tread on serpents and scorpions, and wherever their feet go the powers of hell begin to be broken.[28]

This was the "good news" that Jack was preaching, and people were responding, opening their lives to Jesus.

BEARING WITNESS

Jack's more hopeful view of fallen humanity helped him reach people in the arts and entertainment world of Southern California. As a composer and musician himself, Jack had great appreciation for the talents and gifts of the actors and musicians who were coming to the church. Kathie Lee Gifford remembers how much Jack encouraged those in show business to see the entertainment world as their missionary field. He understood and respected their callings and celebrated their gifts.

The relationships Jack had with entertainment workers brought opportunities to share the good news he was preaching in more personal ways.

He could be very direct, but he always did so with genuine compassion and concern. Singer and actress Stormie Omartian tells of her encounter with Jack before she became a Christian. She was asked by Jimmy and Carol Owens to sing on a recording they were making and was at a rehearsal at their home.

The Owenses were committed members at the Church on the Way and invited Jack to drop by the rehearsal, where they introduced Stormie to their pastor. Jack asked her a few questions regarding her relationship with God. She responded "with a mystical spiel about how my occult practices had taught me to commune with a higher power through meditation and belief in a creative force. My New Age explanation did not impress him in the least, and he made some very direct statements about Jesus being Lord and the only way to God."

Jack told her she was "ignorant," but it wasn't hostile—just direct. As always he was careful to explain his choice of words. "'You are an intelligent person, not stupid,' he said. 'By ignorant I mean you are unknowing of, or ignoring, what it is you need.' His words made me feel better, but the conversation ended when it was clear I was not open to anything he was saying."[29]

Over a year later, Stormie was reintroduced to Jack by a friend. By then, her life had "spiraled downhill" and she was seriously considering suicide. Knowing something of her struggles, Stormie's Christian friend arranged a lunch meeting so they could talk with Jack. The conversation lasted nearly two hours.

This wasn't like her first encounter with Jack. This time, she was honest with him about many of her struggles and she "hung on every word" as he talked about the Lord. Afterward, Jack had them go with him to his church office, where he gave Stormie three books, one of which was C. S. Lewis' famous *The Screwtape Letters*, a satirical take on the devil's deceitful ways.

The book was extremely important in helping Stormie see the reality of the occult and its destructive impact on her life. More importantly, it helped her see how she "could triumph victoriously over the plans of evil and fulfill God's plans for [her] life instead." When her friend took her back to meet with Jack a week later, Jack asked Stormie if she wanted to receive Jesus as her Savior. She said yes and the three of them prayed together as she committed her life to Jesus. After leaving the office, she "felt hope for the first time that I could remember." Although it would be a process in finding healing for her brokenness, her journey in Christ had begun.

She started attending the Van Nuys church and growing in discipleship. Stormie, single at the time, had met musician and music producer Michael Omartian earlier before she was a Christian but ran into him again at a Sunday morning worship service at the Church on the Way. Michael, already a believer, was attending for the first time. The two started dating and were married a year later. Both their careers soared in the years that followed, Michael winning three Grammys in 1980 and Stormie writing bestselling books on prayer with millions of copies sold. For Jack, seeing God's redeeming grace in people like Stormie was at the heart of his ministry and being "agents" of the kingdom of God.

Long before the term *missional* came into wide usage, Jack was leading the Church on the Way to be a missional church that looked to the people to do ministry as they simply lived out their daily lives. People really do matter to God; they are His image bearers and need the redemption offered in Jesus Christ. What Jack modeled in sharing Jesus with Stormie was what God has called every believer to do. Perhaps many at the Church on the Way would not be as bold as Jack had been with Stormie, but they were nevertheless witnesses to their families, neighbors, schoolmates, and coworkers of the good news of Jesus' love for people. For Jack the whole church was to be part of God's redemption business. The Church on the Way kept growing.

Chapter 12

PASTOR *AND* APOSTLE

GROWING INFLUENCE

Although the Church on the Way had remodeled and expanded their sanctuary in August 1974, so that it seated over 500, they still needed three Sunday morning worship services to accommodate the congregation's growth.[1] More services were added, and from 1978 to 1981, five Sunday services were needed.

Even after completing construction of a new building with a 2,200-seat multipurpose auditorium, called the "Living Room," multiple services were still needed. They dedicated the new facility in June 1981, and by 1982 attendance had soared past 4,000. The Church on the Way was the fastest-growing church in the Foursquare denomination for much of the 1970s and into the 1980s.[2]

In the midst of the attention this brought, Hayford was sitting in his office at the church building.[3] He was not in prayer at the time, just staring at the wall, when God spoke to him: "The mantle of the leadership of the Foursquare movement has passed from Angelus Temple to this place." He "just sat there," not really knowing what to do with what he had heard.[4]

Jack told very few about this, always concerned that some might think he was claiming a privileged position for himself or the church. He didn't think what God had said suggested in any way that he was somehow the *de facto* "leader of the movement." Rather, he believed it signaled that the historic grace that had made the Temple a "kind of center of gravity" for so many years was now on the Church on the Way.

Jack also didn't think what God spoke diminished the historic significance of Angelus Temple or its centrality in the Foursquare Church identity. It was more a confirmation of the remarkable growth the Van Nuys congregation was experiencing and the increasing prominence in Foursquare that came with it.[5] Jack realized as well that there were other churches experiencing similar spiritual renewal and growth.

Two good friends were pastoring churches in Foursquare and getting much attention. Roy Hicks Jr.'s congregation, Faith Center in Eugene, Oregon, and Jerry Cook's congregation in Gresham, Oregon, were growing rapidly, as well. The three men talked frequently by phone and spoke with some regularity at conferences and events at each other's churches. Still, the Church on the Way was getting more notice beyond the Foursquare movement, and Jack's influence was expanding in scope.

EXPANDING MINISTRY

By the mid-'70s, Jack Hayford had three arenas of ministry. The natural center of his ministry after the 1974 Reno experience was clearly as pastor of the Church on the Way. The late 1970s and early 1980s were very demanding in that role. In the thirteen years from 1969 to 1982, the tiny congregation of eighteen members had become one of the most well-known churches in America.[6] He and his leadership team were constantly faced with facility and parking challenges. The church was landlocked at their Sherman Way location despite efforts to buy surrounding properties whenever they came available.

In 1972, as the congregation's growth accelerated, they had explored the possibility of purchasing land elsewhere and building on the outskirts of the area, as many growing churches were doing. But in May, the issue was settled when in a meeting of the church council, a prophecy was given that said, "Break out to right hand and the left. You are to stay here."[7] They were called to stay in their Van Nuys location; it would require patience as for years they purchased one piece of property after another to provide parking and a site for the building completed in 1981.

In the spring of 1972, Jack and the church's elders also received a word of prophecy that told them they were to build the church's pastoral and staff teams from within the congregation. Already this had been the case with leaders like Chuck Shoemake and Paul Charter. For years, key leaders who had been discipled under Jack's teaching had been hired and had become vital not only to the church's growth but to Jack's release to serve the broader church. Shoemake and Charter, so important to Jack's first three years at the church, both left in 1972 to pastor other congregations, but others had been trained and were ready to take their place.

By 1975, three men were part of the pastoral staff at the church, each of whom had been at the church almost from when Jack had first come. Darrel Roberts served with Jack until 1985, and John Farmer and Max Lile pastored with Jack until he stepped aside in 1999, and they continued to serve afterward.[8]

These men and the others who would join the pastoral team were essential to the stability and excellence that characterized the ministries at the Church on the Way. The demands of rapid growth would eventually mean that not every member of the pastoral staff would come from within the church, but it was always the primary way the pastoral team and staff expanded.

Jack's second arena of ministry was within the Foursquare Church. With the Church on the Way by far the denomination's largest church, Hayford's voice in the denomination became increasingly significant. Most of the earlier questions about Hayford's loyalty to the movement had faded by 1980. His position on speaking in tongues—not insisting on the experience as validation of Spirit baptism—continued to bother some into the 1990s, but it didn't seem to be an issue for most Foursquare pastors who saw Jack and the Church on the Way as a model.

The majority of Jack's speaking invitations still came from fellow Foursquare leaders who valued his ministry and invited him to speak to groups of pastors. Perhaps he had no greater affirmation than when Foursquare president Rolf McPherson asked Hayford whether he would be interested in the pastorate at Angelus Temple. It was not something he felt called to do, but he was deeply humbled by the inquiry.[9] Because Jack was, in the 1980s, so widely known outside of Foursquare, many independent pastors and churches joined the denomination, mostly because of their regard for Jack and the Church on the Way.[10]

The Charismatic movement was the third arena in which Hayford had a growing profile, both with speaking invitations and opportunities to write for Charismatic publications.[11] Notably, when the Charismatic movement was nearly split by the shepherding/discipleship controversy in 1975 and 1976, Hayford was in the middle of the debate, and his willingness to be conciliatory to both sides was an early sign of his emerging role as both peacemaker and statesman.[12]

Throughout the latter half of the 1970s, Hayford spoke at various Charismatic events and also made a number of appearances on Pat Robertson's Christian Broadcasting Network, Jim Bakker's PTL network, and what became the Trinity Broadcasting Network, led by Paul and Jan Crouch.[13] He was invited to write in popular Charismatic publications *Logos Journal* and *New Wine* magazine and was featured on the cover of the June 1985 issue of *Charisma* magazine. In his entire ministry in Charismatic circles, Jack never played down his commitment to Foursquare, but neither did he let it narrowly define him.[14]

From 1975 to 1980, Hayford traveled to Japan, Australia, New Zealand, Mexico, Panama, Canada, Denmark, England, and the Philippines, speaking at conferences for Foursquare and other Charismatic groups.[15] He also made numerous trips around the nation for conferences and other events.

His travel respite in the fall of 1974 had lasted only a few months. But one thing had changed: Jack now prioritized speaking events for pastors and leaders. Except on rare occasions, he no longer accepted invitations to speak at local churches or for groups like the one in Reno where he'd been invited to start a church.[16] He knew that his commitment was primarily to the First Foursquare Church of Van Nuys and secondarily to pastors and church leaders.

While his increasing visibility in Foursquare and the Charismatic movement was gratifying and important to Jack, he still saw the Church on the Way as his base and the springboard for his expanding ministry.[17] When he settled the question about his commitment to Foursquare in 1971, God had promised, "I'm going to raise up a voice from this church that will speak to the entire Foursquare denomination and to the Body of Christ at large."[18]

Jack has described how he reacted to that promise and others like it. "When the Lord has spoken things like that to me [it is] ... just a fact that was said.... I don't know what to do about it. I don't have any reason to disbelieve it but I don't know what it means. It's just, 'Fine, it's your business [God].'" By the mid-1970s, however, he could see that the promise was becoming a reality.[19] The vibrancy and health of the Church on the Way, along with Hayford's submission to his denomination, had given him great credibility.

Because of this, the Foursquare Church's leadership invited Hayford to return to his alma mater, Life Bible College, as president.[20] Hayford was interested, but he set as the only condition that he would be allowed to remain on as senior pastor in Van Nuys, which was his first priority. The denomination agreed, and Hayford served the college from 1977 to 1982. With his usual determination, he brought vision and direction to the school and helped bring to it "an authentic spirit of revitalization."

Under his leadership, a goal he had recommended years before when he'd served as Dean of Students finally became reality. In 1980, the college was accredited by the American Association of Bible Colleges.[21] He also led the school in the "reconstruction of the Correspondence Department" to better serve local churches in training and discipling their people.[22] Perhaps his greatest contribution was to spur the school to be more forward-thinking rather than languishing in the past.[23] There was a general optimism at the college while Hayford served as president, and when he stepped down in 1982, it was on a solid course.[24]

STRUCTURING FOR GROWTH

While the presidency of the college was a fruitful experience for the school, the demands it placed on Jack were a distraction to his leadership of the church. Throughout his entire pastorate, he had to reckon with how to balance ministry assignments that were in addition to pastoring. Despite Jack's tireless energy and ability to multitask, he struggled to keep focused on the pastorate he knew was giving him the credibility that brought so many opportunities. It proved extremely demanding, but he did his best to keep focused on pastoring the congregation and building big people.

The goal of discipleship, so central to his understanding of pastoral leadership, grew more and more difficult as the church grew and adjustments were needed. Multiple services meant that people were literally lining up on the front steps of the building to find seats in the main auditorium after the previous service ended. People who didn't find seats were guided to overflow rooms, where they had to watch the service on small TV screens (remember, this was the 1970s).

Jack was never interested in simply ministering to "crowds." He knew that developing the ministry of every believer couldn't be accomplished by people attending the larger worship gatherings alone nor did it foster the development of leaders. Prayer circles helped encourage participation and growth in ministry, but multiple services created time restraints that meant prayer circles lasted five minutes at most. This ministry-mindedness emphasis needed new structures that gave more opportunity for practical engagement one to another.

In 1975, the church began developing approaches through which believers could more readily participate in ministry and also form deeper relationships with other believers. The church experimented with various small-group strategies, but the most significant ministry development in this regard resulted from an experience Jack had while on a trip to Japan in 1977.

Hayford was in a Tokyo commuter terminal watching thousands upon thousands of people stream in and out of trains with amazing efficiency. He remembers: "And here my heart began to throb with a sense of the Holy Spirit moving. I felt the heart of God for these multitudes." It was a "pivotal point in bringing about our Home Ministries ... at 'The Church On The Way.'" He perceived that ministering to such masses was impossible with traditional methods.[25]

A radical plan was needed, and he went back to the United States convinced that the Van Nuys church had to expand its horizons so no one was "lost in the crowd." The idea that every member was a minister needed to be more than a slogan and would require major structural changes. Jack believed the answer was to break the church into home groups that *required* every member's participation.[26] This was not going to be optional. Over the summer of 1977, Jack cast vision for "house to house" ministry, calling every church member to join a home group. The plan was to have one quarter of the congregation meet off campus in their home groups one Sunday morning each month while the other three quarters would meet on campus.

To launch the plan and demonstrate the priority they were giving to home ministries, Jack and his leadership team decided to cancel the worship services at their Sherman Way location for Sunday, August 14, 1977. Instead, the entire congregation would gather in home meetings. This was *really* radical—a church with a Sunday worship attendance of over 2,000 canceling its on-site weekend services.

Jack believed it was the only way to go, but the plan also gave him pause. Did he have the courage to do it? Did he really trust the people to respond? Again, God spoke to him: "Will you trust Me to work in people as you have taught them to expect Me to?"[27] The plan went forward, and on that August Sunday, the congregation met in nearly 200 locations in the San Fernando Valley area and other parts of Los Angeles. At the Sherman Way campus, a few pastors and church members were present to greet people and give them directions to one of the home meetings, but no services were provided.

It proved an enormously fruitful decision. By that October, every Sunday morning, a quarter of the congregation met off campus in home meetings. The move gave space for substantial ministry "one to another" and for outreach to family and friends through the home gatherings—each group had a second meeting each month as well at a time they selected. Not only did the change make room for more people to attend the Church on the Way campus each weekend, it also multiplied leadership within the church. Many of the initial home group leaders came out of the men's ministry training from the previous five years.[28] Another blessing was that it expanded the scope of pastoral care for the growing congregation, as ordinary believers found places of significant leadership in caring for their fellow group members.

For the next twenty years, structures supporting the commitment to teach and sustain this every-member ministry would change with some frequency as the church sought to keep in step with the Spirit's leading. During Jack's pastorate of the Church on the Way, he was known for making quick adjustments, sometimes completely reversing course from previous decisions.

On occasion, some of these adjustments were significant enough to be unnerving to the congregation. But, as always, he would carefully explain why he believed the changes were necessary. Usually the reason was "his dogged insistence on hearing God's voice."[29] Still, some decisions shook the church. One story in this regard stands out.

TO "CO-PASTOR" OR NOT?

Perhaps the most telling example of this happened in the fall of 1984. The five-year stint as president of Life Bible College, along with his many ministry travels, had again brought Hayford to a crisis point. He was simply doing too much.

In 1982, Jack had invited Dennis Easter, a former staff member at the Church on the Way, who was pastoring a church in Lancaster, California, to return to the Van Nuys church as an executive pastor with the plan to transition eventually to the congregation's co-pastor.[30] This would allow Jack to more freely engage in his growing apostolic ministry and respond to invitations to minister outside the church.[31]

The transition was announced in November 1984 at a packed Sunday evening congregational meeting. Jack carefully explained the transition plan in a lengthy pastoral letter that he read in its entirety at the meeting. He gave the congregation a history of how the decision was made to appoint Easter as co-pastor and how it was a result of the leadership's prayerful recognition of Jack's call not only to pastor the church but to serve the larger body of Christ.

He would remain the church's senior pastor and primary weekend teacher but Easter, as co-pastor, would "oversee the entire thrust of the congregation's ongoing life internally." As for Jack, he would focus on those things which involve the impact of our church-life as it reaches outward. In particular, the demands of that outreach which … [include] media (radio, television, and multiple other means); through conference ministries both here and elsewhere (by which means tens of thousands of leaders each year are assisted toward more effective ministry); through involvement with interdenominational and denominational activities which influence the global Body of Christ; and through personal involvement with leaders who seek and need counsel from a trusted peer.[32]

Jack affirmed his complete trust of Easter as "a son in the faith" and his prayerful confidence that the plan was the will of God for the church and that he and Anna were at peace about the decision.

Dennis Easter was installed as co-pastor two months later at another packed congregational gathering, on January 6, 1985.[33] At this meeting, Easter spoke at length, laying out his vision for his role and the future of the congregation. Jack fully endorsed Easter's message.[34] At first, the plan went forward and seemed to be working well. Nevertheless, Easter was soon concerned that the co-pastor role might be creating dual allegiances within the congregation, with some hearing his voice as the primary leader and others hearing Jack's, who was speaking on more weekends than Easter was.

Jack had similar concerns. In a memo in March, Jack wrote to Dennis Easter and John Farmer, troubled over confusion related to matters the church faced that called for clear leadership.[35] The confusion had to do with communication more than anything. Jack was trying to let go by leaving things to Easter. At the same time, Easter was concerned about assuming so much leadership that it supplanted Jack's role as senior pastor. There was an uneasy tension, and yet, given the high profile the transition had been given, Jack and Dennis were hesitant to engage their concerns directly to each other. It left a communication vacuum.

Things came to a head in May. Jack was in Edinburgh, Scotland, on a three-week ministry trip.[36] After receiving a call from his daughter Rebecca, Hayford wrote in his journal that her call was "both a confirmation & warning re: my relative 'awayness' from the church at home." Indeed, he'd been away for a total of nearly two months from January through May. Was his absence creating a "means which the adversary would seek to discredit [his] ministry?"

He wasn't inferring anything wrong on Dennis Easter's part, but he was fretting over his frequent absences from church and concerned that it was impacting his ability to serve effectively as senior pastor. He was also now seriously questioning whether having two principal leaders of the church was really workable after all.[37] Anna had expressed similar concerns to Jack for weeks.[38]

With Jack in his hotel room in Edinburgh, in the midst of these thoughts, the Lord spoke and clarified the issues. Jack believed God was calling him to go home and "pastor the church again." On one hand, Jack was gratified to hear this from the Lord, but on the other, he had no idea how to go about it.

Doing so, he knew, could create enormous turmoil. Yet if he was truly hearing from God, he needed to obey, no matter the cost. Much like the crisis in 1974 with the Reno opportunity (chapter 10), he was called to the larger church, certainly, but his first commitment was to the Church on the Way as its senior pastor. This was always a tension point for his leadership in Van Nuys. How would he live out his call to both? He knew that the answer to that question was up to God. He needed to obey but was baffled as to how.[39]

But the Lord had more to say, and Jack wasn't prepared for what he heard: "Dennis isn't supposed to be the co-pastor." Although Jack was wrestling over the whole situation, this left him dumbfounded. He genuinely believed God had led him to appoint Dennis. Now what should he do? He told the Lord, "I cannot go back and tell that to anybody." The prayer put the whole matter in God's hands. The only solace Jack had was that he believed, however this was to be processed, it would have to be the Lord's doing.

He returned to Van Nuys, and within twenty-four hours he knew for certain that God was already processing the situation without his help. The first night back, a trusted elder in the church phoned Jack, telling him that he felt the church was spiritually facing a "shaking." But the most dramatic confirmation was at a meeting the very next morning. Jack met with the pastoral executive team so he could catch up with the things that had transpired during his three-week absence. After meeting for an hour, Dennis Easter told Jack he had a letter he wanted to read to him, having already read it to the others on the executive team.

In his letter, Easter acknowledged that, at first, he had relished his role as co-pastor and looked forward to the times when Jack was away and he was able to speak on the weekends and to steer the church in the way he felt Jack had empowered him to do. Nevertheless, as time went on, he had become confused regarding his role.

He told Jack that, for a season after becoming co-pastor, he had hoped to someday serve as the church's senior pastor, but now, he wrote, "that desire has vanished and I believe God has lifted it from me." Dennis believed that "the yoke of pastoring this church is custom fit, in my estimation, for your shoulders.... You, *and not you and I*, but you alone are the pastor of this congregation."[40]

With that letter, Easter effectively stepped aside as co-pastor and briefly took on another role at the church. The structural changes were processed transparently before the church in a meeting of the congregation on June 2, 1985. Jack told of the events in Edinburgh and the confirmations he'd had upon his return, and Dennis read an edited version of his letter to Jack to the congregation.

Unquestionably, the episode was a "shaking" for the church, but the open manner in which it was processed lessened its impact.[41] Nevertheless, it was a difficult transition for Easter, and he struggled through the summer months. Convinced he was called to serve as a senior pastor, he accepted an invitation to pastor a Foursquare church in Ventura. With Jack's and the congregation's blessing, the Easters left in September.[42]

Jack has always believed, rightly or wrongly, that God had led him to appoint Easter as co-pastor, but God also told him it was a mistake.[43] Whatever the case, because Easter graciously initiated his resignation without Jack requesting it, coupled with the transparency with which Jack and Easter handled the situation, there was no division in the church, and the congregation continued to flourish. In a move that would carry significance for what lay ahead for the congregation, Jack invited his son-in-law Scott Bauer and his daughter Rebecca, who had been sent out in 1982 to pastor in Northern California, to return and join the pastoral team.[44]

By the fall of 1985, Hayford was fully engaged again as senior pastor, and for the next eleven years, there was no question who was leading the church. He continued to travel extensively, but the turmoil that had surrounded appointing a co-pastor had given him a renewed realization that his apostolic voice outside the church had greater credibility because of his pastoral ministry at the church. Jack was back and with fresh energy and vision.

Chapter 13

PASTOR TO PASTORS

A RIVER OF MINISTRY

Commissioning and sending out pastors, staff, and other leaders in the church to serve elsewhere were fairly regular occurrences throughout Jack's thirty years pastoring the Church on the Way. Sometimes, staff pastors were sent to plant new churches or to assume pastorates of other churches. Jack's brother, Jim, after pastoring the youth in Van Nuys, took a pastorate in nearby Glendale. Jim and his wife, Betsy, left Glendale to start a church in Northern California in 1977 that grew to be one of the largest congregations in Foursquare under Jim's twelve years at the church. At other times, the church was sending people to serve as missionaries or in itinerant ministries to the larger church. Jack saw it as a fulfillment of the earlier prophecy "I will make you as the church at Antioch."

Jack's sister, Luanne, and her husband, Duane Chumley, and their two children were examples of missionaries sent from the Church on the Way.

Luanne and her husband, both graduates of Life Bible College, were sent to China as missionaries in August 1976, serving from Hong Kong as their base.[1]

After arriving in Hong Kong, Luanne developed cancer and the Van Nuys church labored in prayer for her healing. She and her family courageously battled the disease for two years, traveling back and forth to the US from the mission field.[2] She died at the age of forty on August 13, 1978.[3] It was difficult for the family, and Jack was the one to tell the children their mother had passed. Both Jack and his brother, Jim, helped officiate her memorial service. It was a moving tribute to her memory and ministry. A prophecy was given during the week of Luanne's passing that said the Church on the Way was and would continue to be a "river of ministry."

Indeed, by the middle of the 1980s, the Church on the Way was a thriving ministry center, with twenty-one full-time pastors overseeing more than 100 ministries. Jack's emphasis on excellence in leadership showed in both the maintenance of the church's facilities and the quality of its ministries, particularly to children and youth. The church also served as a resource to the Los Angeles area.

An example was the 1984 Summer Olympics in Los Angeles, when thousands from the church were involved in outreach and evangelism.[4] The congregation's Extension Ministries numbered well over 100 in 1984 and represented scores of churches that had been planted and missionaries sent out, not to mention all the pastorates that had been filled by former members of the congregation's pastoral staff.[5] It also included contemporary Christian recording artists the 2nd Chapter of Acts and Chuck Girard, a founding member of the early Jesus People movement band Love Song. Extension Ministries would eventually number over 300.

The SoundWord Tape Ministry, created originally for distribution of Hayford's messages for those in the congregation, grew exponentially, mailing tapes around the nation. It grew so fast that a separate corporation was formed, Living Way Ministries, to serve the demand for Hayford's audio sermons, books, and other teaching materials that were requested.

Through Living Way Ministries, the church began a daily radio program in 1981 called *Freeway*. By the late 1980s, the show was called *Living Way* and was being broadcast on over 150 radio stations.[6] Although Jack's teaching ministry already had wide exposure through his various Christian television ministries, the church produced its own weekly television broadcast in the late 1980s that, like the radio broadcast, was available throughout the US on various television stations.[7]

Jack's 1982 book, *The Church on the Way*, later revised and expanded in 1991 under the title *Glory on Your House,* sold well. Both editions told the story of the church in considerable detail, highlighting the teachings on worship, prayer, the kingdom of God, and the ministry of every believer that were so central to the Jack's ministry.[8]

WORSHIP HIS MAJESTY

All through the first decade in Van Nuys, Jack was writing hymns and praise choruses that often became a regular part of the congregation's worship services. Many of his songs were used in churches both in his denomination and in the wider Charismatic movement. Singer and variety television host Tennessee Ernie Ford, best known for his 1955 hit song "Sixteen Tons," recorded Hayford's hymn "Come On Down" in 1975, and it reached #52 on the US country charts. But far and away his most well-known composition was his worship chorus "Majesty."

The song was written while Jack and Anna, along with their daughter Christa, were vacationing in Britain in the summer of 1977, during the celebration of the twenty-fifth anniversary of Queen Elizabeth's coronation.[9] One day as they were sightseeing, they toured the historic Blenheim Palace, where Winston Churchill had spent much of his childhood. Walking through the grounds and massive structure, Jack could understand how its regal character had influenced Churchill's sense of being someone "bred to influence the world."

Convinced as he was "that the provisions of Christ for the believer not only included the forgiveness for sin, but provided a restoration to a royal relationship with God as sons and daughters born into the family through His Majesty, Our Savior Jesus Christ," Jack was moved at the thought of God's high destiny for His children.[10] Later, while Jack was driving the car, the song "Majesty" was born.

Jack asked Anna to jot the words and melody line down in her notebook (Anna loved to tell everyone that she was the one who wrote "Majesty").[11] As Jack recited the lines, he was filled with a powerful

> sense of Christ Jesus' royalty, dignity and majesty.... I seemed to feel something new of what it meant to be *His*! The accomplished triumph of His Cross has not only unlocked us from the chains of our own bondage and restored us to fellowship with the Father, but He has also unfolded to us a life of authority over sin and hell and raised us to partnership with Him in His Throne—Now![12]

Jack completed the song after they returned to California.

> Majesty, worship his majesty;
> Unto Jesus be all glory, honor, and praise.
> Majesty, kingdom authority,
> Flow from his throne unto his own, his anthem raise.
> So exalt, lift up on high the name of Jesus.
> Magnify, come glorify Christ Jesus, the King.
> Majesty, worship his majesty,
> Jesus who died, now glorified,
> King of all kings[13]

Jack introduced "Majesty" in the services at the Church on the Way in late 1977, and the hymn-like song resonated strongly with the congregation and quickly came into use throughout Pentecostal and Charismatic church circles. The popularity of "Majesty" swelled unabated into the 1990s. According to Christian Copyright Licensing International,[14] "Majesty" was the most-used song among churches from 1989 through 1994, and it remained in the top ten into 2001. It resided in the top fifty most-used songs until 2006, and it remains in the top 200 as of this writing.

"Majesty" continues to be used transdenominationally and is published in many denominational hymnals. "Majesty" was also instrumental in introducing Jack Hayford to a much wider spectrum of the church. The song's popularity highlighted Jack's artistic gifts and demonstrated the rich blessing God was giving his ministry.

The wide reach of "Majesty" contributed to Jack's growing recognition as a trusted voice on the subject of worship. One of his bestselling books, *Worship His Majesty,* published in 1987, helped provide theological and biblical foundations for worship practices, doing so with pastoral sensitivity.[15] The book chronicles many of Jack's experiences leading the Church on the Way in the priority of worship.[16] It also affirms the essential practices that characterize expressive Pentecostal-like worship, such as lifting hands, clapping, kneeling, standing, and shouting.[17]

PASTORING PASTORS

For years, pastors were ordering recordings of Jack's sermons, often preaching his messages in their own churches.[18] As his ministry enlarged, he saw that an increasing number of pastors were looking to him as a model for ministry. He realized that God had given him special favor with pastors and church leaders. As early as 1972, the church was getting inquiries from pastors who wanted to visit and learn more about what the Church on the Way was doing that made possible the blessings they were experiencing.

The answer to that question for Jack was simple: the grace on the congregation was foremost a result of God's sovereign bestowal of His glory. Still, he also knew that boldly following the prophetic leadership of the Holy Spirit was a key factor. That was something other pastors could do just as well, and Hayford believed that telling the church's story might serve as a valuable example for other leaders.

However, Jack steadfastly resisted any notion that what God was doing in one church could be automatically replicated in another context, producing the same results. He knew the tendency of church leaders—early in his ministry he had done so himself—to try to copy success by discovering the "secrets" of a successful ministry.

Yet he also realized that the things he learned in his Van Nuys "laboratory" were principles and practices that, while not necessarily leading to similar numerical growth, could bring new life and vitality to any congregation willing to learn them. He knew this from experience in seeing the Church on the Way transformed as they learned together how to grow in ministry to the Lord (worship), ministry to one another (fellowship), and ministry to the world (evangelism). Those were things he could teach.

There was no way to personally address all the inquiries coming Jack's way from pastors. Therefore, a decision was made to host a pastors' seminar. Just under a hundred pastors attended the first seminar, in June 1973. Jack and two colleagues, Roy Hicks Jr. and Jerry Cook, served as the speakers. While clearly identifying with their Foursquare denomination, these three made frequent references to the larger renewal sweeping the nation at the time. They seemed to see themselves and their congregations as a vanguard within the Foursquare Church. That first conference reflected the almost euphoric attitude toward the Charismatic Renewal at the time.

Jack saw the first pastors' seminar as a foretaste of something God wanted to continue, so he followed it up with two conferences in 1974, each larger than the previous. The pastors' conference became an annual event at the Church on the Way through 2010. Attendance grew to over 2,000 pastors and leaders each year.[19] From 1976 on, the conferences, held in November, became a platform for Jack to address leaders, many from outside Pentecostal and Charismatic circles. These leaders not only valued his teaching ministry, they also saw him as a mentor despite having no personal relationship with him.

The fall conferences usually recounted the most important themes that the Church on the Way had learned over the given year or addressed a particular teaching emphasis that seemed important at the time. The conference always featured notable Christian pastors and leaders, over the years including Oral Roberts, John Wimber, Bill Hybels, James Robison, and Robert Morris, to name just a few. Jack also invited speakers from outside Pentecostal and Charismatic circles, like John MacArthur and Robert Schuller. But most pastors came to hear Jack.

Aware of the financial challenges many pastors faced, registration costs were kept low. In the early years, housing was provided in the homes of church members. The pastors' conferences became famous for the fabulous brunches served during the day sessions. For years, these featured a Hayford favorite: alligator bars, a decadent and delicious pecan pie–like pastry. Jack and the Church on the Way lavished gifts on the attendees, as well. Books, Bibles, cassette tapes, and later CDs, were given away, always including any new books Jack had written.[20] He wanted pastors to feel blessed no matter the struggles they faced.

He seemed especially at home with pastors, and his messages to leaders had a similar impact as they had on those in his congregation. Pastors attending the conferences and those who listened to him through audio or viewed his messages on video felt they knew him. Hayford had a special sensitivity to the needs of pastors, particularly pastors of smaller churches who wrestled with discouragement.

His forthrightness about his struggles as a pastor helped leaders identify with him as a fellow traveler who knew how hard pastoring could often be.[21] Jack wasn't trying to seem transparent—he was just being honest. He was also unafraid to talk about his fears and his bouts with depression.

Jack praying with leaders

This vulnerability was sincere and shows up in his journal entries over the years, where he writes with brutal honesty about his self-doubts and insecurities. He never forgot his Fort Wayne experiences and the hardships and disappointments he and Anna had faced there. Although he was wonderfully blessed with what had happened in Van Nuys, he never lost touch with the difficulties most pastors lived with every day.

Because Jack talked about these issues so openly, it helped other pastors realize there was no need to beat themselves up over similar struggles. Pastors attending the conferences, most of whom were pastoring small congregations, were reassured to hear him often say, "Big isn't always better," and he made it clear that pastoring a big church came with its own set of challenges and heartaches.

Jack truly believed that the numerical growth of the Church on the Way and churches like it was not "normal" and he plainly stated that size should never be the goal. That was something easier said than done for most pastors. Jack believed that so-called megachurches—churches of more than 2,000—were exceptions and he knew that when pastors of smaller congregations made comparisons to large churches, it only added to the burden of unfulfilled expectations that plagued them.

Jack didn't dismiss the obvious giftedness of pastors who led megachurches, nor did he discount the innovations and excellence that often marked large churches. But he was convinced that the biggest factor contributing to their growth was that God had something He wanted to say to the whole church that perhaps would only be heard if the church was big. He elaborated what he meant:

> I've never seen a megachurch that wasn't a prophetic statement of some kind. Each setting magnifies an idea—a kingdom concept. Whatever else, you'll find certain timeless verities are spoken by the incarnate reality of huge congregations.
>
> God has ways of making an idea big by growing a large church around it. Usually the leader is an expression of the idea, but the concept is bigger than the person—so note first how God uses that person to advance a kingdom value.
>
> Just a few of these values are: (1) evangelism; (2) mobilizing the laity; (3) creatively penetrating the culture; (4) releasing faith to bring hope and healing; (5) Word-centered discipling; (6) caring for the broken; (7) serving global mission; and (8) prayer passion and outreach. Look beyond the miracle of the ministry's size—see the message.[22]

Jack regularly reminded pastors that no matter the size of the church they pastored, the fundamental aim of pastoral ministry was "to serve the mission of an eternal kingdom, as we serve the interests and growth of eternal souls." It was a familiar theme for Jack. He felt that a church's durability, not its size, was the truest measure of ministry fruitfulness. Too often, large churches emerge and carry a prophetic message that can all too easily fade away because factors that contribute to long-term fruitfulness are not prioritized.

Jack was wise enough not to offer a complete endorsement of all large churches, and neither did he intend to be a critic when he cautioned leaders against a "superficial fascination" with churches or ministries just because they were big. He had witnessed how a great ministry "evaporated as quickly as a morning's mushrooms—and sometimes have been as toxic." He knew from experience that a lasting ministry was more than the dramatic. With his customary candor, he taught leaders what was most important.

> There is an excitement about a place where God is moving mightily. This is not unspiritual, and it is to be expected. But it isn't a spiritual law that God's dynamics are always dramatic. There is a distinct lack of colorfulness to plain, everyday faithfulness.
>
> There is a sameness to living out the basic disciplines of a true disciple. It is just plain work to give oneself to study, to prayer and to building character. These rather mundane traits will not be the most noticeable features of a megachurch, but I guarantee you—where a durable work is in process, the basics are everywhere being applied.
>
> Growth that lasts isn't the result of fancy footwork. So look beyond the dramatic and find what basics are functioning to secure the footings for both substance and size.

I've seen and lived the miracle of a megachurch. My opinion is that they are not normal—but they are prophetic. Thus, I urge church leaders: Capture the concepts of spiritual growth and you will have that degree of church growth ordained for your ministry. If it grows a big congregation, you've got a sometime-pleasant problem. But the real question to ask is this: "Am I growing big people?"

Every leader can do that.[23]

It was refreshing for weary pastors to hear someone talk this way, and there seemed to be special grace on Jack's communication to pastors and church leaders. They often remarked, "He says what I believe but I didn't know how to say it."[24] It was more than Jack's storytelling and illustrations; it had to do with his well-grounded insights biblically and theologically. He was able to get at core issues that were foundational to effective and enduring leadership. Being able to influence and encourage pastors and church leaders was one of Jack's greatest privileges in ministry. He loved pastors and they loved him.

THE SCRIPTURES AND THE SPIRIT

Pastors and church leaders were drawn to Jack Hayford for many reasons.[25] They appreciated his careful and nuanced approach and the way he rooted his teaching first in exegesis of a biblical passage with sensitivity to a text's historical and cultural context. At the same time, Jack was unflinching in his conviction that God wanted to speak prophetically through the Scriptures to the people he pastored, and this often meant seeing new and fuller meanings in particular biblical passages that were inspired by the Holy Spirit. Jack always believed that pastoral preaching had to address the realities and struggles people faced in their daily lives.[26]

While always concerned to not diminish the importance of the historical and contextual issues that informed the biblical authors' original message to their readers, a view treasured by evangelicals, Jack believed the Bible pointed beyond itself to Jesus Christ, the Living Word, and that the aim of biblical teaching and preaching[27] was not first about doctrine but *transformation*.[28] He had articulated this early in his teaching ministry at the Church on the Way in his Mary Miracle messages mentioned previously.

Jack taught that the "contemporary pastor/teacher may expect God to give 'direct promptings' ... concerning what he should preach ... [and] that the Holy Spirit will respond and assist with insight into how a specific text speaks specifically to the present moment."[29] This he believes is prophetic preaching, "an approach to study that helps us capture the life and breath of things within the text."[30]

Hayford is careful to affirm that any prophetic word discerned in Scripture "must be measured against the whole of the Scriptures as to its truthfulness and relative worth and is subject to evaluation by the leadership of the Body (1 Corinthians 14:29; 1 John 4:1–3; 1 Thessalonians 5:21)."[31]

This approach seemed to resonate with those pastors who felt that the role of the Holy Spirit was almost ignored in the process of interpreting the Bible. Jack argued that if the Spirit's role wasn't given its place in message preparation, "meaning can become very academic and our sermons finally distill to only academic presentations, however lucidly and graciously they are delivered." Jack modeled a way that encouraged leaders to be attuned to the Spirit's illumination and to diligently apply interpretive methods so essential to faithful interpretation of Scripture. Both are equally necessary.

Pastors were regularly impressed with Jack's insights into Scripture. It wasn't uncommon to hear them remark, "I've read that passage a hundred times and have never seen what he sees."[32] Jack has an explanation for it. He doesn't think the insights he receives in his study of Scripture are the result of his own creative or interpretive skills but come from insight God gives him. Jack is convinced that his ability to "see" is fundamentally tied to his obedience and openness in his personal pilgrimage with Christ.

In saying this, Jack is careful not to claim some special holiness on his part. Instead, he simply believes that the ability to hear God speak comes from living openly and honestly before God. It's something every pastor/ leader can do. He describes it this way: "My commitment to walk with integrity of heart calls me to refuse to allow the most minor deviations from honesty with my*self*, with the *facts*, and most of all, with *the Holy Spirit's corrections*."[33] Integrity is essential to the development of one's character, and that process depends

> on how willingly I permit His Spirit to continually refine my imperfect capacities for receiving and responding to His will in the moment-to-moment details of my life. My character is not shaped by the sum of my *information,* but by the process of a *transformation* that is as unceasingly needed in *me* as God's word is unchanging with *Him.*
>
> There is more to my character formation than having learned a set of ideas—even if they are God's. I not only need to *turn to the Bible*, but I must keep *tuned to the Holy Spirit*, for with the "grid" of values His Word gives me, He provides His Spirit as the ultimate umpire who comes to apply that Word to my living.... The purpose of His monitoring is not to produce a mystical brand of sup- posed "holiness," but a dynamic quality of wholehearted, clear-eyed people.[34]

This understanding of the importance of integrity is the main aspect in his journey of daily opening his heart to God for scrutiny. Jack has described his devotional pilgrimage "not as an exercise in self-flagellating or berating introspection, but as a practice of maintaining sensitivity to His Spirit's 'voice' keeping integrity with His dealings with my heart."[35]

Consequently, as we have seen throughout his story, Jack has lived his life with a sometimes-brutal honesty. Integrity of heart is the bedrock of his life, and he believes this "way of repentance" not only leaves his heart open to see and hear more clearly what the Spirit is saying in the Bible, but also makes it possible for God's transforming Word to flow through him to transform those who also see and hear through his preaching.[36]

LANDMARK SERMONS

Although his convictions about integrity reached back to his childhood, the particular message Jack commonly shared with pastors was born out of a moral failure at the church when a woman came forward about having been propositioned by a staff pastor. Around that time, Jack was preparing to address a pastors' event and was prompted by the Lord the very morning of the event to do a word study on the term *integrity* in both Testaments. He hastily called his assistant, who brought him the books he needed and then drove him to the event two hours away.

Troubled by what had happened at the church, Jack was wrestling with why leaders who know better still fall so grievously. Sitting in the back seat studying, he made a discovery. It was a confirmation of something he had has always intuited: in Scripture, integrity had to do with wholeness and completeness. Jack recognized that the word *integrity,* when used in the phrase "integrity of heart," was describing an undivided heart before God, a heart entirely open to God in complete honesty.[37] He knew this was an absolute necessity if one was to live in obedience to God's way.

In an article Jack wrote for *New Wine* magazine in 1983, based on his teaching on integrity, he elaborated on its significance for Christian leaders.

Whenever I speak at a conference of pastors, inevitably I am asked, "What is the key to fruitful ministry and a growing personal relationship with God?" It would be easy to list a number of items we usually think of as the crux of spiritual life and growth—the Word of God, prayer, giving, service, gifts and fruit of the Spirit. Yet, I would have to insist that none of them is the key.

What, then, is the key? I believe the single most critical issue we must address in life is *absolute integrity of heart before God.* Integrity is the key.

Perhaps the simplest definition of integrity is "wholeness." Notice I didn't say "holiness"; for holiness flows from wholeness. But the essence of integrity is completion. In mathematics, a *whole* number is an "integer." When several parts are "integrated," they are made into one. But when something is disintegrated, it is fragmented.

Integrity of heart refers to a heart that is complete. It is not splintered by double-mindedness. It is not compromised or eroded by personal dishonesty or self-deception. Having integrity means I don't refuse to hear my own conscience's commentary on my life.[38]

When he preached the message to the pastors that day, Jack could tell it was reverberating through the room. He went on to tell about his mother's lesson long ago about telling the truth "in front of Jesus," something Jack had sought to do ever since. Being honest with God had prevented him from falling into adultery while working at the denomination's central offices in the 1960s. He knew firsthand that the prayer of Psalm 25:21, "May integrity and uprightness preserve me" (ESV), was a promise for those living with integrity.

Jack wrote in *New Wine*, "As Christians we have an enemy—the devil—who militantly organizes his legions against us. But the integrity of our hearts will make room for God to head off our enemies and protect us."[39]

The message on integrity of heart became one of Jack's "landmark sermons," a term he uses to describe sermons that stand out as defining moments of a church or a pastor.[40]

Later, when a worship leader in the church committed suicide, Jack addressed the issue head-on, arguing that suicide for a Christian didn't necessarily mean the person was condemned to hell.[41] After the deadly 1994 Northridge earthquake shook the Southern California area, Hayford openly preached about his own struggle with fear after the earthquake.[42]

More than once after such tragedies, he sought to answer the question: "Why do bad things happen to good people?"[43] Jack's father died of lung cancer in August 1979, just days short of his sixty-sixth birthday. On the day of "Daddy's" memorial service, Jack brought a Wednesday evening message to the church about why people die too soon. He told the congregation that his dad had smoked most of his life and that it no doubt contributed to an early death. His father's cancer diagnosis was shocking, and he was finally able to quit four months before his death.[44] For Jack and the family, it was a belated victory, but they were still glad for it.[45]

It was a difficult message to bring, but Jack was able to honor his father as "a great man," something he often affirmed. In a way that was characteristic of his preaching, he was able to both acknowledge his father's brokenness and celebrate God's redemptive grace in his father's life over the thirty years after rededicating his life to Christ in 1948. It was an especially poignant message.

While some landmark sermons were deeply personal, others addressed difficulties the contemporary church faced. For example, when the popular TV evangelists Jim Bakker and Jimmy Swaggart were caught up in scandals in 1987 and 1988, Jack argued that, while forgiveness for the men could be immediate, fallen leaders must go through a lengthy restoration process that reestablished their trustworthiness for spiritual leadership. The message *Where Have All the Flowers Gone?* and the later book based on the message, *Restoring Fallen Leaders,* earned Jack considerable respect from the evangelical community.[46]

When a prominent pastor in the church fell into adultery, Jack and the church leadership practiced what they preached and addressed the pastor's moral failure openly. The person who fell publicly repented at a congregational gathering and submitted himself to church discipline and the process of restoration. The service was recorded and edited to protect the person's identity. The message, called "A Case of New Testament Discipline," was requested by thousands of pastors who saw it as a model for handling moral failure with a church leader or pastor.[47]

Jack preached with surprising frankness on human sexuality, addressing a range of topics from masturbation to premarital sex to adultery to homosexuality, always affirming biblical faithfulness and yet doing so without ranting or undue moralizing.[48]

In one series of four Sunday evening messages, aptly named *Ex-Rated Sex,* the focus was on God's design for sexual fulfillment as part of a healthy marriage between a man and a woman. He addressed the challenges Christians face in a sex-crazed culture that easily perverts God's intention for human sexuality. In one of the messages, he reminded the congregation that orgasms were God's idea, not Satan's. Jack even addressed the issue of oral sex.[49]

Jack dealt with controversial issues like divorce and remarriage, moderate drinking (though Jack himself practiced total abstinence), what happens to stillborn or aborted children, the creation and evolution debate, the problem of profanity, Christians and politics, and many more. There was no subject he wasn't willing to tackle. He saw the need to address head-on life's issues and challenges as part of being a faithful shepherd to God's people.[50] Dealing with such difficult topics often required him to speak for ninety minutes or more to adequately deal with the complexities of particular issues.

It must be remembered that these "landmark sermons" were in addition to his regular strategic preaching on the key themes essential to disciple a congregation, such as teachings on prayer, worship, the kingdom of God, spiritual warfare, and the ministry of the believer. Jack kept a preaching calendar and systematically mapped out the various message series he planned to preach over the year. If the church was facing an important transition, he would do a series of messages that helped the congregation stay focused and moving together.

Although Hayford's preaching has often been described as "balanced," he never liked the term. To his understanding, what others called *balance* was more a matter of his both/and approach that didn't force biblical texts to fit a prescribed theological system. Jack realized that there are a number of vital truths in Scripture that exist in tension: God is one and three, Jesus is God and Man, and the idea that God's sovereignty and human freedom stand together. He sometimes referred to these and other paradoxes in Scripture as "imponderables" that call for worship, not explanation. Considering all this, it's easy to see why so many pastors admired and even copied his approach to pastoral preaching.

It is not a stretch to suggest that Jack Hayford's teaching ministry fits within the tradition of Christianity's historic pastor-theologians.[51] Too often we forget that Augustine, Luther, Wesley, and others were church pastors who did much of their theologizing in their preaching and not by their writing alone. Gerald Hiestand agrees:

> Historically, the church's most influential theologians were *church*men—pastors, priests, and bishops. Clerics such as Athanasius, Augustine (indeed nearly all the church Fathers), Anselm, Luther, Calvin, Zwingli, Edwards, and Wesley functioned as the wider theologians of their day—shaping not only the theological vision of their own parishes, but that of the wider church. In their day, the

pastoral community represented the most influential, most insightful, and most articulate body of theologians. [italics Hiestand][52]

Hayford's far-reaching influence had much to do with the fact that pastors and church leaders were some of the biggest consumers of his messages, which gave him a much wider audience through his influence to their ministries. His ministry "fed" pastors spiritually while helping them to see the role pastoral teaching had in getting "theology into people, to get it lived out."[53]

Leadership Journal was a publication geared to church leaders. Jack's ministry and his preaching caught the attention of the journal, and he became a frequent contributor to the magazine and to books they published on preaching and worship.[54] This was an important platform to minister to the evangelical community. He also made frequent contributions to *Preaching Today,* a magazine that provides preaching resources to pastors.

In 1988, Jack began writing "Pastor to Pastor," a column in Charisma Media's periodical for leaders, *Ministries Today.* The magazine was another vehicle for Jack to touch pastors. In the one-to-two-page columns, he sometimes boldly addressed "hot button" topics. Charisma House collected a number of columns he'd written over the years and published two books on leadership: *The Leading Edge* and *Sharpening the Leading Edge.*[55]

Jack Hayford's role as a pastor to pastors started small, with that first seminar in 1973, but it blossomed over the years, bringing him wide recognition as a pastor's pastor.[56] His first ministry priority until 1999 remained as pastor of the Church on the Way, but his love and concern for pastors would continue to require significant investment of his time and energy. He was glad to do it.

Chapter 14

BECOMING A PENTECOSTAL STATESMAN

BRIDGE-BUILDER

In 1969, the Van Nuys Baptist Church was one of the fastest-growing churches in the US. Just two weeks after he'd assumed the pastorate in Van Nuys that year, Jack Hayford was driving to the printer to copy bulletins for Sunday worship service. He was stopped at the light at Kester Avenue and Sherman Way, directly in front of the Baptist church, which was located less than a mile from the First Foursquare Church of Van Nuys. As he waited for the light to change, he could feel his face burning on the side toward the Baptist church. He knew why.

He was intimidated by the size of the church that dwarfed his little congregation up the street.[1] Jack was also bothered because he thought the Baptists were judgmental toward him as a Pentecostal.[2] "Through an inner voice, God spoke to him reprovingly: 'You could at least begin by looking at the building.'"[3] Jack reluctantly turned his head and God spoke again: "I want you to pray for the work I'm doing at this church. There's no way the pastoral staff can keep up with it. You are a shepherd to my flock, and though that is not your flock, it's mine and you are mine. Pray for the grace I am working there to advance and be fruitful because the great work needs the care of my shepherds."

Jack began praying and as he did God filled him with a love for the church that just a moment before had intimidated him. It would be a lasting change. The love he was feeling would overflow in the days ahead, not only for that congregation but to other churches he passed while driving in LA, including a Roman Catholic church nearby and other congregations that might be labeled "liberal." It was an important lesson. Despite his interdenominational upbringing, he realized that there had been "an imperceptible sectarian smallness in my soul."

Jack knew sectarianism was wrong, having accepted long ago that no group "has a corner on truth." Still, he had been bruised by the rejection he'd sometimes felt as a Pentecostal. In the years traveling for his denomination, he had, on a number of occasions, sensed a "coolness" in some evangelical leaders after telling them he was a Classical Pentecostal. The rejection in subtle ways made him feel defensive, and that attitude needed to be confronted.

> That morning the Lord called me to love the whole Church.... He reminded me that the church was his and I was privileged to share mutually ... in the work of God's grace in the whole church not just my own denomination. God told me to pray down a blessing for a church that seemed to have more than its share of blessings already while my tiny flock was short on blessings. The Lord told me to bless them when I had nothing in the world and no dream at all of what he was getting ready to do."[4]

From that day on, Jack took the initiative in building cordial if not close relationships with the pastors of the Van Nuys Baptist Church—relationships that would prove more significant than he realized at the time. His openness to the whole church was renewed, and he recommitted himself to carry on his ministry with an interdenominational heart. Throughout his thirty years leading the Van Nuys church, Jack reached out to pastors in the Los Angeles area, arranging breakfast and lunch meetings to build relationships with his fellow shepherds. A few of these meetings led to long-term friendships that positively impacted Christian unity in Southern California.

In the 1980s, Jack and Lloyd Ogilvie, who was then pastor of First Presbyterian Church of Hollywood, started meeting occasionally for breakfast. Both had "large churches, radio and television ministries, and wrote books"—commonalities that helped forge a quick bond.[5] Despite coming from very different traditions, their friendship grew and the two began praying together with some regularity. They were both deeply concerned about the city of Los Angeles, growing racial tensions, the poor, and the suffering in the sprawling metropolis.[6]

Under Jack's inclusive leadership, they started a small interracial group of pastors from high and low churches, rich and poor churches, traditional, evangelical, and Charismatic churches. There was no other agenda than to encourage each other's ministries and pray for Los Angeles. Later, Ogilvie reflected on Jack's role in the group as a peacemaker who "was used by the Holy Spirit to help us grow in a profound love for each other as brothers and sisters in Christ."[7]

From their meetings together came a vision to call together for an extended time of prayer all pastors, church workers, and leaders of missions working in the inner city. A list of 500 was assembled, and invitations were sent out. The morning prayer meeting was held on Valentine's Day in February 1989 and appropriately named "Shepherds Love LA" To everyone's surprise, over a thousand gathered to pray. The ethnically and denominationally diverse group of leaders represented the mosaic that is Los Angeles. Tom Bradley, then mayor of the city, also attended.[8]

Jack with Mayor Bradley and Lloyd Ogilvie, 1991

Jack preached a brief message from Jeremiah 29:7–13, exhorting the group to seek the peace of the city.[9] The meeting lasted four hours as groups of leaders joined in prayer for the city. It was an overwhelming success and just the beginning of ongoing prayer gatherings of suburban and inner-city pastors and leaders in the Los Angeles area that continued for over a decade.[10] The Love LA gatherings would prove especially significant after the 1992 Los Angeles riots, as churches throughout Southern California were able to work together to respond to the crisis.[11]

Hayford rallied the Church on the Way to serve the community following the riots, giving over $150,000 and sending truckloads of food to support relief efforts. It demonstrated that the commitment to seek the peace of the city was more than words. Similarly, after the 1994 Northridge earthquake that killed 57 people and left over 100,000 people homeless, the Church on the Way once again generously gave financially and provided volunteers not only to serve their own members impacted by the disaster but to help others in Southern California recover.[12] Hayford's community service and ecumenical work brought him great admiration and respect in the Los Angeles area.[13]

THE BEAUTY OF SPIRITUAL LANGUAGE

Jack's bridge-building efforts helped him span theological divides that few Classical Pentecostals managed to cross. He never wavered in his commitment to the Foursquare movement or to his convictions about being baptized with the Holy Spirit. His advocacy for the work of the Holy Spirit was always expressed in a winsome manner, and he wasn't afraid to bring fresh ways of understanding Spirit-empowered Christian experience. As we saw in chapter 10, nowhere was this more evident than with the issue of speaking in tongues.

James Robison, then a Southern Baptist evangelist, invited Hayford to speak at his pastors' conference held in Dallas, Texas, early in 1987.[14] Attendance was expected to be in the thousands, mostly Southern Baptists. Robison had experienced a dramatic spiritual deliverance from anger in the mid-1980s and had become very receptive to the Charismatic Renewal. After hearing Hayford discuss speaking with tongues in a television interview, Robison contacted him and asked him to address that very issue at his conference.[15]

Hayford accepted the assignment but was apprehensive at the thought of talking about tongues to an audience filled with leaders who, he thought, would likely be cautious or even opposed to the Pentecostal idea of speaking with tongues.[16] Given the demanding task, Hayford carefully prepared a message he entitled "The Beauty of Spiritual Language," and on January 8 he made his presentation. The message was warmly received by the conferees.[17] A young Baptist evangelist at that meeting was particularly impressed by Jack and his message. "I want to be like that man," he said. That evangelist was Robert Morris, who later would become one of Jack's most loyal friends.

It was this presentation at the Robison conference that developed into Hayford's popular but somewhat controversial book *The Beauty of Spiritual Language* (1992). The book was written as an apologetic and appeal for the importance of spiritual language (his term for speaking in tongues) in the daily lives of believers. It was a very intentional "attempt to recast the image many seem to have of 'tongues,'" challenging notions that associated speaking in tongues with snake-handling fanaticism or emotional religious excess.[18]

Jack was aiming the book at sincere and open believers who were uninformed about the true biblical nature of the gift. The thrust of the book was to present the attractiveness, desirability, availability, and usefulness of spiritual language rather than arguing that speaking in tongues was the sign or evidence that one was baptized in the Holy Spirit.

He knew his Classical Pentecostal friends might see the book as an abandonment of a cherished Pentecostal doctrine. Hayford was well aware that he was treading on sacred ground in changing the emphasis. Nevertheless, his desire to introduce a broader audience to the potential benefits of spiritual language motivated him to risk being misunderstood by his Pentecostal colleagues. In the book, Hayford discusses the challenge faced by the Church on the Way when the Classical Pentecostal congregation was thrust into rapid growth during the Charismatic Renewal of the 1970s.

> When the renewal first came to our church, I felt I was walking a tightrope. I wanted to be sensitive to two things—both of which I felt were of equal importance. First, God was pouring out "new wine" into our midst. The old wineskins of our church's traditions were being stretched with such blessing.... How could I lead in a way that respected the Holy Spirit's earlier workings there and still be receptive to His present works?[19]

Hayford knew the tension well. He acknowledged that Classical Pentecostals are able to argue their initial evidence position through their interpretation of the Acts narratives (at least to their satisfaction). But it is also true that equally devout non-Pentecostals were able to make a biblical case that tongues are not present in every passage where believers experienced the Spirit's fullness in Acts.[20] Consequently, he could no longer "*demand* tongues as an evidence of Holy-Spirit fullness" nor could he "*deny* the availability or value of tongues."[21]

Importantly, Jack believed there weren't sufficient biblical grounds to dispute or affirm someone's claim to have experienced Spirit baptism solely by whether or not they have spoken in tongues, because he acknowledged that there are other "evidences" of being Spirit-filled.[22] Jack also acknowledged that the very term *baptism with the Holy Spirit* is open to varied interpretations exegetically. While he used the term to refer to a distinct, usually subsequent, empowering experience, he admitted at his 1986 pastors' conference that he could understand why many evangelicals see Spirit baptism as Christian initiation/conversion.[23]

This admission is part of why he downplayed tongues as evidence of Spirit baptism in his message at Robison's conference and eventually his book. His reasoning went something like this: if tongues is evidentially linked to "baptism in the Holy Spirit," which meant conversion/initiation to many conferees, then in effect they are being told that tongues are essential to conversion. It was possible that some would hear him saying, "You aren't saved until you speak with tongues." This had to be avoided.

Jack was concerned as well for those who did believe in Spirit baptism as a subsequent empowerment but disagreed about tongues as initial evidence. To argue for initial evidence could potentially reinforce his listeners' (and later readers') rejection of a valuable gift. Consequently, in public ministry situations like Robison's conference, he regularly emphasized the value of tongues apart from its connection as evidence of Spirit baptism, much as he had done since the early years at the Church on the Way.[24]

Jack has never denied that speaking in tongues has important eviden-tial value in Acts. But he saw it as secondary to its continuing value in the life of the believer.[25] Often in his ministry, he observed Pentecostals who wore their experience of tongues speech as a kind of badge to prove they had received Spirit baptism.[26] Yet the exercise of spiritual language didn't continue as an ongoing, daily experience in their lives.[27] He felt this was the result of the near total emphasis on tongues as initial evidence among many Classical Pentecostals in the United States. All of these perspectives came together in his book *The Beauty of Spiritual Language*.

As expected, the book stirred a reaction from some Classical Pentecostals. In an effort to head off further misunderstanding, Jack wrote a January 1993 letter to a number of key Pentecostal leaders. Referring to the book, he wrote:

> I am hoping you will hear my heart in its pages. Because you are a fellow-Pentecostal, I am *very* concerned that you recognize my commitment to our values, and my desire that *every* Christian come to experience the rich benefits we have learned to realize in speaking with tongues.[28]

Despite similar public appeals, Hayford was still seen by some as retreating from a full commitment to a vital Pentecostal distinctive, and he received letters expressing dissatisfaction with the book, one from a high-ranking denominational official in one of America's largest Pentecostal groups.[29] But for Jack, it was a matter of conviction. He was seeking to read the biblical text faithfully and help more believers experience all that God had for them.

He said as much in his letter back to the denominational official who had, along with others, met with Hayford to clarify what he actually believed and whether it matched what he wrote in the book. The official specifically objected to Hayford's statement in the book that God "never intended spiritual language as a proof, but that He had offered it as a provision—a resource for readiness in prayer and praise."[30] Jack, ever the diplomat, made his position clear in his letter:

> In that regard, I hold to the conviction that: (a) *as surely as I see and believe* and embrace the conviction of there being a biblical basis for the argument that "tongues" is to be expected accompanying the baptism with the Spirit, (b) *so surely I do not believe* there is a conclusively airtight argument for this position available in God's Word....
>
> Thus, I affirm: *Yes*—in honest conversation with such, I do concede the possible validity of their argument, according to the way I have expressed in my book. I do this in the spirit of refusing to be a deafened dogmatist unable to hear the sincere and accurate arguments of those who use the text in a way seeming incomplete to me, but appearing to be so to them. And *Yes*—I also accordingly refuse to assert it to be my right to tell *them* that any claim they have to being baptized in the Spirit is invalid. In other words, I will not take a place of judgment against brethren over an issue that I think has room for argument, given the *words* of Scripture, even though I believe the *Word* of Scripture to undergird my differing convictions and practice.

Hayford's letter further clarified that practice. When he pastored the Church on the Way, he was required by the Foursquare Church to submit tallies of how many people had been baptized with the Holy Spirit. Hayford included someone in those totals only if he or she had spoken in tongues.

Regardless of the pushback from some Pentecostals, the book accomplished his goal of persuasively presenting the value and beauty of spiritual language and helping non-Pentecostals be open to Spirit fullness and tongues speech. Whether one agrees with everything Jack argues or not, large numbers of people responded over the years to Hayford's invitations to receive the gift of spiritual language.[31]

It wasn't just a theological argument; his position was informed by his personal, ongoing experience of the gift in prayer and worship.[32] Spiritual language was a vital part of his prayer life, helping him to "expand communication in prayer."[33] Jack's preaching regularly recounted stories of finding himself perplexed and confused until he prayed in tongues, at which point he experienced confidence that the Holy Spirit was inspiring prayer according to God's will. Jack regularly employed tongues for intercession and spiritual warfare.[34] Perhaps as much as anything, it was in worship that he believed spiritual language gave believers the ability to transcend the limits of human speech to praise and glorify God.[35]

He taught his congregation that, if they were having difficulty understanding their heartaches or points of personal bondage, or simply didn't know how to pray for a matter, they should pray in tongues and God would bring answers.[36] Jack's practice was almost sacramental at times.[37] At a time when US Classical Pentecostal denominations were seeing an alarming decline in the number of their constituents who spoke in tongues, over 80 percent of the members of the Church on the Way did so.[38]

PASSION FOR FULLNESS

Jack's articulate way of explaining spiritual experiences like speaking in tongues, coupled with his careful way of validating those experiences in Scripture, brought growing admiration from evangelical leaders in the 1980s.

In 1986, Jack was one the few Pentecostals invited to speak at the Congress on Biblical Exposition (COBE), an evangelical event held in Anaheim, California. The congress received considerable coverage in Christian media at the time, and though the event was highly focused on the task of preaching, much attention was given to hermeneutical issues and concerns.[39] Plenary session speakers included the likes of Charles Swindoll, John MacArthur, James I. Packer, and other pedigreed evangelicals. Jack spoke at two well-attended workshop sessions and was well received.

His esteem in the evangelical community was especially evident when he was invited to deliver a plenary address at the Lausanne II Congress on World Evangelization in 1989, which was held in Manila. It was a follow-up event to the historic 1974 Congress that had met in Lausanne, Switzerland, convening under the leadership of Billy Graham to address the challenges and issues associated with global evangelization and mission. The 1974 event drew 2,300 attendees from 150 nations.

A key outcome of the first Congress was the Lausanne Covenant, which had been drafted by an international committee led by British evangelical John Stott. The Covenant was widely regarded as one of the most significant documents in modern church history. The document defined what it means to be evangelical and challenged Christians to work together to make Jesus Christ known throughout the world.[40] The document made a bold declaration concerning the work of the Holy Spirit.

> We therefore call upon all Christians to pray for such a visitation of the sovereign Spirit of God that all his fruit may appear in all his people and that all his gifts may enrich the Body of Christ. Only then will the whole church become a fit instrument in his hands, that the whole earth may hear his voice.[41]

Lausanne II, like the first Congress, was an invitation-only gathering attended by over 4,300 men and women from 173 nations. Jack was asked to speak on "The Power of the Holy Spirit in World Evangelism" in an evening plenary session.[42] His message that night followed the address of renowned British theologian Dr. James I. Packer. It was a humbling challenge to follow

Packer, but Hayford saw the opportunity as providential. Jack titled his message "A Passion for Fullness," based on these two texts:

> And I know that when I come to you, I will come in the fullness of the blessing of Christ. (Romans 15:29 NRSV)

> I pray that, according to the riches of his glory, he may grant that you may be strengthened in your inner being with power through his Spirit … and to know the love of Christ that surpasses knowledge, so that you may be filled with all the fullness of God. (Ephesians 3:16, 19 NRSV)

Jack read from his manuscript (all the speakers had submitted their papers months earlier), which wasn't his customary way of preaching, but he still conveyed his topic well. Jack asked the crowd to "hear the call of the Holy Spirit to receive His supernatural works and gifts" that are inextricably linked to the proclamation of the gospel. What may have surprised some was that this Pentecostal preacher was so decidedly Christ-centered in his call for the Spirit's work in evangelization.

> Thus described, The Word of God reveals that the gospel indeed comes as a two-edged sword: *first*, by declaring that Jesus died for our sins and rose again according to the Scriptures; and, *second*, by confirming the Word with evidences of power, proving Jesus is still alive and active—saving the lost, transforming the soul, healing the sick, and delivering the demonized.
>
> A passion for fullness in such ministry may well rise in us all. Without such fullness we draw on less than the resources we need to shatter hell's strongholds and answer human need.[43]

Hayford argued that the book of Acts "projects the church's ministry as continuing Jesus' ministry, a ministry defined in Jesus' words: 'The work that I do you shall do ... and greater' (John 14:12 NKJV)."[44] To carry on Jesus' ministry was impossible without the fullness of the Holy Spirit, he told the Congress. Not allowing himself to be defined by parochial Pentecostal terminology, Jack made it clear what he meant.

> *Whatever* "the baptism with the Spirit" may mean to us, *whenever* we may feel it is experienced, or *however* it may be evidenced, this much is sure: Jesus said *that baptism* is to provide us with power to minister everything Jesus has and is to the world He *died to redeem* and *touch* with His fullness.
>
> It is both inappropriate and unnecessary to debate theological differences. These are essentially immaterial in the light of the larger question I must answer: "Is the *power* of God's Spirit as evident in my *works* as the *truth* of God's Spirit is in my words?" No structure or belief should block my passion for *all of Jesus in all of my ministry.* That passion for fullness will open me to the Holy Spirit's constant overflow in my life, welcoming His gifts and transcending my limits with His almightiness....
>
> It is clear that the first church felt no need to argue when or where they had *been* filled with the Spirit. For them, the issue was *being* filled—*this* moment; for God's immediate purposes to be served by the Spirit's present surges of supernatural power.[45]

For Jack, a passion for fullness was much more than a theological position. It was about the experience of God's power and it was about the whole church moving together in "the fullness of Christ's ministry."

A passion for fullness means moving beyond sectarianism or stereotypes. "Christ's prayer for unity, 'that the world may know,' is not his mandate to our total doctrinal agreement any more than to our uniformity in church government."

Jack was appealing for all Christians to hear the Apostle Paul's prayer "that you may be filled with all the fullness of God." The word *pleroma*, translated as "fullness" in the passage, called the church beyond its differences to unity in the "fullness of Christ" and to ministry "filled with the Holy Spirit and His power." He went on to suggest a more unifying view that transcended doctrinal precision: "Since we would be people of the *pleroma*—the fullness—we might be called *pleromatics*; that is, people committed to witness to *all* God's Word with *all* the Spirit's wonders, until *all* the world is reached with *all* Christ's fullness!"[46]

He concluded by reaffirming the call of the 1974 Lausanne Covenant to "pray for such a visitation of the sovereign Spirit of God that all His fruit may appear in all His people and that all His gifts may enrich the body of Christ"; because we agree that "only then will the whole Church become a fit instrument in His hands, that the whole earth may hear His voice." All in all, his Lausanne message was classic Hayford.

The message was warmly received, and after finishing his message, Jack was asked to lead "the assembly ... in a season of worship and prayer." He described what happened as those gathered, only a minority of whom were Pentecostal, responded.

> People were standing everywhere, many extending their hands in earnest—indeed, passionate—prayer and praise. The huge hall was pulsating with genuine emotion as a holy intensity rose to dominate the moment. Clearly there was more than a casual stance of soul among vast numbers of the assembly. I was simply standing at the pulpit, praying quietly—seeking to be careful not to say or do

anything which I thought might offend anyone in the broadly representative audience.

There was a bit of a stir at the conclusion of his message, when a small number present that evening thought Hayford's worship and prayer leadership imposed "a sectarian style of prayer and praise on the Congress." The Congress leadership, however, was supportive of Hayford, and the few who were disgruntled were "handled graciously and tactfully." His Lausanne message became the basis of his 1990 book *A Passion for Fullness*, an important and more expansive articulation of his message in Manila.

Events like COBE and Lausanne II helped broaden the recognition of Jack's intellect and good sense so tied to his childlike passion for God.[47]

RESPECTED STATESMAN

In addition to ministry in Pentecostal and Charismatic arenas, the media exposure in the 1980s brought opportunities to more regularly minister to other Christian traditions. Jack was now receiving invitations to speak at conferences from Lutherans, Free Methodists, United Methodists, the Salvation Army, Seventh-day Adventists, United Brethren, and other denominational groups.

He was invited to speak at non-Pentecostal institutions like Biola University in Los Angeles, and he spoke at a number of events for the Billy Graham Evangelistic Association's Schools of Evangelism.[48] Jack served as co-chair along with Ken Ulmer at the November 2004 Billy Graham Los Angeles Crusade held at the Rose Bowl.[49] Hayford was invited to serve on boards and committees for many organizations, such as the National Religious Broadcasters, the Lausanne Committee for World Evangelization (International Committee), and the National Association of Evangelicals (Executive Committee). All this was in addition to his service to organizations within the Pentecostal and Charismatic arenas.

Billy Graham and Jack, 2004 Billy Graham Los Angeles Crusade

In January 1987, Hayford was asked by the Thomas Nelson Company, at the time the world's largest publisher of Bibles, to serve as General Editor of *The Spirit-Filled Life Bible.* Jack's assignment was to lead in bringing together a broadly representative group of practitioners and scholars from the Pentecostal and Charismatic movements to produce a study Bible that would serve every Christian interested in "the whole counsel of God."[50] The project took four years to complete, and the Bible was released in the fall of 1991. As of this writing, the Bible is in its third edition and has sold over two million copies.

Jack was in demand and was invited to speak in some of America's most famous churches, ranging from Robert Schuller's Crystal Cathedral to Donn Moomaw's Bel Air Presbyterian Church. Internationally, he spoke at the world's largest church, Yoido Full Gospel Church in Seoul, South Korea. In 1985, he was speaker at the famed Hollywood Bowl Easter Sunrise Service. Not bad for a Pentecostal preacher.

Jack and David Yonggi Cho, Seoul, Korea

The Charismatic Renewal and its emphasis on worship helped spark a kind of modern worship renaissance that blossomed in the last decades of the twentieth century. Hayford became an important voice in giving a theology for worship that fit well for Pentecostals and Charismatics.

Integrity Music was one of the vanguard groups serving the worship revival. When they established Integrity Worship Institute, which hosted worship seminars around the United States, they turned to Jack for advice and for help in shaping their curriculum.

In the words of Michael Coleman, founder and then CEO of Integrity Music, "more than any other leader I knew, Jack Hayford could transcend denomination barriers." Coleman thought Hayford was the one person who could best articulate theological and biblical foundations for worship practices and do so with pastoral sensitivity. Jack became a primary speaker at the Integrity worship events. These seminars grew into cohosted courses offered by Liberty University and Regent University School of Divinity.

Worship leader and songwriter Don Moen, who worked closely with Integrity Music from its beginnings, was impressed with Jack's ability to "explain and disarm," calling him "uncanny" in making physical worship expression accessible to non-Pentecostals.[51] "He takes the mystery out of expressive worship without removing the wonder of God's presence." Jack did so by modeling powerful, Spirit-filled worship "without the baggage of excess and extremes that some associate with Pentecostal worship."[52]

Many leaders in the worship music industry believed Jack's greatest contribution to the contemporary worship renaissance was his influence on many worship leaders who read his books and listened to his tapes. Moen later observed, "There is no well-known worship leader today that Jack hasn't had some measure of impact on their understanding of worship and worship leadership."[53]

In many spheres, Jack was seen as a voice of sanity and balance, and he was increasingly viewed as a Pentecostal statesman for his nonstrident tone. In 1994 and 1995 there was heated debate over the legitimacy of revivals and the exotic phenomena people were experiencing at the Toronto Airport Vineyard Church and at the Brownsville Assembly of God Church in Florida, better known as the "Toronto Blessing" and "Pensecola Outpouring," respectively. Jack was a calming voice in the controversy, writing a small pamphlet, *Stanced before Almightiness*, in which he called for an openness to workings of the Holy Spirit while also cautioning wholesale endorsement.[54]

His concerns over ministerial ethics made him the leader of choice to moderate disputes and to facilitate dialogues among leaders.[55] Jack was also called on to give trusted counsel and advice when leaders in Pentecostal and Charismatic circles needed correction or help in establishing restoration processes after serious missteps.[56]

There were too many ministry opportunities to keep up with, and he declined the majority. He also turned down a number of requests to serve in new positions, including Oral Roberts' 1986 invitation to succeed him as president of Oral Roberts University. Jack was in high demand, but the remarkable influence came at a cost. Jack found himself being away from home as many as 120 nights a year and, in the midst of it all, he was still pastoring a church that needed his leadership.

Chapter 15

"MINISTRY ON THE WAY"

THE WEST CAMPUS

Following the co-pastoring episode in 1985, Hayford fully intended to "pastor as if he had never pastored before." Clearly, his vision was renewed and he brought strong leadership to the church, despite his many travels. Even with all the ministry opportunities he had, Jack still managed to preach almost every weekend in Van Nuys. By 1986, the church had over 6,000 members and a worship attendance over 5,000. The congregation faced challenges that came from its ongoing growth.

The Church on the Way's commitment to stay at their Sherman Way location in the heart of the San Fernando Valley was severely stressing their facilities. Parking was a nightmare. They tried a number of creative remedies. One they called "Park and Praise" encouraged members to park remotely and then shuttle to the church campus in buses and vans. Someone on the vehicle would lead the passengers in singing choruses and hymns.

Logistically it was hard to organize and sustain long term. No solution they came up with fully addressed their parking problems.

Jack and his team also continued to pursue acquisitions of any available adjacent or nearby properties and seemed to always be renovating and repurposing the properties and buildings they owned. None of their efforts adequately addressed the challenges growth was bringing, but the church still grew nevertheless. In the midst of it all an unexpected opportunity presented itself.

In June 1986, Hayford was on a trip in the Midwest when he was jolted awake. As he began to doze off again, "suddenly a voice spoke sharply: '*Rise up and lay claim to the Baptist Church property.*'" Jack immediately got up and knelt by his bed for a brief prayer: "Father, in the Name of Jesus Christ of Nazareth, Your Son and my Savior, I lay claim to the Baptist property; that it may become ours according to Your sovereign will and power."[1] Hayford was astonished by what happened next.

> Then—*the very day* [after] the Holy Spirit directed me to lay "claim"—I received a completely unexpected call from the Baptist pastor: "Jack, it looks like our people are seriously ready to discuss a sale. When can we talk?" You can imagine the faith I felt that this indeed was *God's timing!* Shortly, the council leaders of our congregation began conversations with the Baptist Church leaders.[2]

There was a backstory to why Jack saw the wake-up call from the Lord as so significant. Eight years earlier, in 1978,

> the Lord spoke to me one day saying: "Walk around the Baptist church property." The command was clear, but how to obey without appearing presumptuous was another problem. I didn't covet the property and I didn't

want to be seen and misunderstood. But I did know that I was to obey the directive; so, just before sunrise one morning, I took two pastoral staff members with whom I had shared this "word."[3]

The three walked the perimeter of the First Baptist Church of Van Nuys' property, but they did not cross the street to walk the full border that the Baptist church owned at the time. Hayford felt they were not to do so. All they knew was that God was saying something about the future borders of the Church on the Way. After walking and praying, they left it to God to work out.[4]

Though the road would be difficult and would take a number of unexpected turns, the Church on the Way agreed to purchase the property in 1987 and gradually occupied the property over the next three years.[5] When they made the purchase, the property line of the Baptist church was exactly the perimeter that Jack and the two pastors had walked nine years before, since the Baptist church had sold the property across the street where the three had decided not to walk.

Jack had been praying for the Baptist congregation all the years since the Lord had confronted him at the stoplight in 1969. He also had taken the time to build friendly relationships with Harold Fickett, who pastored the church in 1969 and also with Fickett's successor, Jess Moody.[6] The warmth of those friendships no doubt contributed to the Church on the Way's acquisition of the property. Ironically, the Church on the Way now owned the buildings and property of a congregation that had once intimidated Jack by its size compared to his tiny church down the road.

Jack was thrilled that the Baptist church had over 600 parking spaces. The fact that the Baptist campus was located on Sherman Way, just 2,000 feet west of the Church on the Way's main campus, made the idea of a dual campus especially feasible. Multiple campuses were not yet the "thing" in the 1980s, but the acquisition made room for hundreds more to join the congregation over the coming years. It also facilitated "simulcast" services allowing Jack to preach in person on one campus and via video link to the other. It was another innovation that many churches were later to adopt. The new campus helped the Church on the Way thrive into the 1990s.

OUT RACING THE WORLD

God's call for the church to stay in Van Nuys also meant Jack needed to pastor the congregation through the changing demographics of the San Fernando Valley. By the early 1990s, Van Nuys was a different city than it had been when Jack started pastoring there in 1969. It was no longer a predominantly white, suburban community. As Los Angeles had grown, so had its suburban sprawl, ever pushing growth and development to the area's edges, thus changing communities more at its center. In October 1993, Van Nuys and the immediate area around the Church on the Way's San Fernando Valley location had growing Hispanic and African American populations.

Given Jack's leadership involvement with the Love LA prayer meetings, he was more aware than ever of the challenges that inner-city pastors and community leaders faced. His growing relationship with pastors of color was specially attuning Jack to what he believed was America's greatest sin: racism. In response to both the changing demographics of Van Nuys and his growing interest in racial reconciliation, Jack brought to the congregation a series of two messages, each nearly two hours in length, which he titled "Out Racing the World."[7]

Jack affirmed that God had created one humanity, one human race, and although humanity's ethnic differences were real, every person was descended from the original *Adam*, male and female, the first couple. Quoting Paul's sermon on Mars Hill in Acts 17, Hayford declared, "We are all His offspring." It was a familiar theme for Jack, who believed that every human born into the world was created to know and love God. Only through redemption in Christ could humanity achieve God's highest purposes for their lives.

"Out Racing the World" was a call to the Church on the Way and the church at large to address the problem of racism, to "out-love and out-race" the surrounding culture, not in some kind of competition but as a vanguard leading the way. He pointed out that the changing face of the congregation increasingly reflected the diversity that was now their community. Jack also retold the story of the Lord speaking to them in 1972 that the church was to stay where they were and not move. He wondered if part of the reason was to model what he called "trans-ethnicity."

Jack, with his usual honesty, told the congregation that "out-racing the world" would require repentance. He recounted to the church a number of incidents from his own journey, from the time in Fort Wayne years earlier when he'd first acknowledged he'd been "enculturated" with racial prejudice to lessons he'd learned from pastors of color.

He mentioned a paper from 1968, which he'd written while serving as Dean of Students at the college. Jack had taken a graduate class at Azusa Pacific University on ethical problems. The paper, written just four months after Martin Luther King Jr.'s assassination, reflected on racial prejudice and how only then had he come to the realization that, in the language of the era, the "evangelical church has failed the Negro in America." He was referencing what he saw as the failure of evangelicals and Pentecostals to stand with African Americans during the Civil Rights Movement in the 1950s and 1960s. When Jack recounted to the congregation the lesson he had learned, he pointedly included himself in the failure.

> In the season of the Civil Rights Movement, there was great mixture of opinion, first, in the nation. Martin Luther King was, by many, viewed as the ultimate hero, and appropriately so ... he was in terms of affecting a long-overdue rectification of past failures.

In many sectors of the church as in many sectors of the United States general population, there were people who resented what he was doing. He was called everything from a "communist" to words that ought not be used by anybody. And as there were things said about the man, I remember feeling kind of in a mixed posture.... I excused myself from any supportiveness toward what was taking place in terms of the Civil Rights Movement ... [and from] the number of clergy that were becoming involved ... almost exclusively of liberal church background ... the evangelical white church neatly distanced itself. *I was part of that.*

I do not remember consciously saying, "I am an evangelical white, and I will distance myself;" but it is what happened. Why? Because of the blindness of the systemic, unperceived and, really, un-Christian attitudes that existed ... the absence of discernment because of such heavy enculturation in tolerating things as they had been. The absence of discernment that this was a kingdom moment, and that something ought to be done. And I had nothing to do. I did nothing with it. I stood, backed away.

He went on to say that it was only in the last few years, as he had prayed with African American pastors at Love LA meetings, that he was able to see how the failure of the conservative churches had impacted their view of white, evangelical pastors. The white evangelicals' failure to support the Civil Rights Movement only reinforced the distance and distrust many black pastors already had toward sectors of evangelicalism.

Jack acknowledged the long history of systemic racism[8] in America and even seemed to suggest, while not justifying violence and looting, that the 1992 riots in South Central LA were at least in part fueled by the African American community's "reservoir of unresolved pain ... the sense of betrayal, the sense of rejection, the sense of disenfranchisement."[9]

Even before "Out Racing the World," Jack was working at racial reconciliation on a personal level. Nine years before the October 1993 messages to the Van Nuys church, Jack had ministered in Washington, DC, at a conference for inner-city pastors.[10] During the Communion service, he asked a black pastor to minister with him, and Jack served the man Communion, asking forgiveness for his and his fellow evangelicals' "violations" of their African American brothers—a video portion of that service was played in Jack's first "Out Racing the World" message.

Jack appealed to the Pentecostal outpouring narrative in Acts as a sign of God's reconciling intention. The "many nations" (ethnicities) gathered in Jerusalem who heard the disciples speaking in tongues but hearing them speak the wonders of God in their "own languages" (see Acts 2:5–11) pointed to the gospel's transcultural reach. This intention will find its ultimate fulfillment at the consummation of the kingdom with a heavenly multitude "from every nation, tribe, people and language" worshipping God before His throne (Revelation 7:9–10 NIV). He told the congregation that the 1906 Azusa Street Revival, the catalytic beginning of US Pentecostalism, had presented a vision for the reconciling of the races through the work of the Holy Spirit. Sadly, systemic racism would eventually eclipse the vision as Pentecostals ended up forming segregated denominations in the early decades of the twentieth century.

Jack closed his final message in the series by calling the congregation to open themselves to "a new era for the Body of Christ at large" and for the Church on the Way to be a place where a reconciling way could be modeled. Jack told them that it would take a generation for real change to be realized but that they needed to start.

They did start and, although the church didn't achieve the full trans-ethnicity they hoped for, they would within fifteen years have one of the largest Spanish-speaking congregations in Los Angeles and also have Farsi-, Syriac-, Arabic-, Chinese-, and Korean-speaking congregations. They also sought to serve the Los Angeles area in ways that addressed the challenging issues the city faced, ranging from gang violence and housing to urban poverty.

The "Out Racing the World" messages gave Hayford opportunities to speak widely on the topic and to work with Christian leaders toward racial reconciliation. He was an important player in what became known as the "Memphis Miracle," in which white and black Pentecostals met to dialogue regarding reconciliation.

When the Pentecostal Fellowship of North America (PFNA) was organized in 1948, it had included only white Pentecostals, perpetuating a division that stretched from not long after the integrated Azusa Street Mission in Los Angeles. Ever since then, the PFNA and black Pentecostals had been two separate streams.

In 1991, Bishop B. E. Underwood of the International Pentecostal Holiness Church became chairman of the PFNA and, along with the group's leadership, initiated a series of steps that brought together the two streams in October 1994. The PFNA was abolished and reconstituted as the Pentecostal Charismatic Churches of North America, which included both white and black Pentecostals. Jack spoke at the event, and he also brought a prophecy that prompted a foot-washing in which a white pastor washed the feet of Ithiel Clemmons, a black minister and bishop in the Church of God in Christ.[11]

Jack brought the address "An Evangelical Response to Racism" at the 1995 Convention of the North American Association of Evangelicals. He also spoke on racial reconciliation at a number of Promise Keepers events. He continued to prioritize relationships with African American pastors in Los Angeles.

Two important relationships were with Charles Blake, pastor of West Angeles Church of God in Christ, who became the presiding bishop of the Church of God in Christ, and Ken Ulmer, pastor of Faith Central Bible Church. Hayford's relationship with Ulmer became especially close when Ulmer joined Jack and Lloyd Ogilvie as prayer partners after the first Shepherds Love LA event.

STANDING WITH THE JEWISH PEOPLE AND ISRAEL

Hayford's bridge-building extended to the Jewish community, as well. Jack had taken his first trip to Israel in 1970, almost exactly a year after coming to Van Nuys. Little did he know then that he would eventually travel to Israel another forty-two times.

Jack profoundly believed that the church did not replace Israel in God's plan and that Gentile believers were called to love Jewish people and to pray for Israel and for the peace of Jerusalem. It would become an important priority for his ministry. Hayford served on the boards of a number of organizations that supported the Jewish state. The majority of his trips to Israel were in leading tour groups, sometimes as large as 200 people.

Jack and Anna on Israel tour bus

He worked with rabbis and Jewish leaders in Los Angeles and was highly respected as a friend for calling Gentile believers to recognize that the Jewish people were in a unique covenant relationship with the God of Israel that required affirmation by the Gentile Christian world.[12] Jack believed that Gentile believers should lead the way in condemning "anti-Semitism of all kinds, including replacement theology."[13]

> [M]any Christians are subconsciously, if not consciously resonant to the spirit of anti-Semitism that is broadly spread throughout the world....[14] [S]ome Christians oppose prophetic promises regarding the restoration of national Israel. There is a line of teaching called "Replacement Theology"... [which] is essentially a theological system that says when the Jew rejected the Messiah at the time of Christ, that God broke covenant forever with Israel, and now His covenant with all mankind is solely through the church.... Replacement Theology holds then that the church, only the church, is Israel today.[15]

Jack's advocacy was the direct result of pastoring in the San Fernando Valley. He knew well that his Van Nuys congregation was surrounded by a Jewish population numbering nearly 500,000, and he was convinced that the Church on the Way was called to minster to them. During the Jesus People movement in Southern California, many young Jews became believers in Jesus and started attending the church. They often brought friends and family members, and Jack learned not to ask anyone "to become a Christian" when he gave invitations in services.[16]

"I didn't use those words ... because I knew that there were always Jews who came to our church.... In the Jewish mindset, 'becoming a Christian' means something it doesn't mean to the average Gentile. While for Gentiles, it is an issue of faith, to a Jew, it became an issue of sacrificing one's individuality, heritage, and ethnicity."[17] Jack's sensitivity led many Jews to receive Jesus as Messiah over the years, making the Church on the Way what some said was the single largest congregation of Messianic Jews in Los Angeles.

Jack also affirmed Jesus-believing Jews as Jews, expressing his support for those who embrace their Jewish identity, including those who are Torah observant. Jack additionally supported the planting of Messianic synagogues in Los Angeles.[18] He saw his advocacy as part of God's call to Gentile Christians, and Jack became a good friend to the Messianic Jewish community for the rest of his active ministry. He joined with Robert Sterns, serving as co-chair with him for the Day of Prayer for the Peace of Jerusalem, committing to pray every day for Israel and the Jewish people. When Jack was approached about supporting a Messianic Jewish Bible translation, *The Tree of Life Bible,* he threw his full support in as a sponsor.

Jack supported Rabbi Marty Waldman's "Toward Jerusalem Council II (TJCII)," an initiative to pursue repentance and reconciliation between the Jewish and Gentile wings of the church:[19]

> The vision is that one day there will be a second Council of Jerusalem that will be, in an important respect, the inverse of the first Council described in Acts 15. Whereas the first Council was made up of Jewish believers in Yeshua (Jesus), who decided not to impose on the Gentiles the requirements of the Jewish law, so the second Council would be made up of Gentile church leaders, who would recognize and welcome the Jewish believers in Yeshua without requiring them to abandon their Jewish identity and practice.[20]

Jack Hayford's love and support for the Jews and Israel reflected the values of TJCII in many ways. It was something he cultivated while pastoring the Church on the Way as he interacted and worked alongside Jewish friends and colleagues. This was particularly the case with his support of Messianic Judaism.

NEW HORIZONS

Jack was awakened early in the morning on September 21, 1993, when the Lord said to his heart, "This is the first day of autumn."[21] He thought for a moment and realized the date was indeed September 21, the beginning of fall, always Jack and Anna's favorite season.

Jack got up and was walking through the hall to go where he planned to have a devotional time, when the voice continued: "I don't mean this is the first day of the season, I mean this is the first day of the fourth and last season of your life."[22] He was not fearful, but it was sobering. He sensed God was telling him that this season of his and Anna's life would be uniquely blessed. He went into the living room to pray. He wrote in his journal,

> Today, the autumn of my years begins.
> But it is the most beautiful ...
> It is the most bountiful ...
> And the winter which concludes it,
> only breaks unto God's eternal spring!
> I love you Lord.

As he sat on the couch in the living room praying, he soon realized that God was calling him to begin mentoring pastors in new ways, and that this was to be the major thrust for the rest of his life. Though the actual form would come later, the basic concept of the Jack W. Hayford School of Pastoral Nurture was born at that moment.[23]

The Church on the Way had already started a church-based ministry training school in the fall of 1971,[24] which had developed into a full-blown Bible institute by the middle of 1987.[25] Originally called the School on the Way, it was renamed The King's Institute, and Hayford thought his mentoring of pastoral leaders would be offered through it.

In 1992, Bill McCartney, then the head coach of the University of Colorado Buffalos football team, invited Hayford to speak at a rally for men in Boulder, attended by 22,000 men.[26] It began a long season of ministry for Hayford in the Promise Keepers men's movement. Throughout the 1990s, Hayford spoke around the nation at stadium events attended by tens of thousands of men. Jack was asked to serve on the board of Promise Keepers, and he was humbled by the invitation of the predominantly evangelical ministry.

Hayford was asked to serve as the Master of Ceremonies at the historic Promise Keepers Washington, DC, Mall event in October 1997, a gathering that drew an estimated crowd of over one million. Jack ably guided the men through the rally's segments. Although he was not one of the worship leaders at the event, he tactfully and graciously encouraged men to worship God freely.[27] His years ministering to men had prepared him to lead over a million men to love and honor their Lord. It was one of the highlights of his ministry.

Another privilege for him was the February 1996 Promise Keepers National Clergy Conference in Atlanta, at which Jack addressed as many as 40,000 pastors.[28] He preached a message on worship and told a story of hearing the Lord ask him to dance for Him.

It was a funny but tender story of humbling himself before God. As was so often the case, Jack's way of telling the story was disarming. Most of those in the stadium loved it, but Jack received a few letters from clergy who believed he had, like in Manila, unnecessarily imposed his Pentecostal views. But Coach McCartney and the Promise Keepers leadership were pleased with Jack's message and stood with him.

On February 19, 1996, about an hour into the flight back to Los Angeles after the Atlanta conference, God spoke to Jack again. He was gazing out the window when he heard the Lord speak "with the clearest voice … [saying], 'Found a seminary.'"[29] It was a complete surprise, and Jack found himself arguing in response. "If I did that, people would laugh at me."

Jack responded this way because, as a local church pastor most of his life, he believed he had little significant "academic respectability" for such an endeavor.[30] Considering Jack had served for years as the Dean of Students at Life Bible College and as the school's president for five years, even teaching on the faculty as well, it was surprising that he felt so inadequate, but he did. Jack was often insecure over his lack of significant graduate training.

He also knew that, in order to start a seminary, The King's Institute would need to become a formal college. He realized as well that forming a seminary would eventually lead to a transition in his role away from senior pastor of the Church on the Way.

As he always had, he obeyed God's direction. In June 1996, he invited Paul Chappell, a longtime academic administrator and former Dean of the School of Theology and Mission at Oral Roberts University, to lead the founding of the seminary and the transition of the institute.[31] By 1997, The King's College offered its first classes, and in January 1999, the seminary opened. It was just the beginning for The King's College and Seminary.

The vision of mentoring pastors was realized in June 1997 when "The King's" hosted the very first Jack W. Hayford School of Pastoral Nurture Consultation. It convened on the west campus of the Church on the Way, and forty-five pastors attended. Jack spent over fifty hours teaching and dialoging with the group over a seven-day period.[32] By 2000, The King's College and Seminary would host ten to eleven consultations each year.[33] Spending time with pastors was Jack's "sweet spot."

THE FACE OF THE FOURSQUARE CHURCH

With Jack Hayford's rise, the fortunes of the Foursquare denomination had risen, as well. Jack became the face of the movement's resurgence from the late 1970s on.[34] From 1980 to 1991, Foursquare churches in the United States grew in number from 921 to 1,516—a 65 percent increase.[35]

In 1991, Roy Hicks Jr., Jack's longtime friend and fellow pastor, then the director of Foursquare Missions, told a reporter, "When the younger generation thinks of Foursquare now they think of Jack Hayford."[36] It was very true in 1993 when Jack's face was again on the cover of *Charisma* magazine. The article discussed Hayford's and other leaders' influence in reshaping the denomination started decades earlier by Aimee Semple McPherson.

In considering the nearly one-hundred-year history of the Foursquare Church, it is fair to suggest that the person most associated with the movement besides its founder has been Jack Hayford. It makes sense. Both were gifted with superior communication skills and were savvy at adapting their message to their audiences. Both sought a balanced Pentecostal expression yet hungered for the fullest experience of Christ's life-transforming gospel. Both centered their ministries in the local church and were deeply committed to Los Angeles. It is not widely known, but McPherson's son, Rolf, once remarked of Hayford, "That man is so much like my mother it makes me nervous."[37]

Jack was always a fierce apologist for Aimee. In September 1990, he delivered a message at Angelus Temple entitled "The Unending Trial of Aimee Semple McPherson," in which he vigorously defended her ministry, pointing out how Christ-centered her message was.[38] He acknowledged the role of many significant Christian women of the twentieth century but believed that, "in terms of touching the multitudes, healing the sick and establishing a globe-encompassing ministry, none exceed Aimee Semple McPherson."[39]

The 1990 message was given in the wake of the scandals surrounding Jim Bakker and Jimmy Swaggart, both of whose ministries were publicly identified with Pentecostalism. Jack believed that Aimee's life had been unfairly judged, especially in regard to her disappearance. He defended the relentless, unending trial she was forced to undergo regarding her story of being kidnapped. Hayford declared: "There is something to be said for a person whose ministry was so fruitful that ... the devil still hates her sufficiently to spray lying venom at her memory."[40]

It's not surprising that, in a movement started by a woman, Jack has been a strong advocate for women in ministry leadership. He has long argued that women are fully called and capable to serve as pastors, teachers, evangelists, prophets. The only exception for him was apostle.[41]

Jack's advocacy for women in ministry was rooted in his understanding of God's intention before the fall. "At the creation there was no submission of the woman to the man enjoined—only the submission of both to their Maker and to His divine order for the fulfilling of their destiny." He believed, however, that the fall of man had altered God's original intention and, consequently, man was given the responsibility to lead in the "recovery of the original order—of both male and female being restored to equal dominion."[42]

Accordingly, Jack affirmed the traditional complementarian view of many evangelicals that, in marriage, a woman is to submit to her husband's leadership, although Jack always emphasized the husband's role to love and serve his wife. On the one hand, he wanted women to find a full release in ministry leadership, something he saw in Scripture, and yet on the other hand, he believed that in marriage the man was to take his place in leading his wife.[43]

TRANSFERRING THE FLAG

Not long after the Lord spoke to Jack in September 1993, telling him that he was entering the autumn season of his life, he wrote to the church council and a few other elders, suggesting that they begin praying together about a transition in the next few years. He even offered to step aside within two years, but the elders felt that would be too soon. Jack was nearing sixty, and he didn't want to see the church age with the pastor, something he had observed often led to declining congregations. So they began praying together.

After the Lord called him to start a seminary in 1996, Jack wrote the church council again in June to let them know he believed the time was at hand to begin a transition to a new senior pastor. Both Jack and the church council believed his transition out of the senior pastor role would not mean he was leaving the church. Rather, he would continue to provide different but distinct leadership and high visibility, even after transitioning his role, though they were uncertain what that would look like.[44]

He outlined his reasons for the transition. First, the demands of shepherding the congregation while trying to manage his ministry to the larger church, assignments he'd long struggled to balance, were wearing him down. Second, the culture was changing, and the congregation needed vision to serve a younger generation. He didn't want the church to be caught in a "time warp." Third, he felt God now clearly calling him to prioritize his apostolic role and his ministry to pastors. Fourth, he listed several prospects that needed his attention: his writing, his board involvements, and, chiefly, starting the seminary and all it would require.

He recommended to the council that his son-in-law, Scott Bauer, be appointed co-pastor and senior executive pastor of the church, and that he at some point become the church's next senior pastor. The church council met in late June and prayerfully decided to recommend Scott Bauer to the Foursquare district supervisor as the congregation's next senior pastor, although the exact time wasn't yet decided.

Scott and Rebecca had rejoined the pastoral staff at the church in 1985 after Dennis Easter had stepped out of his role as co-pastor. They believed they were to make a ten-year commitment to the church, although they had never mentioned that to Jack. The years passed quickly and in 1995, Scott thought he and Rebecca were ready to move to a new assignment. But the Lord didn't give any direction, so they stayed.

About a year later, in May 1996, at a time when Scott and Rebecca were earnestly asking the Lord what to do, Scott got up very early one morning and went out into his living room to pray. He knew the Lord had awakened him and he asked the Lord, "What do You have to say to me?" The answer was immediate. "I am transferring the flag of responsibility for the Church on the Way to your vessel." Bauer understood the Lord was saying that there was a movement of authority ahead. It was overwhelming and wasn't anything he'd ever thought or talked about with Jack in the eleven years since they'd been at the church.

Three weeks later, Jack invited Scott to his home office and read him the letter he was going to send to the church council, not wanting to recommend Scott unless he was comfortable with the possibility. Only then did Scott relate his story to Jack of what God had spoken. Neither Jack nor Scott told the church council what God had said until after the council had affirmed their sense that Scott was to be the church's next senior pastor, not wanting to influence their decision.

Following the council's decision, Hayford and the leadership team developed a schedule from 1997 through 1999 that would gradually reduce Jack's teaching responsibilities on the weekends.[45] Scott took the weekends when Jack didn't preach, and in 1999 he preached over 50 percent of the time and was received well by the congregation.

Jack had learned from the previous co-pastor episode that he needed to reduce his preaching role in order to make the transition work. He had to give Scott the place of leadership by gradually increasing his preaching in the weekend services. Scott Bauer was presented as co-pastor "without fanfare, ritual, or special announcement" in the church bulletin in the spring of 1997.[46]

Jack also spent considerable time communicating and leading the transition. He wrote pastoral letters and met with the pastoral team, the church staff, and the larger body of key servants in the church. It helped the whole congregation "own" the transition. Jack went out of his way to make it absolutely clear that Scott had neither *sought* the senior pastor position nor "got" it by reason of family ties.[47] He knew for some that would be hard to believe, but it was the truth. He assured the congregation he wasn't going anywhere and would still preach some, but in a secondary role.

Despite all the planning and preparation, it was harder than Jack expected to let go of the church he had led for thirty years, but he knew it was what God was asking and he never said no to the Lord. His focus was to be on training pastors and church leaders, and this required the surrender of a role he loved. He wrote in his journal about struggling with "deep discomfort in my soul over my departing the senior pastorate." He feared confusion might ensue and diminish the possibilities of the seminary and his focus on mentoring pastors and leaders. So much of his notoriety had come from being the senior pastor. What would it be like now?[48]

"Transferring the Flag" to Scott Bauer, October 1999

But Jack obeyed, and on October 24, 1999, Scott and Rebecca Bauer were appointed as pastors of the Church on the Way, with Scott as senior pastor.[49] The news release about the transition reflected the word God had spoken to Scott: "Jack Hayford Leads Church in 'Transferring' the Flag." The release announced that Jack was not retiring but answering a call "to lay foundations for equipping pastoral leaders globally for a new millennium."[50]

Jack assumed the title of Founding Pastor and continued to teach at the church ten or twelve times a year. His priority, however, was now as president of the new seminary God had called him to start. With Chappell's able leadership, the seminary received national accreditation in just two years. The King's College and Seminary was growing in enrollment, and Jack was now spending ten or more weeks each year mentoring pastors through the School of Pastoral Nurture.

The Church on the Way, whose attendance had plateaued for seven years, started growing again under Scott and Rebecca's leadership, its weekend attendance growing by nearly 2,500 by 2003. A year before the transition in June 1998, the Lord had spoken a word to Jack and Scott about The *New* Church on the Way. It wasn't about changing the name, but it reflected the expansive vision God was giving Bauer.

Scott invited Jim Tolle, who had earlier served on the pastoral staff and who was fluent in Spanish, to lead La Iglesia En El Camino, the church's small Spanish-speaking congregation. Under Tolle's leadership, it exploded to several thousand. Bauer also cast a vision for a third campus in Santa Clarita, fourteen miles north of the Van Nuys campuses.[51] It was exactly the kind of leadership Jack believed the congregation needed.

The King's College and Seminary was also flourishing, and Jack was able to travel more widely without the need to be back for weekends. He and Anna also were freer to travel and rest, and they purchased a home in Solvang, two hours north of Los Angeles, a place that had been a favorite getaway spot for them over the years. The blessings God had promised them for their autumn years seemed at hand.

Chapter 16

SERVING THE KING

THE BLESSINGS OF AUTUMN?

In a hospital just miles away, Jack's son-in-law, Scott, the husband of his oldest daughter, Rebecca, and his pastoral successor in Van Nuys, lay brain dead. People around the world were mobilized to pray for a miracle of divine healing. Short of that miracle, the family planned to stop life support that afternoon at two.[1]

The room was dark when Jack woke up on Friday, October 24, 2003. It was 5:00 a.m. and it had been thirty-three hours since forty-nine-year-old Scott Bauer had collapsed at the end of the Wednesday night service at the Church on the Way. Scott was just concluding the Wednesday night prayer meeting when he experienced a terrible headache and asked one of the other pastors to finish for him. He stepped off the platform and collapsed, never fully regaining consciousness from a ruptured congenital aneurism.

Still in bed, Jack heard a whisper, but it was not God's voice. In the dark room the voice snarled, "So these are the blessings of autumn!!" In

Jack's words, "It was the most vicious, hateful, sinister sound I have ever heard in my life." It felt like a knife to his soul.

> The hate-filled, heinous words—threaded with an icy fury—require explanation, for they were spoken as a despicable mockery, spewing back at me a statement I had testified to Father God's having spoken to me several years earlier. Now I was [69], but nearly a decade before, our loving God had clearly impressed me that the autumn years of my life would be filled with and attended by profound promise and hope.[2]

Now "Satan himself was seeking to capitalize on our trial and spit in the face of the gracious 'future hope' that God had declared to be His will for me."[3] And the enemy continued his stinging vitriol: "Everything will collapse along with Scott. The church will not withstand this shock, the seminary vision will falter and fail, and the faith of those who have prayed will turn to futility and abiding doubt!"[4] It was a dreadful and "absolutely crushing" experience. Jack was so exhausted that he did not even fight back but just offered a prayer, "Jesus. You are going to have to handle this." He fell back to sleep.[5]

He woke up two hours later. As the morning light was just beginning to brighten the previously dark room, he realized that something remarkable had happened. He *"was enveloped with an overwhelming sense of the PEACE OF GOD!"* As he got out of bed he felt an "unshakable sense of being totally, mightily and majestically undergirded by the power of God in a manner that transcended any security, confidence or peace I'd ever experienced."[6] It was like standing on "a block of granite stretching a mile in each direction."

A few minutes later, Jack stepped outside to get the morning paper and stared out at the brightness of the sun, which was just coming over the horizon. Many a time in the twenty-five years in which he had lived in the house, he had prayed in his front yard. There were occasions when one or two doves would land nearby, almost as if divinely "arranged." That morning, Jack uttered a prayer: "Lord, Your peace is so wonderful just now—but it would be nice to 'have a dove' this morning." There were no doves, but as Jack turned to go back in the house, something did happen:

> Instantly, there was a distinct and unexplainable movement of wind across the trees in front of our house—a breeze that was as inexplicable, naturally speaking, as it was beautiful in its display. With a smooth, continual "whoosh," the leaves were softly folded back, and an indescribable display of sunlight—like diamonds—sparkled through the trees in our yard. Amid the utter beauty of the moment and its absolute distinct unlikelihood as an occurrence, I was dumbstruck with wonder. Then, a clear, gentle Voice spoke within my heart: "*There are other ways than a dove by which I reveal my Presence.*"
>
> It was so real, so tenderly gracious and so significantly timed—my heart leaped within me, and I stood in the morning sunlight, arms upraised, and I began to sing:
> He is our Peace, who has broken down every wall!
> He is our Peace—He is our Peace![7]

Scott Bauer died that afternoon, exactly four years to the day after he had succeeded his father-in-law. The family was present at his bedside as Scott breathed his last.[8] It was an unimaginable loss to the entire family and painfully difficult for Rebecca and the children, but God, as He so often had in the past, poured out His great grace and led them through the ordeal.

Just hours later, Jack met with the Church on the Way's primary leaders and, at their request, agreed to return in an interim role as the senior pastor and lead the congregation through the crisis. It was one of the most challenging assignments Jack had ever faced, but he did so with courage and honesty, helping the church see God's faithfulness in the midst of the loss.[9]

Jack was asked hard questions following the shocking and sudden death of the church's young shepherd. "Was there not enough prayer?" "Was there not enough faith?" "Had the doctors done enough?" He assured the congregation that it was not a matter of insufficient prayer or faith, telling the church he had never seen such a great response of believing prayer. Jack spoke of the excellent medical care Scott had received.

The greatest comfort was knowing that Scott "was not taken; he was received into the arms of Jesus. He was welcomed as a good soldier who had fought the good fight. He was welcomed as a good shepherd who only lived to hear these words, 'Well done, good and faithful servant.'"[10]

One week after Scott's collapse, his memorial service was held. It was a fitting tribute to his life and ministry. Jack spoke at the memorial along with others. A particularly moving moment was when Rebecca told of holding Scott's hand as he passed: "When I let go of Scott's hand God picked up mine." She would write in the church's bulletin a year later how hard the months after Scott's death were, but also how God had taught her "to run to Him."[11]

In the years after Scott had first succeeded his father-in-law, Jack had been intensely focused on The King's College and Seminary, serving first as president of the seminary and then as the institution's chancellor. He was convinced that "the birth of The King's was the Lord's idea." Hayford wrote in his journal about a prophecy he had received.

> I told you *Why* to begin the Institute/College, and I told you *TO* found the Seminary. Further, you have named them both as Mine. So be assured—I will sustain what I have ordained: I will guard & keep what is Mine.[12]

With Scott's passing, Jack's focus would now be on both the school and the church, but he was confident that God would provide the needed grace. He was reminded of a morning not long after Scott died when he'd seen two doves perched on the house, and the Holy Spirit had whispered: "They represent my provision of a dual anointing for this season you must lead both—The Church and The King's."[13]

For the next eleven months, Jack served the Church on the Way as the senior pastor. But he knew from the moment he came back that it was only temporary. The momentum the church had gained under Scott's leadership continued, and Jack recommended to the church's elders that another one of his sons in the faith, Jim Tolle, the pastor of the church's Spanish-language congregation, La Iglesia En El Camino, be named senior pastor. The elders agreed, and the Foursquare Church affirmed the recommendation.

Tolle would now pastor both the English-speaking and Spanish-speaking congregations. In September 2004, Jim Tolle, a man Hayford had closely discipled years before, was appointed the new senior pastor.[14]

THE KING'S COLLEGE AND SEMINARY

With a new senior pastor in place, Jack refocused on the The King's College and Seminary. The school was founded with an educational philosophy vitally tied to the local church. The vision was to link together ministry education and the practice of ministry, hence the slogan "education and ministry ... better together." When the seminary opened on January 11, 1999, with seventy-eight students, its purpose was "to equip Church leadership with the pragmatics for ministry and the dynamics of enablement to lead God's people in the power of the Holy Spirit."[15] The vision for the seminary was the "blending of spiritual passion with scholarly earnestness."[16]

The school was interdenominational, while intending to serve in partnership with the Foursquare Church. Jack had met with the Foursquare denomination's board of directors in April 1997 to seek their approval, not wanting the new school, so near the denomination's primary school, Life Bible College, to be competing for the same students.[17]

Jack made it clear that he was starting a graduate seminary. Since in 1997 Life Bible College did not offer graduate education, there was no reason to be concerned that students would be drawn away from the Foursquare college. And while it was true that the Church on the Way would be transitioning The King's Institute from a two-year training school to a full four-year undergraduate college offering degrees, it would be focused on recruiting older, non-residential students, whereas Life Bible College was focused on younger, residential students. After the meeting, the Foursquare leadership gave their blessings to Jack in starting The King's College and Seminary.

Hayford wanted the new school to be accessible and affordable.[18] Online education was an important part the school's programs from the very start. They also made a significant investment in marketing that capitalized on Jack's notoriety, putting full-page advertisements in a number of Christian periodicals. The investment paid dividends and by 2006 the school had grown to over 600 students.

Jack teaching at the School of Pastoral Nurture

Teaching at the seminary's School of Pastoral Nurture (SPN) was what Hayford most enjoyed. Spending time with forty to forty-five pastors energized Jack. The relaxed, conversational sessions allowed Jack to be himself.

He bantered with the leaders and fielded hard questions and would teach six to eight hours each day. He was in an environment that allowed him to challenge "sacred cows" and push leaders to reflect deeply and biblically and, occasionally, controversially.

For example, Jack always emphasized the church's mandate to reach out to a world in need of a Savior. He expressed his conviction that believers avoid overidentification with any particular political party, concerned that such identification might become an obstacle to the gospel. His understanding of the kingdom of God was decidedly apolitical, referencing Jesus' words, "My kingdom is not of this world." He sometimes quipped that God wasn't a Republican or a Democrat.

Jack wasn't suggesting that Christians shouldn't act responsibly as citizens, always affirming the need to vote, seek public office, and influence culture as salt and light. Jack was pro-life, affirming the sanctity of life, and he believed the Bible taught the sanctity of marriage as the union between a man and woman, an institution created by God. He always communicated his convictions graciously and wisely and never in combative language.

He believed the church had a responsibility to speak prophetically to culture, but he taught that it must be done with a redemptive posture motivated by love. He did not want the church to be perceived as hostile to the very people who need God's salvation. His concern was that people not see the church as against them. "You can't win the culture by being its enemy," he said. "The church isn't called to raise a standard of righteousness *to* the world. We are called to proclaim the gospel to the world and to live a standard of righteousness *before* the world." He saw Jesus' ministry as the model; He was a "friend of sinners."

It wasn't unusual in the SPNs for Jack to share his concern about some advocates of young earth creationism who saw their position as the only biblically faithful option. Jack, ever the bridge-builder, argued there were several legitimate options in how the Genesis creation accounts could be interpreted, including young earth creationism but others as well.[19] Jack's own view aligned more closely to astrophysicist and Christian apologist Hugh Ross's "old earth," progressive creationism, positing the earth was billions of years old. Jack was always curious and read widely on topics like string theory and quantum physics while never questioning God as Creator.

But what Hayford talked most about at the different SPNs was what one would expect. It was about how he lived out his private walk with God and how he thought about the people he pastored. He taught on worship, prayer, and the kingdom of God, the themes that developed when he first came to the Church on the Way. Jack never tired of these subjects and loved the opportunity to push deep with the pastors and leaders. His teaching on Paul's letter to the Ephesians and what the book had to say about God's high purpose for His church were some of his favorite SPN sessions.

PRESIDENT OF THE FOURSQUARE CHURCH

Twice, Jack Hayford was considered for the presidency of the Foursquare movement, in 1987–88 and 1997. But in both instances, he didn't believe he should leave the Van Nuys church to serve full-time as president, something that was expected of anyone serving in the position.[20] Hayford had never sought to lead the denomination and, if anything, he stayed in the background whenever possible, though he was never shy about voicing his perspectives.

Things changed in 2004 when Paul Risser, the movement's president, resigned following inappropriate investments in a Ponzi scheme that lost the denomination millions of dollars. John Holland, Risser's predecessor, also had been forced to resign for questionable financial management. Although in both cases nothing illegal was done, nor did either man ever profit personally, the resignations brought to the surface long-standing questions over financial secrecy that had characterized the corporate offices of the Foursquare Church.[21]

In the spring of 2004, Hayford was approached by a nominating committee asking to submit his name as a candidate for the presidency. Since his service as the pastor of the Church on the Way was only temporary, he agreed to do so.[22] At the June 2004 annual convention held in San Francisco, Hayford was overwhelmingly elected to a five-year term as the fifth president (excluding those who served interim terms) of the International Church of the Foursquare Gospel.[23]

Jack's installation service was held on October 1, 2004. Rick Warren, one of America's most respected evangelical leaders and pastor of Saddleback Church, asked to be part of his installation "because of the influence Jack Hayford and his ministry [has had] on my life." Warren brought a brief but glowing tribute to Jack lauding his heart for the kingdom, his authenticity, his integrity, and his obedience to God. The words of such a highly regarded fellow pastor, respected for his integrity, were profoundly humbling for Jack.

It was also humbling to find himself leading the entire Foursquare movement, a scenario he would never have imagined in 1974 when he'd sat in his office hearing the Lord say, "The mantle of leadership has moved."[24] He would carry out his leadership of the Foursquare Church with the same ecumenical grace that was evident while leading the Church on the Way.[25]

In view of the issues that had forced the resignations of the two previous presidents, Jack wanted to establish a culture of trust. He instituted changes at the movement's central offices, requiring full disclosure of financial matters. Jack believed that greater transparency would help heal some of the residual distrust regarding the handling of the movement's resources. He also began regular times of prayer and worship at the central offices, and he promoted a more relational working environment through occasional joint meals and fellowship times.

An important move was restructuring the movement's national leadership team to reflect a more collegial approach to decision-making.[26] Another strategic and far-reaching move was his appointment of Tammy

Dunahoo as Vice President of Women in Leadership Ministry. She would go on to serve as the denomination's General Supervisor, overseeing all the movement's churches in the US.

Hayford began to correspond regularly with the movement's ministers about "family matters." Never known for an economy of words, Jack wrote multipage letters at least quarterly for most of his five-year term. Motivated by a desire to resource pastors, he expanded the role of the movement's central offices. During his presidency, the denomination also went through a complicated restructuring of how it oversaw its churches in the US.

In 2002, the movement had multiplied its district structure of churches from nine districts to over seventy. It proved to be an unwieldy structure that failed to achieve its goals. Under Hayford's watch the movement undertook a "consolidation" of the districts, reducing the seventy-plus districts to fourteen. The consolidation restructuring has served the movement well ever since.

The biggest challenge for Jack's presidency was the denomination's struggle with the consequences of the Great Recession of 2008–2009, when the world financial markets collapsed. The Foursquare Church's equity investments lost heavily and, coupled with the spending during the early years of Jack's presidency in expanding the role of the central offices, the movement lost approximately 26 million dollars. Hayford and the executive team worked hard to help the denomination recover financially, but it would be a long road and was not entirely successful during his last year as president.

As his term was ending, Jack submitted his name for another five-year term. He had some uncertainly about a second term but felt a "constraint to serve anyway."[27] The movement's polity allowed for a second five-year term that only required ratification by the convention body at the 2009 Foursquare annual meeting.

Early Sunday morning the day before the 2009 convention was to begin, Jack awakened feeling a "profound unrest." He got up and as he prayed he saw in his mind a placard with the words "Let the peace of God rule in your heart" written on it. He also recognized that part of what had motivated him to offer himself for another term was "a sense of duty."

Anna woke up and Jack told her what he was feeling. As Jack recounted his thoughts to her, the idea of not serving another term flooded him with a sense of the peace of God. By 5:30 a.m., Jack and Anna had prayed and decided he needed to withdraw his name. He would serve out his term but not serve a second. Even though it was still very early, he asked two members of his executive team to come to his hotel room, where he shared the decision with them.

With Jack's nomination withdrawn, the denomination's board of directors was left to make quick decisions about how to proceed. They decided to appoint Glenn Burris, the General Supervisor of the national church, as interim president with the election of a new president to be held at the 2010 convention. The 2009 convention had started with most people expecting Hayford to be ratified for a second term, so it was shocking when his decision was announced to the convention body.[28]

Some in Foursquare were not happy with the denomination's financial woes and with Hayford's expansion of the role of the central offices. There was talk that he withdrew his name for a second term out of fear that he wouldn't be ratified.[29] Nevertheless, Jack was still highly regarded by the majority of ministers and members of the movement and would likely have been ratified. Jack was aware of the questions about his decision but affirmed it was simply a matter of obeying God's peace in his heart.

In his journal, Hayford admitted that there were some who would likely see his presidency as a failure and others who might say, "Nice try, but give him a D or C grade for his service." He continued,

All this brings me to the confession of my human vulnerability and this is my sin, in having judged others
the same way … [having] privately expressed opinions
that—however accurate or inaccurate—have only been
that—opinions. And all of them from that limited viewpoint that every person has.…

Forgive me for all my sins—committed in ignorance,
in haste or blindly, and release every "knot" tied with
words or thoughts that presumed I was right.…

Your son and servant,

Jack[30]

When Jack concluded his term four months later, it would be the
final time he would serve the Foursquare family in any official capacity. In
the years since, Jack has been relatively uninvolved with the movement in
which he spent his entire ministry. He still saw Foursquare as his beloved
family and still had a voice, but not as before.[31]

He later observed that, in every instance—as National Youth Director,
Dean of Students at the college, president of the college, and then as president of the denomination—his service always lasted five years.[32] Jack always
believed symmetry revealed something of God's design, but he also realized
that his presidency of Foursquare was one of his very few assignments that
hadn't been remarkably blessed.

JACK, THE KING'S, AND GATEWAY CHURCH

Jack's presidency of Foursquare had taken so much of his time and energy
that he had been little able to provide the kind of leadership The King's
College and Seminary had needed. It had also given him less time for his
ministry to the larger church. In the fall of 2009 Jack was seventy-five and,

as the university chancellor, he had to address a number of issues at the school. The recession created difficulties for smaller, tuition-based schools, and the college and seminary needed his leadership.

Early in Jack's Foursquare presidency, there had been serious discussions over the possibility of The King's and Life Bible College merging, but the plan had never materialized. The denomination had, as part of the potential merger of the two schools and also as part of a broader ministerial education plan, assumed a $14 million loan for The King's College and Seminary's purchase of a nearby hospital, which they had planned to repurpose as a new campus.

The project proved unfeasible over costs necessary for abatement and renovation, and the idea was abandoned. Now with Foursquare's financial challenges, the building had to be sold, and the responsibility for the sale fell to The King's. It took over a year to find a buyer. Selling the building was an important step in helping stabilize the institution's financial difficulties, but what would secure the future of the university was the budding relationship between Jack and Robert Morris.

Morris was that young evangelist who had first been introduced to Jack Hayford at James Robison's 1987 conference. After being impressed with Jack at the conference, Morris started watching Jack on television, listening to many of his sermons, and reading his books.[33] The more he did so, the more he respected Jack.

In 2000, Morris started Gateway Church in Southlake, Texas. Later that same year, he was at a conference at which Jack was speaking and took the opportunity to introduce himself. They talked only briefly, but shortly after, Morris invited Jack to one of Gateway Church's first pastors' conferences. He also attended one of the School of Pastoral Nurture Consultations. It was the beginning of a growing friendship and ministry partnership.

By 2004, Gateway Church had become one of the fastest-growing churches in America. In Jack, Robert Morris saw a spiritual father and someone who knew the blessings and difficulties that came with the rapid growth of a church and the recognition that comes with it. The two spoke frequently by phone, and Jack spoke with some regularity at Gateway, usually including the first Sunday of the year. Hayford was named an "apostolic elder" to Gateway Church.

Jack invited Morris to serve as a trustee for The King's College and Seminary, and in 2009, in the midst of enrollment and financial issues the school was dealing with, Morris was asked to serve as chairperson of the trustees. Jack, also at the request of the trustees, stepped back into the role of president to help steer the school through troubled waters and to find a new permanent president.

On the first Sunday of January 2010, Hayford spoke at Gateway Church. Morris took Jack to see the church's 4,000-seat sanctuary building, which was still under construction. As the two stood in the balcony looking down at the large bowl where the main floor seats would be, Jack asked Morris if he would consider taking responsibility for The King's. His question was motivated by a recognition of his age and that the Lord had directed him to ask.

Robert Morris told Jack that, just two months earlier in his quiet time, the Lord had spoken and said: "If Jack Hayford asks you to take The King's, would you do it for him and Me?" Morris had said yes to the Lord then, and now told Jack yes, as well.

It was a momentous decision that would eventually move the university's main campus from Van Nuys to Southlake, Texas, and would lead to both financial stability and a strategic future, assuring Jack's legacy as a pastor to pastors. In 2019, the Jack Hayford Endowment was established for The King's Seminary, a distinct divinity school to train future leaders of the church.

Jack at The King's Seminary

The King's University would increasingly reflect Hayford's strong support of the Messianic Jewish community. In the fall of 2007, the university started the Messianic Jewish Studies (MJS) Program "for the formal training of Messianic rabbis and other leaders who are called to serve as bridges between the Church and the Jewish people."[34] The MJS Program has grown significantly in the years since and is an approved training school of the Union of Messianic Jewish Congregations for rabbinical ordination.[35]

Robert Morris and Gateway shared the same commitment to the Jewish people as Jack, something that only served to strengthen their bond. The church started Gateway Jewish Ministry "to proclaim God's love to the Jewish community and connect Christians to Israel and the Jewish roots of the Christian faith."[36] Once monthly, a Friday Shabbat service is attended by hundreds.

After the September 11 terrorist attacks, Hayford traveled to Israel early in 2002. While in prayer there, he saw a vision of a barrier being raised to protect Israel and realized it was a barrier of prayer. In response, Jack established four prayer altars in Israel that became prayer points and would be visited by every tour group he led thereafter. The altars were located in the northern, southern, eastern, and western parts of the land. Gateway Church sponsors a number of tours to Israel each year. After Jack stopped traveling internationally, they committed to visit the prayer altars with their tours.

Robert Morris and Gateway Church were enormously generous to Jack and Anna. They moved his media ministry to Texas and, in partnership with donors who supported Jack's ministry, made a significant investment in digitizing his audio and video messages, creating sermon outlines and transcripts, and then making hundreds available through the Jack Hayford Digital Library.[37] Morris and Gateway wanted Jack's voice to be heard by new generations of leaders.

A commitment was made by Gateway Church's leadership to care financially for Jack and Anna for the rest of their lives and to provide counsel and support as they aged. Morris personally worked with Jack in making decisions regarding his ministry travels in light of the challenges that come with aging.

FAMILY MATTERS

Jack and Anna had their share of the pain and heartache that come with the ebb and flow of life. Certainly, Scott's death was very difficult, and there had been other tragedies. Jack had lost his sister, Luanne, to cancer in 1978.[38] Jack had for a long time experienced back problems, but his back pain became especially acute in his forties. He avoided surgery for as long as possible and was known for carrying a back cushion everywhere he went. Jack was always up front with the congregation about health issues and how they affected his ability to serve the church.

Anna faced the ordeal of a diagnosis of colon cancer in 1988, but early detection, followed by immediate surgery, caught the disease before the cancer had spread. Both Jack and Anna later admitted to the fears they struggled with in facing the terrible reality of cancer, but they were buoyed by the support they received from the congregation.[39] After her surgery, Jack and Anna wrote the church in the Sunday bulletin, thanking the church for the prayers, cards, and letters they had received.

> With all of us, there are probably only two or three dozen events that actually constitute the fashioning of our lives. They are the "impact events"—the earthquake shake-ups, the unforgettable moments, the birth of children, wedding day, a Christmas gift when you're 9 years old, etc. Some are joyous, some tragic, some testing and others incredibly stretching, and the shape of what we become is how we respond to these times. I think Anna and I are doing well at *this* unforgettable time in our life together, and your love and prayers are so much of the reason.[40]

After Jack Sr.'s passing in 1979, Dolores Hayford moved to Los Angeles and became active in ministry at the Church on the Way, even leading the congregation's women's ministry for a season. Dolores experienced over twenty fruitful years of Christian leadership after leaving Oakland, speaking and traveling nationally and publishing a nationally distributed book on child rearing, entitled *As for Me and My House*. Dolores died of cancer on October 31, 1997.[41] For much of her last year, she lived with Jack and Anna. Other than Anna, Dolores was the most influential person in Jack's formation, shaping his approach to life and ministry.

Jack and Anna continued to grow in their marriage through the three decades he pastored at the church. Both were called to ministry, but Anna became the one who held down the household in the midst of Jack's many travels.[42] She went about it in a way that helped the kids still sense Jack's presence even when he was gone.

Although Anna wasn't as visible in public ministry as her husband was, she also wasn't "the woman behind the great man." Jack always acknowledged that Anna was his indispensable ministry partner and that so much of the recognition he received was due to Anna's partnership with him. Besides fulfilling her call to love the people in the church, Anna always played a role ministering to women at the church, but even there she left the primary leadership of women's ministry to others.

The Hayfords' marriage was a very public matter at the Church on the Way. Jack regularly told stories about their home life and even talked about their arguments as teaching illustrations. They worked their way through the struggles that result from two strong people in an intimate relationship.

Jack grew up in a home where words were plentiful (Jack was often roasted for his verbosity), whereas that wasn't the case for Anna. Not long after coming to Van Nuys, Anna wrote a very honest letter to Jack telling him, "I cannot talk with you."[43] When they had disagreements or arguments, Jack would always "outtalk" her, something that was very painful to Anna. He could talk circles around her and she felt like he was critiquing every word she said. As with so many other issues in his life, Jack was confronted when God spoke to him about how to understand and care for his wife.

Once, also early in their days in Van Nuys, the two were on a trip together in Colorado when, in what Jack calls a life-changing experience, the Lord clearly told him that he was not properly caring for Anna. Jack and Anna had just counseled a couple who were struggling in their marriage, and they were praying for them as they drove.

> Suddenly I saw myself as the one in need of prayer. My mind flashed to that passage in Genesis where God tells Adam to "subdue the earth and replenish it." Actually, God was telling Adam that he was responsible to bring earth to its fullest potential—no manipulation, no exploitation.

Adam was responsible to maximize the earth's potential. *Anna is my "earth,"* I thought to myself. *And I have failed to encourage her to be all that she can be.*[44]

He recalled how he used to hear Anna play piano and sing around the house, but he realized she wasn't doing it anymore. In that moment, he knew why. Given his musical abilities, he would often correct her and tell her how to better sing the song, or he would get angry if she didn't hear a harmony part. This was just one of many ways he saw that his focus was on trying to change Anna rather than nurturing her. Jack prayed, *"Lord, I don't know how to bring my world—my Anna—to fruition, but I'm willing to learn."*[45]

Both Jack and Anna have always acknowledged that their marriage has dramatically shaped the people they became. It may have become a "marriage made in heaven," but it was forged by hard work and honesty with God and each other.

Jack's children remember their childhood years as normal and happy. Their dad could be very demanding, and he expected them to do their best whether it was in school or doing their chores. They learned that "the Hayford way" of doing things came with high expectations. They received spankings, but these weren't an everyday thing. When Jack wasn't traveling, the whole family shared dinner together, often playing Bible memory games while eating or talking about all kinds of things. Their dad's travels were just a normal part of their lives, attesting Anna's ability to make home life stable when Jack was gone.[46]

The daughters, Rebecca and Christa, both married pastors, and son Mark for many years was in ministry. Jack III pursued a career as a chemist and teacher and also completed a graduate degree in religion. Jack and Anna were not clingy with the kids, allowing them to live their lives, although they offered counsel and support when it was asked for. Anna was always the glue that kept the family together, something she loved to do.

SLOWING DOWN AND A NEW FRIEND

In 2011, Jack was still speaking nationally and internationally, and now he was also serving The King's University as chancellor again, following the appointment of a new president. Though he had always planned to slow down, he found it hard to do. Well into his seventies, Jack kept the pace of a man half his age, though he still struggled with sometimes severe back and neck pain.

During that spring, Jack began experiencing a progressive numbness in his hands, and he underwent extensive tests. He was diagnosed with congenital spinal stenosis that had worsened over the years.

His neurologist was alarmed by Jack's condition and plainly told him that a traffic accident or fall could leave him paralyzed from the neck down—or even take his life. He recommended surgery as soon as possible, but he told Jack it would be a risky surgery. Jack was at first hesitant to have the surgery so soon, since it would mean canceling many ministry trips that were already scheduled.[47] Persuaded by the urgency of the neurologist, he decided to go forward with the surgery, and it was scheduled for the end of June.

A few days before surgery, Jack was on a walk in his neighborhood when he thought, *I want a dog. I want a Lab.* He had a picture in his mind of a Labrador retriever curled up with its head on his foot looking up at him. In his mind, he saw himself sitting in an overstuffed chair next to a fireplace.

When he got back to the house, he called one of his granddaughters who, along with her husband, had raised Labs. He asked her if she could find one for him that was "neutered—I want a boy—housebroken, and trained." She told Jack that would be nearly impossible.

The day of his surgery he wrote in his journal a prayer affirming that the "living God has intervened to express an urgent need in my body." He told the Lord, "I feel Your nearness today. My peace—You!—is complete, this the momentary process of my surgery could argue against that...." But

Jack was confident that he was "circled by many witnesses" and surrounded by God's presence.[48]

The surgery took place on June 27, two days after Jack's seventy-seventh birthday and one week before his and Anna's fifty-seventh wedding anniversary. The complicated surgery lasted seven hours but was successful. Jack was hospitalized for four weeks, and recovery and rehabilitation were difficult. They required rest and recuperation, and this time he didn't fudge. For the rest of the year, speaking engagements were few and far between. After nearly six decades in ministry, Jack slowed the pace, and he and Anna found a needed respite.[49]

During the recovery, Jack and Anna spent a lot of time at their home in Solvang. One afternoon in November, they were on a drive—one of their favorite things to do together—not far from their home. They were driving down a narrow road when they saw a man ahead stop his car and put a dog out. As they passed, the man got back in his car and drove off, leaving the dog behind. They turned their car around and went back, and by that time another car had stopped.

"That man just abandoned this dog," a woman said frantically. She was petting the dog—a Labrador retriever—and still steaming over the incident. The dog was just standing there wagging his tail when she remarked, "What a happy dog." She wasn't from the area, so Jack and Anna volunteered to take the dog and try to figure out what to do. By now, Jack was beginning to wonder, "Is this the dog I asked for?"

They took the dog to their house. Anna gave him something to eat while Jack went into the living room and started a fire in the fireplace. As Jack was sitting in his overstuffed chair, the dog came and lay down by him, put his head on Jack's foot, and looked up at him. It was the exact picture Jack had seen five months earlier.

Though they made several calls to see if there had been any reports of a lost dog, no one ever claimed their new friend, and the Hayfords became his happy owners. Jack named the dog Mak, from the first three letters of the Greek word *Makarios,* translated variously as *happy* or *blessed.* It turned out that Mak was male, housebroken, neutered, and trained as a rescue dog, exactly what he had asked his granddaughter to find for him. Jack and Anna had found a companion that Jack was absolutely certain was God's gift.

Jack and Anna with Mak

Jack returned to a relatively busy schedule in 2012, but nothing like his past years. Anna wanted him home more, something that wasn't easy for Jack to do, having spent almost his entire life ministering around the world. By 2013, as Jack neared his seventy-ninth birthday, he made the decision in counsel with Robert Morris to no longer travel internationally. He was slowing his pace even more.

In 2014, the Hayfords were honored with a special celebration of their sixtieth wedding anniversary and Jack's eightieth birthday. Held at the Ambassador Auditorium in Pasadena, the celebration featured the Los Angeles Jewish Symphony directed by Noreen Green. The program was produced by Lee Mimms, who managed many Hollywood artists and whose production credits included several Super Bowl halftime shows and television specials for ABC and NBC.

The elaborate gala was hosted by Martha Williamson, executive producer of the hit television show *Touched by an Angel*. Williamson, a longtime member of the Church on the Way, was joined by Kathie Lee Gifford, Gavin MacLeod, Pat Boone, and other artists who had been part of the church over the years. It was a moving tribute to Jack and Anna's marriage and ministry.

Jack and Anna, 2004

Jack and Anna loved to travel and go on cruises in their later years. They took several trips to New York City to take in Broadway plays and musicals. Jack's love of the arts continued to help him make friendships in the entertainment world. Jack and actor Craig T. Nelson, famed for his role as Hayden Fox on the television show *Coach* and as the voice of Mr. Incredible in the *Incredibles* movies, had developed a friendship, often sharing lunch together. Many years prior Jack had influenced Nelson's journey in becoming a Christian when Nelson had listened to Jack on the radio.

In 2014, Tim Clark was appointed as the new senior pastor of the Church on the Way (Jim Tolle had pastored the church from 2004 to

2010, and Ricky Temple served as the congregation's senior pastor from 2011 through 2013). Clark, who had worked at the Church on the Way in his younger years, named Jack as the congregation's Pastor Emeritus, honoring the man who had transformed a fading congregation into one of America's great churches. Jack preached there on occasion but was mostly in the background, attending regularly and providing supportive counsel when requested, something Tim Clark deeply appreciated. Tim was never threatened by Jack's presence in the church, and he needn't have been. Jack honored his leadership, telling others, "Tim is my pastor."

ANNA'S HOMEGOING

In late February 2016, Anna was diagnosed with advanced pancreatic cancer. It was devastating news, but they faced it with courage and faith. Anna immediately underwent treatment for the disease and for the first few months did relatively well. Jack stopped everything and spent all of his time with his wife of sixty-two years. During this time, they had dinner with friends and family, took two cruises together, and carried on their lives as best they could.

Jack reached out to his first ministry partner at the Church on the Way, Chuck Shoemake, who, along with his wife, Ruby, offered Jack and Anna friendship and honest counsel in the midst of the struggle. Jack and Anna were surrounded by people who loved them, especially their children, Rebecca, Jack III, Mark, and Christa. It was an ordeal, but they were strengthened by the tens of thousands of people around the world who prayed for Anna and Jack every day.

Early in 2017, Anna's condition deteriorated quickly. Their older daughter, Rebecca, moved in to help provide care, along with hospice. Their youngest child, daughter Christa, and her husband, Doug, were pastoring nearby at the Church on the Way Santa Clarita and were able to help in many ways. Jack III and Mark and their spouses lived in other parts of the country but were able to visit with their mother during her illness. In the last two weeks of her life, Anna had to be heavily sedated because of pain, and she slept most of the time.

On March 7, Jack was asleep in their bedroom. Anna was sleeping nearby in a hospital bed with the hospice nurse awake next to her. Jack heard Anna call his name, and he got up and went to her bedside, asking the nurse if Anna had called. She told him gently, "No, she hasn't said anything, but I think the time is close."

Jack sat down and took Anna's hand, watching her labored breathing. He said to himself, "I can't believe this is real. I'm watching my wife die." Not long after, Anna took one long, deep sigh and passed into God's presence, just before 3:00 a.m. Only then did Jack fully realize that it hadn't been Anna who called his name; it had been the Lord calling him to be with her.

Early that same morning, Jack called Robert Morris to tell him that Anna had passed. When they talked again later that evening, Morris told Jack of a dream he'd had the night she died. In Morris' dream, he saw Anna walking down a street. She was young and all dressed up, with crowds cheering for her on both sides. Anna was dancing to the Roy Orbison song "Pretty Woman" and twirling the long beads she wore.

When Morris woke up and looked at the clock, it was 5:00 a.m. (3:00 a.m. in California) and he thought, *I think Anna just went to heaven.* When he told Jack the story that evening, Jack was deeply moved, and he told Robert that "Pretty Woman" was one of Anna's favorite songs.[50]

A celebration of Anna Marie Hayford's life was held at the Church on the Way on Saturday, March 18. The service lasted over three hours and included touching tributes from family, close friends, and ministry partners. Jack spoke only briefly, and it was obvious that her passing had hit him hard. Nevertheless, he was certain she was with the Lord. Anna was buried in a private ceremony at Forest Lawn, Hollywood Hills cemetery. Jack and Anna were just four months short of their sixty-third wedding anniversary.

A MAN OF TWO WORLDS

Jack Hayford's life is the story of a man who from childhood faithfully followed Christ. His commitment to always "tell the truth in front of Jesus" helped him avoid the pitfalls that sometimes derail highly successful leaders and ministries.

Jack was often asked what the secret was to a fruitful, lifelong ministry. His answer was always the same. It is about

> fidelity to God's eternal Word, faithful devotion to one's wife and family, personal purity and self-discipline in all things, loving Christ's people and humbly and respectfully acknowledging the worth of all who honor Christ (even though they may differ from your theology). And the real secret—"Where I spend most my time" ... is keeping a life of personal worship and intimate prayer fellowship with Jesus.[51]

A life of worship and intimacy with God was the heart of the matter. This wasn't just something Hayford said but something he lived. His journals reveal a man who lived in profound dependence on God. They show someone who constantly confessed his sins and weaknesses and lived with complete openness to God's correcting hand. He regularly called on God to deliver him from pride and presumption. He prayed for help in living a disciplined life and readily admitted that he often fell short of what he believed was needed. His journals show a man who frequently took inventory of his life in asking if it aligned with God's will.

His journals also reveal his deep love for God, expressed in frequent expressions of praise-filled verse and prose honoring God's faithfulness in his and Anna's life and ministry. Jack would write lists of things he was thankful for and frequently acknowledged that whatever success he had was a gracious gift from God's hand.

Jack Hayford never made any claims of perfection, and those closest to him and who worked for him knew he could become angry and be overly demanding. He journaled about his impatience, perfectionism, and his outbursts, and he asked God's help to change. Max Lyle, one of his closest associates, talked of how Jack "mellowed" over the years.

When many people think of Jack Hayford, they think of his teaching and preaching, his books, his hymns and songs, his role as a pastor to pastors, and his statesmanship. His thirty-year pastorate at the Church on the Way more than anything demonstrated his balanced and fruitful ministry. He founded a university that carries his legacy to new generations.

But for all the things that have endeared Jack to so many, one is sometimes overlooked. Jack lived in a God-charged, open universe that challenged the reductionism of the modern world. At a time in which reality came to be defined in purely naturalistic terms, dismissing the supernatural as antiquated folklore, Jack Hayford's life and ministry offered a recovery of the biblical world, a world in which God is active and present in His creation.

In Jack's world, God spoke to His children and was present in material ways that could be observed in natural phenomena, whether it was in wind, doves, rainbows, or the worship His people gave Him. There was no sacred/secular divide and no division of physical and spiritual realities. Jack's stories invited people to enter that world.[52]

For pastors of all stripes, whether Pentecostals or evangelicals, Jack made the voice of God and the supernatural world of the Bible seem so normal. He carefully explained the way he heard God speak, as his mother had to him, in terms that modern minds could make sense of. He also gave permission to pastors to see the work of the Holy Spirit in enlivening the biblical text so that it spoke to the present in meaningful ways.

Hayford had his feet planted in two worlds. One foot was in the modern world, which called him to provide thoughtful and articulate—and sometimes lengthy—explanations that made the supernatural sensible to those suspicious of claims of mystical experiences. His other foot was firmly planted in a Spirit-saturated, God-drenched world that people read about in their Bibles, and his life of integrity and history in ministry validated the reality of that world. For so many pastors who looked to Jack as their mentor, his humility and self-effacing manner beckoned them to expect God to do the same in their lives.

THE STORY CONTINUES

Following Anna's death, Jack has lived comfortably at the parsonage the Church on the Way provided for the Hayford family in late 1981.[53] The immediate months after Anna's passing were very hard for Jack as he acutely felt the loss of his life partner of sixty-two years. Jack described it as if he were living in a fog. He at first believed he would only live another year or two, but God again spoke to Jack, telling him he had "one more season." Significantly, the Lord told Jack, "I'm going to put a woman in your life."

Fourteen months after Anna passed, Jack Hayford married a long-time family friend, Valarie Lemire—or "Valarie with an 'a,'" as he liked to quip. As the saying goes, "love has no age," and the two were married on May 18, 2018, in a wedding officiated by a Catholic priest, given Valarie's Catholic background. It was a fitting testament to Jack's interdenominational heart.

Jack Hayford is now fully retired and seldom travels. After sixty-five years of ministry, he no longer speaks publicly.

One thing hasn't changed: he still prays and worships his Lord daily. His handwriting is now shaky, but he is still writing in his journal and telling the truth in front of Jesus. His is a life well lived.

There is perhaps no better epitaph to his life than the words of his 1984 hymn, "Jesus My Savior":

Jesus my Savior, I rise to praise You.
Jesus my Master, to You I bow.
Jesus my Leader, This day I'll follow.
Jesus my captain, calling me now.

Lord I now listen, tuned to Your Spirit.
Lord I am waiting; looking above.
Lord I am waiting; Speak I will follow.
Lord I am open, fill with Your love.

Christ be my conqueror, Victor in battle.
Christ be my freedom, truth making free.
Christ my provider, bread for today's need.
Christ be all fullness, overflow me.

Sun of salvation, God of all glory
Fountain of life, the well-spring of joy.
Lord Jesus Christ now king above all kings.
Your highest praises I now employ.

Glory and honor, praise, adoration.
Wisdom and riches, all majesty.
Strength, power and blessing: of all You're worthy.
Jesus the Lamb reigns eternally.[54]

Appendix

AN UNEASY ALLIANCE

What kind of evangelical would we say Jack Hayford is? What kind of Pentecostal? Where do we put him on the spectrum of Protestant belief and doctrine?

World Christianity has dramatically changed in the last century. I am pointing to what some call the "Charismatic Century" or the "Century of the Holy Spirit," in which diverse groupings of Christians around the world experienced the renewing work of the Holy Spirit in the contemporary church.

These groups accent the empowering presence of the Holy Spirit in the lives of believers and the ongoing presence today of spiritual gifts like prophecy, divine healing, miracles, and speaking in tongues. Often referred to as the modern Pentecostal and Charismatic movements, they constitute the growing edge of world Christianity, with some demographers suggesting there are over 650 million renewalist adherents today.[1]

When considering the geographical, social, theological, economic, and ethnic breadth of these movements, simple categorizations are hard to make. Still, some explanation is needed to help us locate Jack Hayford on the contemporary evangelical and Pentecostal landscape.

Three broad expressions of Pentecostalism have characterized the last 120 years: Classical Pentecostals, the Charismatic movement/renewal, and Neocharismatics. In the United States, Classical Pentecostals emerged early in the twentieth century as a unique expression of modern Pentecostalism. Most Classical Pentecostals trace their genesis—sometimes in an almost genealogical fashion—to the revivals in Topeka, Kansas, under Charles F. Parham, and even more so to William J. Seymour and the Azusa Street Mission in Los Angeles.[2]

Largely, Classical Pentecostals formed into denominations in the first three decades of the twentieth century. These groups put great emphasis on Jesus' ministry as the one who baptizes believers with the Holy Spirit, an empowering experience they see as distinct and usually subsequent to conversion/regeneration. Many Classical Pentecostals believe speaking in tongues is *the* initial evidence of Spirit baptism.

While the Charismatic movement's (also referred to as the Charismatic Renewal) roots reach back to the post–World War II period in America, with the emergence of the Healing and Latter Rain movements and their emphasis on healing and prophecy, respectively, the Charismatic movement's popular beginning is usually associated with the story of Episcopalian priest Dennis Bennett's 1960 Palm Sunday announcement to his congregation that he had spoken in tongues.

The rancor in his parish that followed forced him to resign and he was reassigned to a small parish in Seattle that later became a center of Charismatic activity. The story drew national attention, and it soon became clear that many other mainline church traditions were also experiencing a similar renewing work of the Holy Spirit.

Roman Catholics and members of Protestant denominations of all stripes embraced a dynamic encounter with God through the Holy Spirit, as had Classical Pentecostals, but these newcomers interpreted the experiences, particularly Spirit baptism, within their respective church theological traditions. Rather than leave their denominations to attend Pentecostal churches, most stayed in their churches to work for revitalization and renewal.

Neocharismatics are by far the largest and most diverse expression of modern Pentecostalism. They are found all over the world. They often avoid calling themselves Pentecostal or Charismatic, although their theology and practices are "Pentecostal-like" with emphases on healing, prophecy, speaking in tongues, and other spiritual gifts.

Neocharismatic groups include numerous indigenous and independent groups and denominations in both the majority and developed worlds. Neocharismatics include those groups often identified as "Third Wave," like the Association of Vineyard Churches founded by John Wimber, as well as churches in the United States and Europe that eschew association with the terms Pentecostal or Charismatic. Postdenominational groups and their networks that have formed around particular leaders of large megachurches and/or large media ministries are also best described as Neopentecostals.

These classifications of modern Pentecostalism are important to understanding the complexity and diversity of what has transpired in just over 100 years. It is now widely acknowledged that the astounding growth of the Pentecostal and Charismatic movements is a seismic shift of enormous proportion. The growth of Pentecostals in the majority world in the twentieth and twenty-first centuries has moved the center of the Christian world from the Northern and Western hemispheres to the Global South and East. Pentecostal-like Christianity has literally exploded in sub-Saharan Africa, in Latin America, and parts of Asia.[3]

Just as difficult to define, and harder to classify, is modern evangelicalism. Like Pentecostalism, evangelicals come in all stripes and sizes and include denominations ranging from Southern Baptists to Nazarenes to Church of Christ.

In 2015, hoping to find common ground among diverse groups, the National Association of Evangelicals (NAE), based on a large survey, published a broad definition of what it means to be evangelical. It is presented in four statements: (1) The Bible is the highest authority for what I believe; (2) It is very important for me personally to encourage non-Christians to trust Jesus Christ as their Savior; (3) Jesus Christ's death on the cross is the only sacrifice that could remove the penalty of my sin; and (4) Only those who trust in Jesus Christ alone as their Savior receive God's free gift of eternal salvation.

These statements closely mirror British historian David Bebbington's definition of historic evangelicalism reaching back to the revivals associated with John Wesley, George Whitefield, and Jonathan Edwards. Bebbington has argued that evangelicals are identified by conversionism—belief in the necessity of personal conversion; activism—the gospel needs to be actively proclaimed; biblicism—a high regard for biblical authority; and crucicentrism—salvation and atonement are provided by the death and resurrection of Jesus. Jack Hayford and most Pentecostals can identify with evangelicalism defined this broadly.[4]

Historically, this has not always been the case. When Classical Pentecostalism emerged in the United States early in the twentieth century, it faced severe opposition from evangelical churches. At the time, the majority of evangelicals were cessationists, believing that spiritual gifts like healing and speaking in tongues had ceased when the New Testament was canonized. Evangelicals and other Protestant churches viewed Pentecostals as emotional enthusiasts lacking theological sophistication. As Classical Pentecostalism matured, it sought the acceptance of evangelicalism and moderated its extremes, and by the mid-twentieth century it was forming an uneasy alliance with evangelicals.

When the NAE organized in the 1940s, in part to distinguish itself from the more sectarian Fundamentalist groups, a few Classical Pentecostal denominations were charter members. Nevertheless, tensions remained between evangelicals and Pentecostals over the latter's emphasis on experience, the lack of a more fully articulated theology, and a continuing advocacy for the contemporary exercise of spiritual gifts.

With the advent of the Charismatic movement in the 1960s, however, nearly all evangelical churches then had to deal with their own members being baptized with the Holy Spirit and practicing spiritual gifts. With the recognition of the missionary and evangelistic effectiveness of global Pentecostalism in the last fifty years, cessationism has faded to the margins as many evangelicals now acknowledge the legitimacy of a more experiential encounter with God through the Holy Spirit and the ongoing exercise of spiritual gifts.

In addition to acknowledging spiritual gifts, other practices associated with Pentecostalism have impacted evangelical churches. There is no greater example of this than the contemporary worship experience, wherein many evangelicals have adopted expressive worship practices, raising hands, vocalizing praise, and so forth, once almost exclusively the privilege of Pentecostals. Some call this the "pentecostalization" of evangelicalism. Just as surely, Pentecostalism is itself being "evangelicalized" as it has accommodated its Pentecostal practices, subduing what some have seen as emotional excess. Jack W. Hayford stood in the middle of these changes, and his brand of "reasoned Pentecostalism" no doubt contributed in both directions to the changing landscape of North American Christianity.

On the one hand, Hayford is an example of the middle-of-the-road moderation that has characterized Pentecostalism since World War II (Aimee Semple McPherson, the founder of Hayford's denomination, was helping mainstream Classical Pentecostalism as early as the 1920s).[5] Jack's carefully thought-out explanations of the Pentecostal experience along with his social decorum and intellectual sophistication hardly fit the way Classical Pentecostals were commonly perceived. He was certainly not a ranting, raving Pentecostal.

On the other hand, Jack is driven by what he calls a "passion for fullness," understood as the dynamic experience of Spirit baptism and a cultivation of a Spirit-empowered life. For him, everything hinges on the recovery of the New Testament experience as described in the book of Acts and embodied in Paul's passion for the centrality of the Holy Spirit in every believer's life, expressed when he wrote, "If anyone does not have the Spirit of Christ, they do not belong to Christ" (Romans 8:9b NIV).

Foremost, Jack Hayford is a Pentecostal because of his profound identification with the Pentecost event as fundamental to Christian experience. In the final analysis, Jack Hayford's identification with evangelicalism is found more in its Pietist and Wesleyan roots where the emphasis was on "religion of the heart." He would also affirm the NAE's recent four statements on what it is to be an evangelical. Hayford, however, has chafed at the highly rational theological rigidity of some evangelicals that, in his view, "chokes the life out of Scripture." Doctrinal expression is important to Hayford, but it is secondary to a transformational encounter with Jesus Christ, actuated and empowered by the Holy Spirit.

INTERVIEW LIST

The following is a list of the people interviewed in preparation for this biography:

Anderson, Christa and Doug, 31 October 2019.

Bauer, Rebecca, 18 June 2018.

Bird, Vincent, 22 April 1993.

Boeckmann, Bert and Jane, 19 December 2018.

Boone, Pat, 20 December 2018.

Brown, Daniel, 26 May 2018.

Burmeister, Jan, 21 October 2019.

Burris, Glenn, 15 September 2017.

Chappell, Marilyn, 7 February 2008.

Charter, Paul, and Chuck Shoemake, 7 September 2007.

Coleman, Mike, 14 January 2016.

Curtis, Gary, 1 November 2019.

Davis, Russ, 19 March 2012.

Dawson, Keith, 20 August 2008.

Easter, Dennis, 6 March 2019.

Farmer, John, 23 April 1993; 19 August 2008.

Gifford, Kathie Lee, 8 August 2019.

Hamilton, Jack, 5 March 2018.

Hayford, Anita Dolores, 21 April 1993.

Hayford, Anna, 27 September 2002; 27 December 2007.

Hayford, Jack W., 22 April 1993; 10 January 2003; 17 April 2003; 15 September 2003; 1 July 2004; 10 May 2006; 2 December 2006; 1 September 2007; 13 November 2007; 4 December 2007; 27 December 2007; 19 January 2008; 31 July 2008; 22 January 2009; 16 June 2009; 18 May 2010; September 2010; 12 April 2011; 16 April 2013; 19 December 2013; 30 December 2013; 17 January 2014; 21 August 2014; 11 November 2014; 11 February 2015; 26 January 2016; 1 May 2016; 31 August 2017; 30 January 2018; 22 June 2018; 8 August 2018; 16 November 2018; 7 March 2019.

Hayford, Jack W. and Anna, 27 December 2007.

Hayford, Jack W. and Valarie, 6 March 2019.

Hayford, Jack III, 6 November 2019.

Hayford, Jim, 4 December 2007; 27 June 2019.

Hayford, Valarie, 6 September 2018.

Huntzinger, Jonathan, 4 December 2018.

Locke, Louie, 30 September 2007.

Lyle, Max, 19 August 2008.

Lynch, Michael, 15 November 2019.

Moen, Don, 26 February 2016.

Morris, Joshua, 15 November 2019.

Morris, Robert, 5 December 2018.

Mimms, Lee, 7 December 2018.

Nelson, Craig T., March 2019.

Overman, Steve, 29 May 2018.

Rachinski, Howard, 26 February 2016.

Scott, Jim, 25 May 2018.

Shoemake, Chuck, 6 March 2019; 22 June 2018.

Stabbe, Keith, 16 May 1994.

Stabbe, Keith and Peggy, 19 August 2002.

Stedman, Carolyn, 5 November 2003.

Shumate, Bill, 2 December 2006.

Swett, Ken, 11 March 2009.

Synan, Vinson, 23 August 2007.

Zeleny, Steve, 21 August 2008; 1 November 2019.

NOTES

Introduction

1. Throughout this book we have chosen to capitalize terms like Pentecostalism and Pentecostal(s).

2. Jack W. Hayford, *The Church on the Way* (Lincoln, VA: Chosen Books, 1982), 28. This book provides the most detailed, though now dated, narrative of the story of the Church on the Way and Hayford's role pastoring the congregation from 1969 through the book's publication in 1982. The book was later expanded in a new edition: Jack Hayford, *Glory on Your House* (Tarrytown, NY: Chosen Books, 1991).

3. Hayford, *The Church on the Way*, 29-30.

4. Hayford, *The Church on the Way*, 30.

5. Although he waited some time to tell of the experience, it would become a repeated part of the telling of the Church on the Way story. By the summer of 1973, the "glory story" was becoming part of the folklore of the thriving congregation. Jack Hayford, *The Building of the Church on the Way* (Van Nuys: SoundWord Tape Ministry, June 1973), audiocassette.

6. Hayford, *The Church on the Way*, 31.

7. In the church's literature, the entire name, "The Church On The Way," was always entirely capitalized, including the articles and the preposition.

8. "Dr. Jack W. Hayford: Biographical Sketch/Fact Resource," Living Way Ministries, 2003.

9. S. D. Moore, "Jack Williams Hayford Jr.," in Stanley Burgess, *The New International Dictionary of the Pentecostal Charismatic Movement* (Grand Rapids, MI: Zondervan, 2002), 692-93. This brief 2002 article is now obviously dated.

10. Tim Stafford, "The Pentecostal Gold Standard," *Christianity Today*, July 2005, 25-29.

11. Hayford, *Glory on Your House*, 139.

12. Hayford, *Glory on Your House*, 140.

13. Jack Hayford, "Girding for Greatness," Church Bulletin, The Church on the Way, May 2, 1976, 2.

14. Hayford, *The Church on the Way*, 21. "God speaks to everyone," Hayford affirms.

15. For one of Hayford's more carefully argued defenses for the importance of the "voice of God" in the pastor/leader's life, see Jack Hayford, *Pastors of Promise* (Ventura, CA: Regal, 1997), 168-82.

16. John Dart, "His Way: Valley's 'Pastor Jack' Revives Church," *Los Angeles Times*, December 15, 1991, B1, B16 (B1).

17. Stafford, "The Pentecostal Gold Standard," 28.

18. Stafford, "The Pentecostal Gold Standard," 26.

19. Jack Hayford, School of Pastoral Nurture: Consultation 1 Notes, page 1, private holding.

20. The statement was made in an audio recording by Roy Hicks Jr., a close friend and ministry colleague of Hayford. Although I could not locate the recording, a close associate who was a part of the original presentation confirmed the statement as written. Steve Overman, personal interview with the author, May 29, 2018.

21. One of the things discovered in reading his written materials is that Jack Hayford likes to use italics and other devices to add emphasis, so much so that it would be redundant constantly to use brackets with "italics Hayford" at every occurrence. Consequently, any time italics, underlining, or all capitals appear in the body of the manuscript, in every case they are Hayford's unless otherwise noted. This helps keep the text uncluttered.

22. Although Hayford's published materials contain stories of his childhood and early life, they tend to be more fragmented and spotty accounts. Consequently, the early parts of the story lean significantly on personal interviews since not as much written documentation is available.

Chapter 1: A Proper Child

1. This story was told by Dolores Hayford in a 1993 interview. The plan was to record a video interview and she asked that the video recorder be turned off before she related the story. The account is also written with vivid detail in a 1980 journal entry. Anita Dolores Hayford, interview with the author, April 21, 1993; Anita Dolores Hayford, journal entry, 1980, 1-3, private holding. In a series of successive journal entries that begin with the designation "recorded in 1980," Hayford's mother gives lengthy descriptions of her first son's critical early life experiences. With her husband's death in August 1979, Dolores was likely doing a lot of reflection and wanted to provide written accounts of key events. The particular story told above ended with this statement: "In humility, O Lord, I share this with my own."

2. D. Hayford, interview.

3. Hebrews 11:23.

4. D. Hayford, interview.

5. She first told her son about the vision in the 1960s. Jack Hayford, interview with the author, January 10, 2003.

6. Kevin Starr, *Endangered Dreams: The Great Depression in California* (New York: Oxford University Press, 1996), vii.

7. 1930 Census records show Jack Williams Hayford serving as Navy Seaman stationed in San Diego, California.

8. Jack Hayford Jr. believes the marriage was the result of a very sincere love the two had for each other. The naive and proper Dolores Farnsworth would never have had a physical relationship with the streetwise Hayford Sr. without marriage. Jack W. Hayford, interview with the author, September 1, 2007, transcript, 4.

9. Jack W. Hayford, interview, September 1, 2007, transcript, 4.

10. Marguerite Farnsworth, interview with Jack W. Hayford Jr., February 12, 1985.

11. Neither Jack Sr. nor Dolores ever completed high school.

12. 1920 Census documents show Allyn and Margaret Hayford with four children living in Missoula, Montana. Jack Williams Hayford is listed as a six-year-old son.

13. Jack Hayford, interview, September 1, 2007, transcript, 3. Jack Hayford's brother, Jim Hayford, has written a different account of why their father was sent to live with his brother in Oakland in his Kindle published ebook, *"Daddy": Memoirs of My Father*. Since the two stories conflict, I have chosen to use the above account since this is the one Jack communicated in the cited interview. I have not located any independent or written source that substantiates one account over the other.

14. Dolores Hayford, journal entry, 1980, 3.

15. Jack Hayford, School of Pastoral Nurture: Consultation I, May 2007, digital audio recording, 1.21.

16. Memorial Service for Dolores Hayford, handout, November 6, 1997, 4.

17. Dolores Hayford, *Introduction to Parenting God's Way* (Van Nuys: SoundWord Tape Ministry, September 9, 1992), audiocassette.

18. Jack Hayford, interview, April 1993, transcript, 2.

19. Jack W. Hayford, *Blessing Your Children* (Ventura, CA: Regal Books, 2002), 18. In the book, Hayford says the date was September 28 in 1935. That year, the 28th was a Saturday. So the most likely date of their conversion was September 29, 1935.

20. Jack Hayford, interview, September 1, 2007. Hayford said that Hanson regularly attended another church in the area. Hanson considered the Long Beach Foursquare Church to be the strongest church in the area, however, and wanted to invite the couple there because of the church's evangelistic focus on the unsaved. In her journal, Dolores Hayford wrote that she and her husband had no idea that the church was

Pentecostal and likely would not have attended if they had known. In her words, the church was "in order"; there was something at the church that was both "convicting & appealing." Dolores Hayford, 1980, journal entry, October 1935, 1.

21. Jack Hayford, interview, April 1993, transcript, 2.

22. Jack Hayford, interview, April 1993, 3. Evelyn Thompson, a longtime Foursquare Church missionary, was a deaconess in the church at the time and later told Jack Hayford Jr. that Teaford did not regularly pray for a child to be called into ministry. She felt it was a prophetic prayer given by the Holy Spirit to Teaford.

23. This narrative is drawn largely from two sources. The first is a 1973 message Jack Hayford delivered to The Church on the Way, in which he gave his testimony for the first time since coming to the church in 1969. Jack Hayford, *A Personal Testimony of Learning Obedience,* transcript (Van Nuys: SoundWord Tape Ministry, June 24, 1973), 5-6; Dolores Hayford, journal entry, 1980, 1. Much the way she had in the birth story that begins this chapter, in 1980 Dolores details this story in a journal entry. The entry, though recorded in 1980, is dated December 1934. The story has been told in many ways over the years by Jack Hayford. See also Jack Hayford, *The Beauty of Spiritual Language* (Nashville: Thomas Nelson, 1996; originally published by Word Publishers, 1992), 69-70; Jack W. Hayford, *Blessing Your Children* (Ventura, CA: Regal Books, 2002), 179.

24. Hayford, *The Beauty of Spiritual Language,* 69.

25. Hayford, *Testimony of Learning Obedience,* 5.

26. Dolores Hayford, 1980 journal entry, dated December 1934, 2.

27. This narrative is drawn from another of Dolores Hayford's 1980 journal entries, this one simply titled "Jack is about 2½."

28. Dolores Hayford, 1980 journal entry, 1.

29. Dolores Hayford, 1980 journal entry, 2.

30. Dolores Hayford, 1980 journal entry, 2; see also Hayford, *The Beauty of Spiritual Language,* 70.

31. Dolores Hayford, 1980 journal entry, 2.

32. Jack Hayford, *Blessing Your Children,* 174. Jack Hayford Jr. and his mother always refer to Jack Hayford Sr. as "Daddy."

33. Jack Hayford, *Blessing Your Children,* 174. Jack Hayford says this story stimulated his faith until he and his wife, Anna, would have their own stories of God's provision.

34. Jack Hayford, *The Key to Everything* (Orlando: Creation House, 1993), 95-96.

35. Jack Hayford, interview, September 1, 2007. Part of this interview was transcribed; other parts were not. Whenever the transcription is used, it is noted.

36. Hayford, *Blessing Your Children,* 66-67.

37. Hayford, *Blessing Your Children,* 67.

38. Jack Hayford, *His Eternity and Our Transiency: My Father's Death* (Van Nuys: SoundWord Tape Ministry, 1979), audiocassette; Hayford, interview, September 1, 2007, transcript, 7. Hayford, interview, April 22, 1993, transcript, 6.

39. Dolores Hayford, *As for Me and My House* (Lake Mary, FL: Creation House, 1995), 184.

40. Dolores Hayford, *As for Me and My House,* 183-84.

41. Years later, Dolores would say "the devil feared" that her husband, who, despite his failings, "had a genuine passion for the Word of God," would deeply impact his children's sense of calling to ministry. This whole account is detailed in D. Hayford, *As for Me and My House,* 183-85.

42. Jack W. Hayford, *Taking Hold of Tomorrow: Realizing God's Promise for a Bright and Hopeful Future* (Ventura, CA: Regal Books, 1989), 29-30.

43. Hayford, interview, April 22, 1993, transcript, 6.

Chapter 2: In Front of Jesus

1. Hayford, *Taking Hold of Tomorrow,* 29.

2. This account is taken from a 1991 "By the Way" column in The Church on the Way weekend service bulletin. Jack Hayford, "A Christmastime '41 Memory (… and a Christmastime '91 Decision)," Church Bulletin, The Church on the Way, December 22, 1991, 2.

3. Jack Hayford, interview with the author, September 15, 2003.

4. Hayford, interview, September 1, 2007.

5. Jack Hayford, School of Pastoral Nurture: Consultation I, Session 21, May, 2007, digital audio recording.

6. He had his role, but it was more about keeping the house repaired and properly maintained. Housework belonged to Dolores.

7. Dolores always believed that God's sovereign choice was on her family, and the involvement of all three children in vocational Christian service (Luanne as a missionary and Jim as a pastor) confirmed this in her mind. D. Hayford, *As for Me and My House,* 8.

8. Jack Hayford, *Daybreak: Walking with Christ Everyday* (Van Nuys: Living Way Ministries, 1984), 46-47.

9. Jack Hayford, "The Power of Words," *Spectrum* (Fall 2007), 7. In this article, Hayford says he was fourteen when this incident occurred. In the September 1, 2007, interview he says he was fifteen.

10. Hayford, interview, September 1, 2007, transcript, 11.

11. Dolores Hayford, interview, April 21, 1993.

12. Jack Hayford has openly discussed his father's anger while growing up. Though it was not a regular occurrence, he remembers seeing his dad "raising hell in the home" and throwing things in the years he was "away from the Lord." Jack W. Hayford, *Submission in the Family*, Part 1 (Van Nuys: SoundWord Tape Ministry, 1973), audiocassette.

13. Jack Hayford, interview with the author, April 17, 2003.

14. Hayford, interview, September 1, 2007.

15. Hayford, interview with the author, April 22, 1993, transcript, 8.

16. Many of Jack Hayford Sr.'s problems were a result of a sense of unworthiness that stretched back to the rejection he experienced as a thirteen-year-old when he was thrown out of the home by his father and sent off to fend for himself. He also struggled with a sense of guilt for the way he lived during his Navy stint. Hayford, interview, September 1, 2007; D. Hayford, *As for Me and My House*, 184.

17. D. Hayford, *As for Me and My House*, 185.

18. Hayford, interview, September 1, 2007, transcript, 8. Jack's younger brother, Jim, believes that his mother at times excused and unnecessarily defended her husband's inappropriate behavior. Jim Hayford, phone interview with the author, December 4, 2007.

19. Jack Hayford, "My Christmas Bike," Church Bulletin, The Church on the Way, December 23, 1979. It was a black and red bike his father and mother gave the nine-year-old for Christmas in 1943.

20. Dolores Hayford, interview, April 21, 1993.

21. Dolores Hayford tells how, just weeks after they were saved, she learned of the principle of the tithe at their Long Beach church. She went home and told her husband. He said, "We can do that." He "took three cups out of the cupboard" and told his wife: "A tenth of whatever we earn will go in the cup.... Then we will divide the rest into the other two cups." They tithed the rest of their lives and taught the kids to do so as well. D. Hayford, *As for Me and My House*, 238-39.

22. Hayford, interview, September 1, 2007. Hayford, *Submission in the Family*, Part 1.

23. D. Hayford, *As for Me and My House*, 149.

24. D. Hayford, *As for Me and My House*, 149.

25. Hayford, interview, September 1, 2007, transcript, 13-14.

26. Hayford, interview, September 1, 2007, 11.

27. This includes what can only be described as visions.

28. Jack Hayford, "Meet My Mama," *Daystar: Women on the Way* (May 1982), 3.

29. Hayford, "Meet My Mama," 2.

30. Hayford, "Meet My Mama," 2.

31. Hayford, interview, September 1, 2007, transcript, 1.

32. D. Hayford, *As for Me and My House*, 120.

33. When Jack was sixteen, he felt he should no longer attend movies since he was planning eventually to go into vocational Christian service. A few months after the decision, Jack was going to go to a movie with a friend. Dolores reminded him of his previous decision and asked if he was keeping his conscience honest with what was right. Hayford, interview, transcript, 14.

34. Hayford, interview, September 1, 2007, transcript, 1.

35. Hayford, interview, September 1, 2007, transcript, 11.

36. Jack Hayford, *The Power and the Blessing: Celebrating the Disciplines of Spirit-Filled Living* (Wheaton, IL: Victor Books, 1994), 118. See also Jack W. Hayford, *Integrity of Heart* (Van Nuys: SoundWord Tape Ministry, 1979), audiocassette.

37. Hayford, *The Power and the Blessing*, 118-19.

38. Hayford, *The Power and the Blessing*, 119.

Chapter 3: Called to the Ministry

1. D. Hayford, interview, April 21, 1993.

2. Dolores' vision at Jack's birth had to influence her sense that there was a special purpose for Jack Jr.

3. Hayford, interview, April 22, 1993, transcript, 4.

4. Hayford, interview, April 22, 1993, transcript, 3-4.

5. Hayford, interview, April 22, 1993, transcript, 3. In his 1973 message *A Personal Testimony of Learning Obedience*, Hayford says two magazines were missing, worth a total of thirty cents.

6. Hayford, interview, April 22, 1993, transcript, 4.

7. This Foursquare church was started out of the 1944 crusade held by Foursquare founder Aimee Semple McPherson in Oakland. It was following that crusade that she was found dead.

8. Hayford, interview, April 22, 1993, transcript, 4. Jack on occasion has mistakenly referred to the year of his conversion as 1944. It was in 1945 he has repeatedly written in his journals. For example, Jack Hayford, journal entry, March 25, 2012.

9. Jack Hayford, *2001 Alaska Cruise Personal Testimony* (Van Nuys: Jack Hayford Ministries, 2001), audiocassette, transcript, 7.

10. Hayford, *2001 Alaska Cruise Personal Testimony*, 10.

11. D. Hayford, interview, April 21, 1993.

12. He was so good at recognizing notes by ear that some mistakenly thought he had the gift of perfect pitch.

13. Hayford, *Celebrating Jack's Birthday with Music and Testimony* (Van Nuys: SoundWord Tape Ministry, June 12, 1983), audiocassette, transcript, 1.

14. Unfortunately, these notes were lost.

15. Hayford, *Daybreak*, 28-29.

16. Hayford, *Daybreak*, 55.

17. Jim Hayford, interview, December 4, 2007.

18. Jack W. Hayford, *Pursuing the Will of God* (Sisters, OR: Multnomah, 1997), 8. The date was March 19, 1950, according to his journal, as well as other sources. Jack Hayford, journal entry, March 20, 1967, private holding, 1. Hayford notes in his journal entry "that yesterday was the 17th anniversary of the day I surrendered to the Lord's call on my life." Jack often says he was sixteen when he surrendered to Christian ministry. If the above journal entry is correct, then he was three months short of his sixteenth birthday.

19. Jack W. Hayford, *Pursuing the Will of God,* 8.

20. Hayford, interview, April 22, 1993, transcript, 10; Hayford, *The Beauty of Spiritual Language*, 29.

21. Jack W. Hayford, *The Beauty of Spiritual Language*, 26.

22. The crusade was held in San Leandro, California. Hayford, *The Beauty of Spiritual Language*, 26.

23. D. Hayford, interview, April 21, 1993.

24. Hayford, *The Beauty of Spiritual Language*, 25.

25. The whole account is vividly told in *The Beauty of Spiritual Language* over several pages; see pp. 25-35.

26. Hayford, *The Beauty of Spiritual Language*, 27.

27. Hayford, *The Beauty of Spiritual Language*, 28.

28. Hayford, *The Beauty of Spiritual Language*, 28.

29. Hayford, *The Beauty of Spiritual Language*, 29.

30. Hayford, *The Beauty of Spiritual Language*, 29.

31. Jack W. Hayford, *Spirit-Filled: Anointed by Christ the King* (Van Nuys: Living Way Ministries, 1985), 38-39; Hayford, *The Beauty of Spiritual Language*, 41-43. Hayford in *Spirit-Filled* says unequivocally that he was filled with the Holy Spirit at that time. In *The Beauty of Spiritual Language* he says that on that morning when he

went forward he heard in his mind syllables that had he spoken out would have been tongue speech. He did not speak them at that time. We will say more about this in the next chapter.

32. Hayford, *The Beauty of Spiritual Language,* 33-34.

33. Hayford, *The Beauty of Spiritual Language,* 34.

34. Hayford, *The Beauty of Spiritual Language,* 35. This was a reference to the Pentecostal experience as recorded in Acts 2.

35. The acronym L.I.F.E. stood for Lighthouse of International Foursquare Evangelism. Hereafter I will refer to the school as Life Bible College, reflecting the change made decades later to the school's name. As of July 1, 2019, the school is named Life Pacific University.

36. Jack W. Hayford, *E Quake* (Nashville: Thomas Nelson, 1999), 123-24; Hayford, interview with the author, April 17, 2003.

Chapter 4: The College Years

1. Jack Hayford, Notes from chapel message, Life Bible College, April 16, 2003. The college was initially started as the Echo Park Evangelistic and Missionary Training Institute and held its first classes on February 6, 1923. The institute would later be called the Lighthouse of International Foursquare Evangelism (L.I.F.E.) Bible College, and in this study simply Life Bible College. See Nathaniel Van Cleave, *The Vine and the Branches: A History of the International Church of the Foursquare Gospel* (Los Angeles: The International Church of the Foursquare Gospel, 1992), 49-52. In 2003, the college was renamed Life Pacific College and remains the primary ministerial training institution for the denomination.

2. 5,300, to be exact.

3. Because Hayford entered at midterm he was unable to take language classes at the college. While in Fort Wayne, Indiana, from 1956 to 1960, he studied *Koine* Greek at Fort Wayne Bible College.

4. Jack W. Hayford, King's College/Seminary Chapel, Van Nuys, n.d., transcript, 2; D. Hayford, interview, April 21, 1993.

5. D. Hayford, interview, April 21, 1993.

6. In 1952, the role of the dean was essentially the equivalent of serving as president of the college. Dolores Hayford wrote that Teaford "was a great Bible teacher and very family oriented." D. Hayford, *As for Me and My House,* 41.

7. D. Hayford, interview, April 21, 1993.

8. Matthew Avery Sutton, *Aimee Semple McPherson and the Resurrection of Christian America* (Cambridge, MA: Harvard University Press, 2006), 13; in addition to

Sutton's biography on McPherson, see Daniel Epstein, *Sister Aimee: The Life of Aimee Semple McPherson* (New York: Harcourt Brace Jovanovich, 1993); Edith Blumhofer, *Aimee Semple McPherson: Everybody's Sister* (Grand Rapids, MI: Eerdmans, 1993). Earlier works include Aimee Semple McPherson, *The Story of My Life* (Hollywood: International Correspondents' Publication, 1951); Raymond Cox, *The Verdict Is In* (Los Angeles: Research Publications, 1983); Lately Thomas, *The Vanishing Evangelist* (New York: Viking Press, 1959).

9. Aimee moved her family to Los Angeles in 1919. Blumhofer, *Everybody's Sister,* 238. For two accounts of the dedication, see Blumhofer, *Everybody's Sister,* 232-37; Epstein, *Sister Aimee,* 247-52.

10. Van Cleave, *The Vine and the Branches*, 23, 30-31.

11. Sutton, *Aimee Semple McPherson*, 43. Sutton says: "At heart, McPherson was never anything but a Pentecostal." Nevertheless she "downplayed the controversial elements of the movement and instead took a moderate position that facilitated broad alliances."

12. Sutton, *Aimee Semple McPherson*, 267. Blumhofer points out that McPherson was already using "Foursquare Gospel" before the meetings began. Blumhofer, *Everybody's Sister*, 191-92.

13. For the historical antecedents of the fourfold formula see Donald Dayton, *The Theological Roots of Pentecostalism* (Grand Rapids, MI: Zondervan, 1987). Aimee drew the name Foursquare Gospel in part from this message but also as a synonym for "full gospel." In the 1920s, the word was used as an adjective for "complete" or "thorough." Van Cleave, *The Vine and the Branches,* 75.

14. Sutton, *Aimee Semple McPherson*, 277. The first part of the sentence is quoted from Sutton. I have added to this what was the Hayfords' experience at the Long Beach Foursquare Church, in 1934 and 1936, when the church twice prayed for the boy.

15. Sutton, *Aimee Semple McPherson*, 42-45. Sutton argues that Aimee sought in the 1920s to identify herself as much with fundamentalism as with Pentecostalism.

16. Sutton, *Aimee Semple McPherson*, 185.

17. Van Cleave, *Vine and the Branches,* 165. This was the church in Oakland in which fourteen-year-old Jack Hayford Jr. received Christ in 1945.

18. Sutton, *Aimee Semple McPherson,* 267; Van Cleave, *Vine and the Branches*, 164-65.

19. Jack W. Hayford and S. David Moore, *The Charismatic Century: The Enduring Impact of the Azusa Street Revival* (Nashville: Warner Faith, 2006), 152.

20. Van Cleave, *Vine and the Branches,* 170. There was an initial decline after McPherson's death but the movement soon recovered.

21. Matthew A. Sutton, "'Between the Refrigerator and the Wildfire': Aimee Semple McPherson, Pentecostalism and the Fundamentalist-Modernist Controversy," *Church*

History 72.1 (March 2003): 159-88. Sutton provides a helpful survey and discussion on McPherson's ecumenical struggle.

22. For discussion on the NAE and American culture, see Edith Blumhofer, *Restoring the Faith* (Urbana: University of Illinois Press, 1993), 188-90.

23. Patrick Allitt, *Religion in America Since 1945: A History* (New York: Columbia University Press, 2003), 31-34. The post–World War II resurgence among Christians in America has been referred to as the "evangelical awakening." See George Marsden, *Reforming Fundamentalism* (Grand Rapids, MI: Eerdmans, 1987).

24. Vinson Synan, *The Holiness-Pentecostal Tradition* (Grand Rapids, MI: Eerdmans, 1997), 212; Edith Blumhofer, *The Assemblies of God*, vol. 2 (Springfield, MO: Gospel Publishing House, 1989), 54.

25. David E. Harrell, *All Things Are Possible: The Healing and Charismatic Revivals in Modern America* (Bloomington: Indiana University Press, 1975); Richard M. Riss, *Latter Rain* (Etobicoke, Ontario: Honeycomb Visual Productions, 1987); Blumhofer, *The Assemblies of God*, vol. 2, 62.

26. D. Hayford, interview, April 21, 1993.

27. D. Hayford, interview, April 21, 1993, 5.

28. Hayford, interview transcript, April 22, 1993, 5.

29. Jack Hayford, Life Bible College Chapel Message, March 31, 2004, digital audio recording; Hayford, *Testimony of Learning Obedience*, transcript, 14. The summer of 1952 would be the last semester Jack would go home for the summer. His job in Los Angeles gave him summer employment for the rest of his college years.

30. Watson Teaford resigned his position as dean at the end of the spring term to work as a co-pastor at Angelus Temple. After Teaford's departure, Clarence Hall served as the college's new dean with the fall 1952 term.

31. Jack W. Hayford, *A New Time and Place—Ruth's Journey of Faith* (Portland, OR: Multnomah, 1997), 47.

32. *25 Years of Silver Service* (Van Nuys: The Church on the Way, 1994), 6; *30th Anniversary* (Van Nuys: The Church on the Way, 1999), 10.

33. Anna Hayford, interview with the author, September 27, 2002.

34. Hayford, *A New Time and Place*, 47-48; *30th Anniversary*, 10.

35. *25 Years of Silver Service*, 6.

36. *25 Years of Silver Service*, 6. Hayford discusses what led up to the proposal and other thoughts about their relationship in Hayford, *The Beauty of Spiritual Language*, 151.

37. *25 Years of Silver Service*, 6-7. This was the first time Jack Hayford ever flew. Both Jack and Anna had to work on Christmas Eve and the only way they could get to Oakland before Christmas was to fly. They flew out of Burbank, California, on Pacific

Southwest Airlines. Hayford's parents met them at the ramp of the plane out on the tarmac. Jack Hayford, telephone interview with the author, January 19, 2008.

38. *30th Anniversary*, 10.

39. Ruth Senter, "Jack & Anna Hayford: When Words Were Not Enough," *Partnership*, November/December 1985, 25; *Fifty Years of God's Amazing Grace: The 50th Wedding Anniversary of Jack and Anna Hayford* (Los Angeles: The King's College and Seminary, March 2004), 26.

40. *30th Anniversary*, 7. Among the jobs over the years, Emma cleaned hotel rooms, worked as a cook, and worked in a nursing home.

41. Senter, "Jack & Anna Hayford," 25.

42. *30th Anniversary*, 7.

43. Anna Hayford, "A Good Man Leaveth an Inheritance to His Children," Church Bulletin, The Church on the Way, June 18, 1978, 2; Julia C. Loren, "Anna Hayford: Quiet Confidence in Action," *Aglow*, March/April 1990, 8.

44. A. Hayford, "A Good Man Leaveth," 2; Loren, "Anna Hayford," 8.

45. A. Hayford, "A Good Man Leaveth," 2; Anna Hayford, "A woman who fears the Lord, she shall be praised," Church Bulletin, The Church on the Way, May 12, 1985.

46. Loren, "Anna Hayford," 8.

47. *Fifty Years of God's Amazing Grace*, 26; "Anna Marie Smith: Biographical Sketch/Fact Resource" (Van Nuys: The Church on the Way, July 1990), 1.

48. "Anna Marie Smith: Biographical Sketch/Fact Resource," 1.

49. Jack Hayford, *Fatal Attractions: Why Sex Sins Are Worse Than Others* (Ventura, CA: Regal, 2004), 72-73. This book is drawn from an earlier message Hayford preached at The Church on the Way.

50. Hayford, interview, April 22, 1993, transcript, 12.

51. Hayford, interview, April 22, 1993, transcript, 12-13.

52. Jack Hayford Sr. had already decided that if intercourse was involved in the couple's relationship immediate arrangements for a marriage would have to be made.

53. Hayford, interview, April 22, 1993, transcript, 13.

54. Jack worked as a courier for Security First National Bank. Hayford, interview, April 22, 1993, transcript, 18. He was an excellent employee and was commended because he "had not been absent for a single day." C. C. Lincoln, Vice President, Manager, Personnel Department, letter to Mr. Jack W. Hayford, March 15, 1955, private holding, 1.

55. *30th Anniversary*, 11.

56. Hayford, interview, April 22, 1993, transcript, 17.

57. Hayford, interview, April 22, 1993, transcript, 18.

58. A. Hayford, interview, December 27, 2007.

59. *Carry On* (Los Angeles: L.I.F.E. Bible College, 1956), 24. A review of the college yearbooks from 1953 to 1956 reveals an involved Jack Hayford. The 1954 yearbook shows a picture of Jack and Anna sitting together with the caption: "Someday?"

60. Jack Hayford, *A Passion for Fullness* (Dallas: Word Publishing, 1990), 118.

61. Hayford, *A Passion for Fullness*, 119.

62. Hayford, *A Passion for Fullness*, 119.

63. Hayford, *A Passion for Fullness*, 120.

64. Hayford, *The Beauty of Spiritual Language*, 49.

65. For details of his Spirit baptism experience, see Hayford, *The Beauty of Spiritual Language*, 42-43.

66. Jack's sister, Luanne, came home from a summer camp speaking with tongues while Jack was still in high school. Witnesses at the summer camp prayer altar told Luanne that she was speaking Chinese, which she believed to be a call from God to be a missionary there. Jack wondered about her experience but accepted it as legitimate. Hayford, *The Beauty of Spiritual Language*, 37-39.

67. Hayford, *The Beauty of Spiritual Language*, 49.

68. Hayford, *The Beauty of Spiritual Language*, 49.

69. Hayford, *The Beauty of Spiritual Language*, 50.

70. Hayford, *The Beauty of Spiritual Language*, 50.

71. Hayford, interview, April 22, 1993, transcript, 17-18.

72. "Swordbearers Commencement," *Foursquare Magazine*, March 1956, 28. The article about commencement included a picture of Hayford; see also L.I.F.E. Bible College program for the January 26, 1956, commencement service, 2.

Chapter 5: Launching Out in Ministry

1. Hayford, *A Passion for Fullness*, 8.

2. Hayford, *A Passion for Fullness*, 8.

3. Hayford, interview, April 22, 1993, transcript, 8.

4. Hayford, interview, April 22, 1993, transcript 8-9.

5. Vincent R. Bird, letter to Jack Hayford, June 14, 1955, private holding, 1. Bird regularly corresponded with Hayford until his graduation and then throughout his Fort Wayne pastorate. His letters were always affirming and encouraging.

6. Jack Hayford, *Pastors of Promise* (Ventura, CA: Regal, 1997), 33.

7. Hayford, *Pastors of Promise*, 35.

8. Hayford, *Pastors of Promise*, 34.

9. For example, Dr. Bird wrote that "I have heard some very fine reports from the ministers where you have already been." Later in the letter Bird mentions "the sad news in regard to your automobile." He continues: "Many are the testings of the righteous, it seems, but God certainly will see us through." Vincent R. Bird, letter to Rev. and Mrs. Jack Hayford, March 9, 1956, private holding, 1.

10. Hayford, *Pastors of Promise*, 33; Vincent R. Bird, letter to Jack Hayford, July 6, 1955, private holding, 1; Hayford, *Pastors of Promise*, 33-34.

11. Fort Wayne had a population of about 135,000 in 1956 and was home of the Fort Wayne Pistons professional basketball team. Team owner Fred Zollner later moved the team to Detroit.

12. Vincent R. Bird, letter to Rev. and Mrs. Jack Hayford, May 29, 1956, private holding, 1. Jack communicated to Bird the inflated attendance report given by the Muncie pastor, "Bro. Clark." Bird wrote Hayford that he was "disappointed" that his report had counted the Muncie people coming to the meetings.

13. A. Hayford, interview, December 27, 2007.

14. Hayford, *Pastors of Promise*, 131-32.

15. Only one letter from Hayford to Dr. Bird was located, written just three months after taking the church. It clearly shows the effort he and Anna were putting into the new congregation. Saying that "things are progressing slowly," Hayford charts the Sunday school attendance over four consecutive Sundays, as six, eight, nine, and ten. He adds, "So we are growing." Jack W. Hayford, letter to Dr. Vincent R. Bird, August 1, 1956, private holding, 1.

16. Vincent R. Bird, letter to Rev. and Mrs. Jack Hayford, June 7, 1956, private holding, 1; Vincent R. Bird, letter to Rev. Jack Hayford, November 9, 1956. In the November letter, Bird suggested to Hayford that they offer the "Lutheran people" $1,700.00 for the building. The building was purchased in early 1957 by the denomination.

17. Hayford, *Testimony of Learning Obedience*, transcript, 14-15.

18. *30th Anniversary*, 13.

19. *Fifty Years of God's Amazing Grace*, 27; Hayford wrote Bird that they were "doing much door to door work again and think this will be a means by which we shall contact the most folk." Hayford, letter to Dr. Bird, August 1, 1956, 1.

20. Hayford, interview, April 22, 1993, transcript, 22.

21. Hayford, *Testimony of Learning Obedience*, transcript, 15-16.

22. Hayford, *Testimony of Learning Obedience*, transcript, 16.

23. Hayford, *The Beauty of Spiritual Language*, 109. Hayford also tells this story in his message *Testimony of Learning Obedience*. Since the book *The Beauty of Spiritual Language* is more readily available, I have chosen to use it as the primary source in recounting this story.

24. Hayford, *The Beauty of Spiritual Language*, 109.

25. Hayford, *The Beauty of Spiritual Language*, 110.

26. Hayford, *The Beauty of Spiritual Language*, 110-11. In a 1973 account of this story, Hayford says he shouted "Sin! Is like!" Hayford, *Testimony of Learning Obedience*, transcript, 16.

27. Hayford, *The Beauty of Spiritual Language*, 111.

28. Hayford, *The Beauty of Spiritual Language*, 112.

29. At the time the building was purchased from the Lutherans, the Foursquare organization, in a separate contract, purchased the parsonage adjacent to the church building. Vincent R. Bird, letter to Rev. Jack Hayford, October 7, 1957, private holding, 1. In the polity and governance of the International Church of the Foursquare Gospel, all local church properties are deeded to the denomination, not to the local church.

30. Of this incident Jack wrote: "In fact, if God had warned me in advance, I must confess with embarrassment that at that time in my ministry, I would have probably been tempted to opt out." Hayford, *The Beauty of Spiritual Language*, 112-13.

31. Hayford, *Testimony of Learning Obedience*, transcript, 17.

32. Hayford, *Testimony of Learning Obedience*, transcript, 17.

33. The book is still available but now titled E. M. Bounds, *Power through Prayer* (Westwood, NJ: The Christian Library, 1984).

34. Hayford, *A Passion for Fullness*, 4.

35. Hayford, *A Passion for Fullness*, 3.

36. Hayford, *Pastors of Promise*, 48.

37. Hayford, *Pastors of Promise*, 48.

38. Hayford, *Pastors of Promise*, 48.

39. Hayford, interview, April 22, 1993, transcript, 23.

40. Jack Hayford, *The Key to Everything* (Orlando: Creation House, 1993), 126-27.

41. *30th Anniversary*, 14.

42. Jack Hayford, *A Man's Walk with God* (Van Nuys: Living Way Ministries, 1993), 33.

43. Rev. W. B. Stadler, Letter to Rev. and Mrs. Jack Hayford, April 2, 1957, private holding, 1; Rev. W. B. Stadler, Letter to Rev. and Mrs. Jack Hayford, April 16, 1957, private holding, 1. The churches sent the family $163.50. Stadler was the

divisional superintendent for the Fort Wayne church. The International Church of the Foursquare Gospel in the United States was divided up into a number of districts, each led by a district supervisor. The supervisor of the Great Lakes District was Dr. Bird, who acted as the overseer/bishop for the area. In turn the district was divided into divisions of a smaller number of churches. Stadler led one of these divisions.

44. Hayford, *A Man's Walk with God*, 34.

45. *25 Years of Silver Service*, 9. Since Jack Hayford was a teenager, he has used poetry and songwriting to express his faith in often difficult situations.

46. Jack W. Hayford, *Manifest Presence* (Kent, England: Sovereign World, 2005), 158-59.

47. Hayford, *Manifest Presence*, 159.

48. Hayford, *Manifest Presence*, 159.

49. Jack W. Hayford, *An Evangelical Response to Racism: An Address to the 1995 Convention of the National Association of Evangelicals*, edited transcript (Van Nuys: Living Way Ministries, March 1995), 5. Hayford provides a vivid description of the experience, even recalling the exact time of the day.

50. *25 Years of Silver Service*, 8.

51. Hayford, interview, April 22, 1993, transcript, 22.

52. Hayford, interview, April 22, 1993, transcript, 23. The poor attendance never kept Hayford from hoping and planning. He often sketched out how they could expand their little building. He kept himself engaged in writing youth material for the Foursquare denomination. During his entire four years in Fort Wayne, Hayford did youth meetings and provided youth leadership for the Great Lakes District. When he left the church, the average attendance was around forty.

53. Hayford has kept all his message notes for the time in Fort Wayne. For this study I reviewed them and was impressed with their detail. His notes were generally typed, though many are handwritten. They reflect the homiletic style of the 1950s with alliteration and structured three-point outlines. The introductions have "grabbers" with illustrations that Hayford found somewhere. His message notes do not show the personal, self-revealing style of his years at The Church on the Way. To the contrary, they appear quite formal and stilted.

54. Jack Hayford, "What Is a Pentecostal Church?" sermon notes, private holding, 2.

55. Hayford, "What Is a Pentecostal Church?," 1-2.

56. In notes for a Fort Wayne message, Hayford wrote: "I am a Pentecostal preacher. I wasn't always that bold to say so." Jack Hayford, "Patterns Preceeding [*sic*] Pentecost," sermon notes, private holding, 1.

57. Hayford, *Testimony of Learning Obedience*, transcript, 17.

58. Hayford, interview, April 22, 1993, transcript, 23.

59. Van Cleave, *The Vine and the Branches*, 66. Bird was appointed to the role in 1959 and served for eighteen years.

60. The position would later be named the International Youth Director, a more prestigious title.

61. Hayford, interview, April 22, 1993, transcript, 23; Hayford, *Testimony of Learning Obedience*, transcript, 18.

62. Hayford, interview, April 22, 1993, transcript, 23.

63. M. E. Nichols, letter to Rev. Jack Hayford, March 17, 1960, 1. The letter acknowledges, with regret, a March 16 letter from Hayford resigning as pastor of the Fort Wayne church. The letter says that the office is "rejoicing with you that God has given this expanded service for Him."

64. A. Hayford, interview, December 27, 2007.

Chapter 6: Serving the Denomination

1. Hayford, interview, April 22, 1993, transcript, 24.

2. Like other Pentecostal denominations in the first decades of their existence, the Foursquare Church preferred to be known as a movement instead of a denomination.

3. Soon after Hayford arrived in Los Angeles, his name began appearing in the *Los Angeles Times*, usually associated with ads or articles for youth or musical events. For example: Display Ad 34, *Los Angeles Times*, September 3, 1960, B6; "Youth Rally Set at Foursquare Gospel Parley," *Los Angeles Times*, February 16, 1964, 18; "Church Lists Speaker," *Los Angeles Times*, July 24, 1964, SF8; Display Ad 32, *Los Angeles Times*, June 24, 1967, B7; "Pershing Square Site of Post-Sunrise Rite," *Los Angeles Times*, April 13, 1968, B9.

4. Vincent Bird, interview with the author, April 22, 1993.

5. Hayford, interview, April 22, 1993, transcript, 25. Outside meetings included the Pentecostal Fellowship of North America (PFNA), National Association of Evangelicals, and the National Sunday School Association. In 1962, Hayford served as chairman of the Youth Committee for the PFNA. Virginia Cannon, letter to Mr. John Wilson, November 28, 1962, private holding, 1. On many occasions Hayford was a presenter at conference workshops. Harold H. Etling, letter to Mr. Jack Hayford, June 15, 1964, private holding, 1. Etling was the president of the National Sunday School Association and wrote Hayford regarding two workshops at which he would speak.

6. Howard P. Courtney, letter to Rev. Jack Hayford, September 9, 1960, private holding, 1. Courtney, then serving as the General Supervisor overseeing all Foursquare churches in the United States, commended Hayford for his message and said,

"Your thorough preparation both in study and prayer was clearly evident, and I was genuinely proud of you." Significantly he added, "I rejoice in the fruit that your life is bearing wherever you go."

7. Jack's years in Los Angeles were fruitful for his writing in ways that went beyond the materials he produced for the youth department. Among his published articles and poems were "Her Congregation Is Numbered," *Foursquare Magazine*, June 1963, 9-10; "The Word Is Light," *Christian Life*, July 1964, 22-23; "A Very Humble Christmas," *Pentecostal Evangel*, December 25, 1965, 21; "The Conundrum of Consecration," *Lighted Pathway*, November 1965, 20-21; "Chapel Time: This Is Your Hour," *Campus Call*, Winter 1965, 6; "Youth Involved," *Teach*, Summer 1966, 14-15; "Booklet Sales Spiral with Outlines," *Christian Bookseller*, November 1964, 20-21; "The New Man," *Decision*, July 1968, 2.

8. Some of these materials have been located: *Christian Doctrine: Comparisons and Contrasts*, Foursquare Crusader Camp Study Course (Los Angeles: Foursquare Publications, 1963); *Christian Standard: The Call to Live from Above to Live Beyond*, Foursquare Crusader Camp Study Course (Los Angeles: Foursquare Publications, 1963); *Christian Life: Life … in the Will of God*, Foursquare Crusader Camp Study Course (Los Angeles: Foursquare Publications, 1964); *Christian Morality: Wholly His … Today*, Foursquare Crusader Camp Study Course (Los Angeles: Foursquare Publications, 1966); *Q. T. Handbook: A Practical Guide for Youth's Private Devotions* (Los Angeles: Foursquare Publications, n.d.); *Q. T. Handbook: A Practical Guide for Youth's Private Devotions* (Montrose, CA: Rusthoi Publications, 1964).

9. Hayford, *Christian Doctrine: Comparisons and Contrasts*, 1-22.

10. Hayford, *Christian Doctrine: Comparisons and Contrasts*, 19.

11. Hayford, *Christian Doctrine: Comparisons and Contrasts*, 19.

12. Bird, interview, April 22, 1993. Correspondence up until 1963 shows that Hayford referred to his job title as National Youth Representative. Afterward, he refers to his role as International Youth Director: Jack W. Hayford, letter to Robert Walker, editor, March 21, 1964, private holding, 1; 1965 stationery for the Department of Youth and Christian Education lists him as Director of Youth.

13. Jack W. Hayford, School of Pastoral Nurture: Consultation I, King's Seminary, May 2007, digital audio recording, 1.18.

14. Jack W. Hayford, letter to Dr. Rolf K. McPherson, May 8, 1963, private holding, 1. Hayford had talked with McPherson, president of the International Church of the Foursquare Gospel, about the invitation to Portland, expressing his appreciation for "the privilege of talking with [sic] you as frankly and confidentially as I did." Apparently, McPherson helped handle the matter in some way. Hayford also adds: "As only one of hundreds of younger ministers in our group, it is refreshing to be assured that our future is indeed upon the hearts of our leadership"; Jack W. Hayford, letter to Dr. N. M. Van Cleave, May 8, 1963, private holding. Dr. Van Cleave, who

would later play a key role in Jack getting to Van Nuys, had extended the invitation to come to Portland.

15. Van Cleave, *The Vine and the Branches*, 187.

16. Bird, interview, April 22, 1993; Hayford, interview, April 22, 1993, transcript, 24.

17. Jack W. Hayford, untitled paper, January 26, 1963, private holding.

18. Jack W. Hayford, letter to Dr. Rolf K. McPherson, December 28, 1963, private holding.

19. Hayford, letter to McPherson, December 28, 1963, 1. Jack Hayford is known for his "wordiness."

20. Hayford, letter to McPherson, December 28, 1963.

21. The term "headquarters" for the denomination main offices was in vogue at the time but came to be highly unpopular in later decades. In the late nineties, the term was changed to the "central offices."

22. Hayford, letter to McPherson, December 28, 1963, 2-3.

23. Hayford, untitled paper, January 26, 1963, private holding, 1. It is unclear just how many read this paper. There are two copies in Hayford's personal files.

24. Hayford, untitled paper, January 26, 1963, 2. In some measure this suspicion would linger for over thirty years in the denomination. Financial mismanagement, all without illegality, brought the resignations of the two successive presidents that followed McPherson's retirement in 1988. Only after Hayford assumed the Foursquare presidency in 2004 has there been fuller financial disclosure.

25. Hayford, untitled paper, January 26, 1963, 2.

26. Hayford, untitled paper, January 26, 1963, 6.

27. Hayford, untitled paper, January 26, 1963, 5.

28. Hayford, untitled paper, January 26, 1963, 8-14.

29. Van Cleave, *The Vine and the Branches*, 75. Besides Moline, the other two churches were the ones in Portland, Oregon, and Decatur, Illinois.

30. Bird, interview, April 22, 1993.

31. Jack W. Hayford, *Above and Beyond* (Van Nuys: Living Way Ministries, 1986), 10-11. This booklet was a reprinted and slightly edited version of Hayford's Moline message, which was published not long after the 1965 convention. An entire original edition was not located during research other than a few pages of the booklet that was printed in 1965 just a few months after the Moline convention. It may have been self-published. The copyright page shows J. W. Hayford, *Above and Beyond* (B. N. Printing: n.p., 1965). Hayford mentions the booklet in a letter to a friend in September 1965. Jack and Anna Hayford, letter to Rev. and Mrs. J. L. Babcock, September 2, 1965, private holding, 2.

32. Hayford, *Above and Beyond*, 13.

33. Hayford, *Above and Beyond*, 14.

34. Hayford's use of the term "great society" makes one wonder if he was borrowing President Lyndon Johnson's term, given the time period.

35. Hayford, *Above and Beyond*, 21-22.

36. These three words recur throughout Hayford's literature and sermons. Hayford, "The Church on the Way," *Logos Journal*, 39.

37. Hayford, "The Church on the Way," *Logos Journal*, 22.

38. Hayford, "The Church on the Way," *Logos Journal*, 22.

39. Hayford, "The Church on the Way," *Logos Journal*, 23.

40. Hayford, "The Church on the Way," *Logos Journal*, 27.

41. Hayford, interview, April 22, 1993, transcript, 27.

42. Hayford, interview, April 22, 1993, transcript, 27.

43. Lawson, "Pastor 'on the Way,'" 25.

44. Jack recognized the Moline convention's significance. In a later journal entry dated May 7, 1966, he writes: The "Lord reminded me of what He said to me, about this duty [prayer and praise] in 1963. 'If you'll pray for 2 years—I'll show you what I can do.' It was 2 years later that the Moline convention took place."

45. Vincent Bird, handwritten letter to the Life Alumni Association, n.d., private holding, 3.

46. Jack W. Hayford, letter to Dr. Vincent R. Bird, March 12, 1965, private holding, 1. Hayford told Bird he would be willing to stay until the fall if necessary.

47. Jack W. Hayford, letter to Dr. Clarence Hall, April 16, 1965, private holding, 1. Dr. Hall was dean of the college.

48. Although Hayford has not written publicly about exactly how he made the decision to go to Life Bible College, his journal suggests that an important factor was the voice of God. In a June 2, 1965, entry he wrote of his confidence that he had "followed the voice of the Lord." Jack W. Hayford, journal entry, June 2, 1965, private holding, 1.

49. Hayford, journal entry, June 2, 1965, 1.

50. Hayford, interview, April 22, 1993, transcript, 27.

51. Cannon, letter to Mr. John Wilson, November 28, 1962, 1.

52. Jack Hayford, "Sing Thankfully with Me," Church Bulletin, The Church on the Way, 2.

53. Hayford, *Celebrating Pastor Jack's Birthday with Music and Testimony*, transcript, 2.

54. Hayford, *Celebrating Pastor Jack's Birthday*, transcript, 2; Hayford, interview, April 22, 1993, transcript, 31. The hymn context came about following Cliff Barrows' address at the 1961 National Church Music Fellowship in which he lamented the lack of

hymnody originating in the contemporary church. Barrows felt that the theological integrity that hymns generally provided was being lost to the church. The National Church Music Fellowship had the hymn contest the following year. Don Hustad, "Award-Winning Hymn," in *Decision*, March 1963, 10.

55. Dr. Rene Frank, Chm., letter to Mr. Jack Hayford, October 23, 1962, 1. Frank was the chairman of the National Church Music Fellowship and notified Hayford that he had won the contest.

56. Hustad, "Award-winning Hymn," 10; "Hymn Winner Is Los Angeles Youth Worker," *Minneapolis Morning Tribune*, October 31, 1962, 20; "Foursquare Minister Wins Nat'l Hymn-Writing Contest," *Foursquare Magazine*, January 1963, 10.

57. Hayford, *The Key to Everything*, 171.

58. Hayford, *The Key to Everything*, 172.

59. Hayford, *The Key to Everything*, 172-73.

60. I am purposely vague here in dating this account to avoid offering specific information that might expose the identity of this woman. For a detailed telling of the story that follows, see Jack W. Hayford, *The Anatomy of Seduction* (Ventura, CA: Regal Books, 2004). This book is drawn from "The Anatomy of Adultery," a message of Hayford at The Church on the Way that was presented on April 23, 1993. Hayford had told the story before but never in as much detail.

61. Hayford, *The Anatomy of Seduction*, 30.

62 Hayford, *The Anatomy of Seduction*, 31. Many Christians who see the Bible as authoritative and literal believe that it depicts an invisible world inhabited not only by angels but by demonic beings as well. Pentecostals are particularly inclined to believe that Christians are regularly involved in spiritual battles. They take the Apostle Paul's words in Ephesians 6:12 literally when he says: "For our struggle is not against flesh and blood, but against the rulers, against the authorities, against the powers of this dark world and against the spiritual forces of evil in the heavenly realms" (NIV). In addition, Paul writes in 6:11 about the "devil's schemes" (NIV) which for Hayford and many other Pentecostals refers to specific strategies of Satan to defeat Christians. This is what he means by "the Adversary's designs." In the book *The Anatomy of Seduction* Hayford provides significant attention to this whole concept of spiritual warfare. See pages 24-39.

63. Hayford, *The Anatomy of Seduction*, 38.

64. Hayford, *The Anatomy of Seduction*, 41.

65. Hayford, *The Anatomy of Seduction*, 46.

66. Hayford, *The Anatomy of Seduction*, 42.

67. Hayford, *The Anatomy of Seduction*, 43.

68. Some time before Jack ever discussed the relationship with Anna, she began to be concerned, sensing his growing admiration for the woman. On one occasion he came home from the office and remarked to Anna about something his female coworker had worn. Although Anna did not let Jack know at the time, it hurt her. She said, "I remember thinking to myself, *Yes, she can look nice, because she's not home changing diapers!* [italics Anna Hayford]" A. Hayford, "Jack and Anna Hayford: When Words Were Not Enough," 60.

69. Hayford, *The Anatomy of Seduction*, 46-47.

70. Hayford, *The Anatomy of Seduction*, 47.

71. Hayford, *The Anatomy of Seduction*, 47.

72. Hayford, *The Anatomy of Seduction*, 51.

73. Hayford, *The Anatomy of Seduction*, 52.

74. Hayford, *The Anatomy of Seduction*, 53. In "The Anatomy of Adultery," Hayford expresses his "embarrassment" in revealing the depth of his deception. He pressed beyond his hesitation to share the experience "because I deeply desire that no one else would ever experience surrender to such deceit."

75. Hayford, *The Anatomy of Seduction*, 54.

76. Hayford, *The Beauty of Spiritual Language*, 58.

77. Hayford, interview, April 22, 1993, transcript, 25; Hayford, *The Beauty of Spiritual Language*, 58.

78. Hayford, *The Beauty of Spiritual Language*, 58.

79. In his 1993 message to The Church on the Way congregation, Hayford said he believed he was giving place to a "spirit of murder" in indulging thoughts of Anna possibly dying. Jack W. Hayford, "The Anatomy of Adultery" (Van Nuys: Living Way Ministries, 1993, audiocassette).

80. Hayford, *The Anatomy of Seduction*, 55.

81. A. Hayford, "Jack and Anna Hayford: When Words Were Not Enough," 60. Anna never told her parents at the time what had happened. She had asked them to pray and believes it helped her because she knew "they were praying constantly."

82. Hayford, interview, April 22, 1993, transcript, 26.

83. Jack W. Hayford, *Exalt His Name Together* (Gospel Publishing House: SESAC, 1966).

84. Jack W. Hayford, "Exalt His Name Together" in *Day of Thy Power: A Devotional Hymnal* (Van Nuys: Living Way Ministries, 1987), 2.

85. Jack W. Hayford, interview, September 15, 2003. In a journal entry just after his repentance and deliverance Hayford wrote: "The last year held the greatest challenge against my ministry that I have known—and the record here and in heaven shows the greatness of Jesus' conquering ability: complete in grace, power, and restoration.

January 12, _____." The year of the entry is not added to help protect the identity of the woman involved.

86. In the same journal entry of January 12, Hayford writes: "The deepest experiences of the last five months have been to the strengthening of my conviction that the heart of the Father is yearning today for men who will accept the burden and responsibility of a supernatural ministry."

Chapter 7: New Horizons

1. J. and A. Hayford, letter to Babcock, September 2, 1965, 1.

2. Jack W. Hayford, journal entry dated September 13, 1965, private holding, 1.

3. Hayford's responsibilities included all matters that concerned student relations, extracurricular activities, and student dormitory life. His responsibilities in promotion required him to develop an otherwise almost nonexistent outreach for enrollment. J. and A. Hayford, letter to Babcock, September 2, 1965, 1.

4. L.I.F.E. Bible College Enrollment Information, Life Pacific College, San Dimas, CA, photocopy, 1-2. 1964 spring FTE enrollment had fallen to 367 students, compared to 681 at the beginning of 1952 when Hayford first enrolled.

5. Jack Hayford, letter to Vincent R. Bird, September 2, 1965, private holding, 1.

6. Hayford, letter to Vincent R. Bird, September 2, 1965, 2. The quote is written as Hayford included it in his letter to Bird. To have placed *sic* throughout would have been distracting.

7. Hayford, letter to Vincent R. Bird, September 2, 1965, 2.

8. Hayford, interview, April 22, 1993, transcript, 26-27.

9. Hayford, interview, April 22, 1993, transcript, 28. Ironically, Hayford first resisted teaching the course named Song Direction at the college. It proved to be an important assignment because through teaching it he began to grow in his understanding of worship in the local church. The next chapter will discuss this further. Jack W. Hayford, *Worship His Majesty* (Waco: Word Books, 1987), 43-44.

10. L.I.F.E. Bible College Enrollment Information, 2. By 1968, FTE enrollment in the fall semester was 545 students, nearly 200 more students than in 1964.

11. Hayford, interview, April 22, 1993, transcript, 28.

12. Jack W. Hayford, letter to Dr. Rolf K. McPherson, October 7, 1966, private holding, 3-4; Hayford, *E Quake* (Nashville: Thomas Nelson, 1999), 123.

13. Hayford, letter to Rolf McPherson, October 7, 1966, 3.

14. Hayford, letter to Rolf McPherson, October 7, 1966, 5.

15. Hayford, letter to Rolf McPherson, October 7, 1966, 2.

16. Hayford, letter to Rolf McPherson, October 7, 1966, 1-2.

17. Hayford, letter to Rolf McPherson, October 7, 1966, 2.

18. Hayford, letter to Rolf McPherson, October 7, 1966, 5.

19. Jack Hayford, "We're Incomplete without a Heart of Integrity," *New Wine* magazine, May 1983, 27; Hayford, interview, April 22, 1993, transcript, 28.

20. Jack W. Hayford, School of Pastoral Nurture: Consultation II, March 2007, King's Seminary, digital audio recording, 2.1.

21. Jack W. Hayford, School of Pastoral Nurture: Consultation II, March 2007, King's Seminary, digital audio recording, 2.3.

22. Some may object to using the word "revelation" in describing his new insights, but this is how he understood the experience. Typically, evangelicals refer to the inspiration of the Bible as revelation, and to the present work of the Spirit to secure contemporary understanding of texts as illumination. Is it possible to refer to present-day illumination as revelation? A few have given a qualified yes, including Wayne Grudem and J. Rodman Williams. Williams calls it subordinate revelation to imply its lesser authority and subordination to the overall biblical message. This is how Hayford would describe such experiences. J. Rodman Williams, *Renewal Theology*, vol. 1 (Grand Rapids, MI: Zondervan, 1988), 43-44; Wayne Grudem, *The Gift of Prophecy in the New Testament and Today* (Westchester, IL: Crossway Books, 1988), 30, 87. Amos Yong expands on this by noting that revelation can be understood as a verb and is "progressive and dynamic." Amos Yong, *The Spirit Poured Out on All Flesh: Pentecostalism and the Possibility of Global Theology* (Grand Rapids, MI: Baker Academic, 2005), 296-99.

23. Hayford, *The Church on the Way*, 63-64. Hayford, *Glory on Your House*, 111-18.

24. Paul Charter and Chuck Shoemake, interview with the author, September 7, 2007. Charter and Shoemake were two Life Bible College students who went on to work with Hayford at the Church on the Way.

25. Hayford, interview, April 22, 1993, transcript, 29.

26. Hayford, interview, April 22, 1993; Charter and Shoemake, interview, September 7, 2007.

27. Charter and Shoemake, interview, September 7, 2007.

28. Hayford, interview, April 22, 1993, transcript, 26. John and Jean Firth were Foursquare missionaries to Colombia.

29. For perspectives on the deliverance ministry controversy that swirled in the 1970s, see S. David Moore, *The Shepherding Movement: Controversy and Charismatic Ecclesiology* (London: T & T Clark, 2003). Hayford has steadfastly avoided declarations that "Christians can have a demon" and focused more on the idea that Christians are unquestionably subject to demonic influence.

30. Hayford, *The Church on the Way*, 47-48.

31. Hayford, interview, April 22, 1993, transcript, 35.

32. Hayford, interview, April 22, 1993, transcript, 49.

33. Hayford, interview, April 22, 1993, transcript, 49-50.

34. Jack W. Hayford, "A Man's Worship and Witness," 75.

35. The first speaker at the conference was Dr. Gene Scott, the controversial Southern California television pastor, then an Assemblies of God credentialed minister. Jack W. Hayford, interview with the author, November 13, 2007. The outline Scott presented shaped the ministry priorities of the Church on the Way for the thirty years Jack Hayford served as its senior pastor.

36. Jack W. Hayford, *Building a House of Worship*, Autumn Leadership Conference (Van Nuys: King's College and Seminary, 2004), audio recording, transcript, 3.

37. Jack W. Hayford, "A Man's Worship and Witness," 75.

38. Hayford, *Building a House of Worship*, 4.

39. Hayford, *Building a House of Worship*, 4.

40. Hayford, "A Man's Worship and Witness," 77.

41. Hayford, interview, April 22, 1993, transcript, 35.

42. In late 1968, Hayford was nearing completion on a bachelor's degree at nearby Azusa Pacific University. While working as Dean of Students, he took courses whenever possible. He did not need to take many courses because he was able to transfer credits from Life Bible College and Fort Wayne Bible College. He officially graduated in 1970. His second bachelor's degree (the first was his 1956 BTh from Life Bible College) was financed by a scholarship granted him by the United Foursquare Women. Later, once at The Church on the Way, Jack started on a master's degree at Pasadena Nazarene College but was forced to stop with the explosive growth of the Van Nuys church. Hayford, interview, April 22, 1993, transcript, 33; Cynndie Hoff, "1996 Alumnus of the Year: Jack Hayford," *APU Life*, Fall 1996, 4-5.

43. Hayford, interview, April 22, 1993, transcript, 25; Hayford, *The Mary Miracle* (Ventura, CA: Regal Books, 1994), 103-5; Hayford, *Prayer Is Invading the Impossible* (Alachua, FL: Bridge-Logos, 1977, 2002), 81-82. Christa was born seven years after the other siblings. The Hayfords saw her birth as a herald to the coming transition to pastor The Church on the Way.

44. Hayford, interview, April 22, 1993, transcript, 27. The school's "dean" was the functional equivalent of a college president.

45. For the Charismatic Renewal, see Michael Harper, *Three Sisters* (Wheaton, IL: Tyndale, 1979); Peter D. Hocken, "The Charismatic Movement," *The New International Dictionary of the Pentecostal and Charismatic Movements* (Grand Rapids, MI: Zondervan, 2002), 477-519; Harrell, *All Things Are Possible: The Healing and*

Charismatic Revivals in America; Kilian McDonnell, ed., *Presence, Power, Praise: Documents on the Charismatic Renewal*, 3 vols. (Collegeville, MN: Liturgical, 1980); Richard Quebedeaux, *The New Charismatics II* (San Francisco: Harper & Row, 1983); Vinson Synan, *In the Latter Days: The Outpouring of the Holy Spirit in the Twentieth Century* (Ann Arbor, MI: Servant Publications, 1984); Vinson Synan, *The Twentieth-Century Pentecostal Explosion* (Altamonte Springs: Creation House, 1987). Perhaps the most comprehensive and recent study on the Charismatic Movement is: Stephen Hunt, *A History of the Charismatic Movement in Britain and the United States of America*, 2 vols. (Lewiston, NY: Edward Mellen Press, 2009). There are many important period pieces that are more specific studies on groups and movements. For example, see Donald E. Miller, *Reinventing American Protestantism* (Berkeley: University of California Press, 1997); Moore, *The Shepherding Movement: Controversy and Charismatic Ecclesiology*; Bill Jackson, *The Quest for the Radical Middle* (Cape Town, South Africa: Vineyard International, 1999); Vinson Synan, *Under His Banner* (Costa Mesa, CA: Gift Publications, 1992).

46. Dennis J. Bennett, *Nine O'Clock in the Morning* (Plainfield, NJ: Logos International, 1970).

47. Hayford, interview, April 22, 1993, transcript, 34.

48. Hayford, interview, April 22, 1993, transcript, 35.

49. Dorothy Jean Furlong, "Viewpoint: Looking Over Three Decades of Change: An Interview with Jack W. Hayford, D.D.," *Foursquare World Advance*, September 1978, 4.

50. Furlong, "Viewpoint," 5.

51. A number of Hayford's college papers written for courses taken at APU were kept in his files. In a paper for an ethics class he expresses his disappointment with the Angelus Temple church attended by the Hayford family, because they were unwilling to speak out socially. He wrote a very honest paper on "Racial Prejudice," expressing his shock at what blacks endured after reading John Howard Griffin's *Black Like Me*. In a paper on the Vietnam War, Hayford shows sympathy to those who were arguing for withdrawal while also affirming the need for America to keep its defense pledges and commitments. Jack W. Hayford, Reflection Paper: Review "How Free Am I?" unpublished paper, July 28, 1968; Hayford, "Racial Prejudice: A Personal Reflection," unpublished paper, August 13, 1968; Hayford, "Vietnam Crisis: A Review," unpublished paper, n.d.

52. Hayford, *Testimony of Learning Obedience*, transcript, 19.

53. Hayford, interview, April 22, 1993, transcript, 29; Hayford, *Testimony of Learning Obedience*, 19. An especially valuable file folder was located, entitled "Word – Era I – 1970–1984." In this personal folder was a handwritten set of pages that carried the heading "Basic Guidelines received from the Lord concerning the work here at the church: Christmas Night 1973, and the Lord would have me review His dealings." It is a remarkable document that gives specific dates to events regarding Jack's leadership

in the early years at The Church on the Way. The first date he lists is the day on which he claimed that God spoke to him, given as December 6, 1968.

54. Hayford, interview, April 22, 1993, transcript, 29; Jack W. Hayford, *Confessions of a Wandering Pastor* (Van Nuys: SoundWord Tape Ministry, November 1974), audiocassette.

55. Hayford has said that God also spoke to him in December 1968 from the passage in Isaiah 58 regarding the call to see people set free from demonic bondage and oppression. This would prove to be significant when in the early 1970s The Church on the Way began to emphasize the ministry of deliverance as an ongoing part of the church life. Hayford, *Confessions of a Wandering Pastor.*

56. This time Hayford was not formally offered the Portland church.

57. Jack Hayford, journal entry, February 4, 1969, private holding, 1.

58. Hayford, *Testimony of Learning Obedience*, transcript, 20.

59. Jack Hayford, "I Thank God upon Every Remembrance … of Nathaniel Van Cleave," Church Bulletin, The Church on the Way, July 25, 1982, 2.

60. Hayford, interview, April 22, 1993, transcript, 30; Hayford, *Testimony of Learning Obedience*, 20.

61. Hayford, interview, April 22, 1993, transcript, 30.

62. Jack W. Hayford, "The Church on the Way," *Logos Journal*, March/April 1972, 20-22, 39; Hayford, *The Church on the Way*, 11-12. The *Los Angeles Times* carried a small article announcing Hayford's appointment to the church. "Church Greets New Pastor," *Los Angeles Times*, March 16, 1969, SF A4.

63. Hayford, *The Church on the Way*, 12.

64. Hayford, *The Church on the Way*, 13.

65. Hayford, *The Church on the Way*, 13-14.

66. Hayford's journal reflects the hunger he felt for the pastorate while serving the denomination the nine years after Fort Wayne. For example, in an April 2, 1966, entry, he writes, "God knows I have yearned for the pastorate so many times." Jack W. Hayford, journal entry, April 2, 1966, private holding, 1.

Chapter 8: "You Are Home Now"

1. Hayford, *Worship His Majesty*, 53.

2. Lawson, "Pastor 'on the Way,'" 24.

3. Hayford, *Glory on Your House*, 159.

4. Hayford, *Glory on Your House*, 160; Hayford, *The Church on the Way*, 16.

5. The idea of unlearning things is heard in early teaching tapes by Hayford at the Church on the Way. Jack W. Hayford, *Spiritual Worship* 1973 Pastors Seminar (Van Nuys: SoundWord Tape Ministry, 1973), audiocassette.

6. Hayford, *Glory on Your House*, 160; Hayford, *The Church on the Way*, 16-17.

7. Synan, *The Holiness Pentecostal Tradition*, 96; for a concise overview of the Charismatic movement in the 1960s, see Moore, *The Shepherding Movement*, 21-25.

8. Hayford, *Glory on Your House*, 161.

9. "Brief History of the First Foursquare Church of Van Nuys" (1966), Church on the Way holding, Van Nuys, 2. The one-page article is included in a church bulletin typed handout. It lists all the church's "ministers" up to 1966.

10. "75 Years of Fruitful Harvest," The Church on the Way: 75th Anniversary (Van Nuys: The Church on the Way, Van Nuys, November 24 and 25, 2001), 5.

11. John L. Amstutz, "The Portrait of a Church on the Way: A Proposal for Church Growth Submitted to the Pastoral Staff of 'The Church on the Way,' The First Foursquare Church of Van Nuys, California," unpublished paper, Church on the Way holding, Van Nuys, 7; John L. Amstutz, *Church Growth in the San Fernando Valley: A Study of Three Churches*, DMin diss., Fuller Theological Seminary, 1976 (Ann Arbor, MI: UMI, 1976), 34-35. Amstutz's paper on The Church on the Way is based on his dissertation but with more detail on The Church on the Way.

12. Amstutz, "The Portrait of a Church on the Way." The building was officially dedicated on April 30, 1952. Certificate of Dedication: The International Church of the Foursquare Gospel, April 30, 1952, Church on the Way holding, Van Nuys.

13. Lois and Dr. Van Cleave, letter to Jack and Anna Hayford, April 4, 1992, Church on the Way holding. Van Cleave briefly pastored the Van Nuys church from 1951 to 1952. Although Van Cleave was the pastor when the Sherman Way building was dedicated, it was built under the ministry of the previous pastor, Rev. A. B. Cowie. "75 Years of Fruitful Harvest," 2.

14. Amstutz, "The Portrait of a Church on the Way," 7.

15. Amstutz, *Church Growth in the San Fernando Valley*, 34.

16. Hayford, *Alaska Cruise Testimony* transcript, 2001, 13.

17. "75 Years of Fruitful Harvest," 4.

18. Charter and Shoemake, interview, September 7, 2007. Many of the details from the 2007 interview with Shoemake and Charter were corroborated in Jack W. Hayford, *Those Wedding Bells Are Breaking Up That Old Gang of Mine* (Van Nuys: SoundWord Tape Ministry, March 23, 1975).

19. Jack W. Hayford, School of Pastoral Nurture: Consultation I, May 2007, digital recording 1.7.

20. Charter and Shoemake, interview, September 7, 2007.

21. Hayford, *A Man's Walk with God*, 7, 23-24.

22. Amstutz, "The Portrait of a Church on the Way," 1. Both Amstutz's paper and his dissertation give helpful, nearly contemporary perspectives on the San Fernando Valley.

23. "Brief History of the Valley," Nov. 24, 2005, America's Suburb, www.americassuburb .com/brief_history.html.

24. Amstutz, "The Portrait of a Church on the Way," 1.

25. Amstutz, "The Portrait of a Church on the Way," 3.

26. For perspectives on the 1960s, see David Farber, ed., *The Sixties: From Memory to History* (Chapel Hill: University of North Carolina Press, 1994); Todd Gitlin, *The Sixties: Years of Hope, Days of Outrage* (New York: Bantam Books, 1993); Steven M. Tipton, *Getting Saved in the Sixties* (Berkeley: University of California Press, 1982); Robert S. Ellwood, *The 60s Spiritual Awakening* (New Brunswick, NJ: Rutgers University Press, 1994).

27. Jack W. Hayford, journal entry, September 20, 1969, private holding, 1.

28. "Worship His Majesty: That's the Root of Kingdom Life Says Jack Hayford," *Redemption*, October 1987, 45.

29. Hayford, interview, April 22, 1993, transcript, 15. A journal entry later in 1970 records that God told Hayford, "This is it—go to Van Nuys." Jack W. Hayford, journal entry, November 30, 1970, private holding, 1; Hayford, School of Pastoral Nurture: Consultation I, session 1.18.

30. Hayford, interview, April 22, 1993, transcript, 15.

31. Hayford, *The Church on the Way*, 18.

32. Jack Hayford, *Taking Hold of Tomorrow*, 19-20; The Hayfords moved fifteen miles to their new home in five hours exactly. Anna Hayford called it "her horror story." What made it so difficult is that Jack had scheduled a meeting in their new home with couples from the church the day after they moved in.

33. Hayford, interview, April 22, 1993, transcript, 15.

34. A journal entry in the first week of January shows that Hayford was wrestling with the issue of pride and position before his trip to Oakland. He wrote: "When I tho't my experience had produced the knowhow to achieve something, I was puffed up and proud in a deceived way that does not recognize the act as prideful." He called himself "a stupid child!" Jack W. Hayford, journal entry, January 9, 1970, private holding, 1.

35. Hayford, *Testimony of Learning Obedience*, transcript, 22; Hayford, interview, April 22, 1993, transcript, 16. The term used in this narrative is "position" because the 1973 message *Testimony of Learning Obedience* says that was the word on the trophy. His November 30, 1970, journal entry also confirms this. Hayford said in the 1993

interview that the trophy was labeled "leadership." Jack W. Hayford, journal entry, November 30, 1970, 1; see also Lawson, "Pastor 'on the Way,'" 25.

36. Hayford, interview, April 22, 1993, transcript, 16.

37. "An Interview with Jack Hayford and Dallas Willard," *Leadership*, Fall 1994, 18-24 (22).

38. "Hayford and Willard," 22.

39. Hayford, *Testimony of Learning Obedience*, transcript, 23. Hayford says in this testimony message that at the point when he surrendered to God in Oakland he expected that the Van Nuys church would likely never exceed "100–120" people.

40. Hayford, interview, April 22, 1993, transcript, 16.

41. Hayford, journal entry, November 30, 1970, 1; Jack W. Hayford, "Basic Guidelines received from the Lord concerning the work here at the church: Christmas Night 1973," private holding, 2.

42. Lawson, "Pastor 'on the Way,'" 25. Some of Jack's struggle with needing "position" may have come from a sense of needing to live up to his father's high standards that were very much a part of his childhood.

43. Lawson, "Pastor 'on the Way,'" 17.

44. Hayford, *A Personal Testimony*, 23.

45. Hayford, interview, April 22, 1993, transcript, 17.

46. Hayford, *The Mary Miracle*, 26-28. In *The Mary Miracle*, Hayford gives a vivid and detailed description of the Lord speaking to him on the freeway.

47. Hayford, interview, April 22, 1993, transcript, 17.

48. Hayford, *Testimony of Learning Obedience*, transcript, 23.

49. Hayford, *The Mary Miracle*, 27.

50. Hayford, *The Mary Miracle*, 27; Hayford, *Testimony of Learning Obedience*, transcript, 23.

51. Hayford, interview, April 22, 1993, transcript, 17.

52. The few church bulletins that exist from 1969 show that the Van Nuys congregation was fairly traditional in its worship service. There were generally two or three congregational hymns, followed by a Bible reading, the offering, the sermon, and a benediction. Church Bulletin, The Church on the Way, November 2, 1969, 2-3; Church Bulletin, The Church on the Way, November 16, 1969, 2-3; Church Bulletin, The Church on the Way, November 23, 1969, 2-3.

53. Hayford, School of Pastoral Nurture: Consultation I, session 1.18.

54. Charter and Shoemake, interview.

55. Hayford, *The Church on the Way*, 16.

56. Hayford, *The Church on the Way*, 17.

57. Hayford, School of Pastoral Nurture: Consultation I, 1.18.

58. Hayford, *The Church on the Way*, 78.

59. Hayford, *Spiritual Worship,* 1973 Pastors Seminar. Hayford started this practice of questioning why certain worship expressions were used while at Life Bible College. Hayford, *Worship His Majesty*, 44-45. He wrote in 1987 that the "approach worked wonders, and I still recommend it to people seeking renewal in the church traditions. When any of us search for the valid reasons our traditions may have had at their inception … we must set out to find what generated 'spiritual life forms,' when and how they were born, and what biblical grounds supported or interpreted them."

60. Many of the earliest teachings on worship and other subjects were not recorded prior to 1972. For later examples, see Jack W. Hayford, *Spiritual Worship* (Van Nuys: SoundWord Tape Ministry, April 1, 1973), audiocassette. This is a different message from the pastors' seminar message in June 1973; idem, *The Power of Praise* (Van Nuys: SoundWord Tape Ministry, March 6, 1974), audiocassette; idem, *On Lifting Up of Hands to the Lord* (Van Nuys: SoundWord Tape Ministry, March 17, 1974), audiocassette; idem, *The Gift of Song* (Van Nuys: SoundWord Tape Ministry, December 11, 1974), audiocassette.

61. Hayford, School of Pastoral Nurture: Consultation I, 1.18.

62. Hayford, *Worship His Majesty*, 153. Hayford tells of the frustrations he experienced with trying to form a choir after he first came to Van Nuys. He came to the conclusion that he first needed to teach the congregation to truly worship God.

63. Hayford has written several books on worship. Especially for this book were: Hayford, *Worship His Majesty*; Jack W. Hayford, *Foundations of Worship* (Virginia Beach: Christian Broadcasting Network, 1988); Hayford, *A Man's Worship and Witness*; Jack W. Hayford, *Manifest Presence: Expecting a Visitation of God's Grace through Worship* (Kent, England: Sovereign World, 2005); Jack Hayford, John Killinger, and Howard Stevenson, *Mastering Worship* (Portland, OR: Multnomah, 1990). In addition, Hayford has written devotional books that are worship- and praise-focused: Jack Hayford, *The Heart of Praise: Daily Ways to Worship the Father with Psalms* (Ventura, CA: Regal Publishing, 1992); Jack Hayford, *Praise in the Presence of God* (Nashville: Countryman/Thomas Nelson, 2003).

64. Hayford, *Worship His Majesty*, 54.

65. For an exposition on worship from the early time period, see Jack W. Hayford, "The Kind of People God Is Looking For," unpublished paper, The Church on the Way, n.d.

66. For Jack Hayford, worship is a lifestyle to be cultivated that goes beyond participation in worship services, as important as that is. Much of his early material on worship is focused on worship within church services.

67. Hayford, *Worship His Majesty*, 54.

68. Jack W. Hayford, School of Pastoral Nurture: Consultation I, May 2007, King's Seminary, digital audio recording 1.6. Through all the various ministries of the church over his pastorate, there were over 80,000 decisions for Christ. Obviously, many of these were rededications to Christ from lapsed believers. Nevertheless the figures are remarkable by any measure.

69. Hayford, School of Pastoral Nurture: Consultation I, 1.6.

70. Hayford, *Glory on Your House*, 63.

71. Hayford, *Glory on Your House*, 64.

72. Hayford, *The Church on the Way*, 82-83.

73. Shoemake and Charter, interview, September 7, 2007.

74. Hayford, "Basic Guidelines received from the Lord concerning the work here at the church: Christmas Night 1973," 2. In the 1982 book *The Church on the Way*, Hayford recalls that the incident happened on "Reformation Sunday."

75. Hayford, *Manifest Presence*, 99.

76. Hayford, *The Church on the Way*, 83-84; Hayford, *Glory on Your House*, 66.

77. Hayford, *The Church on the Way*, 84; Hayford, "Basic Guidelines received from the Lord concerning the work here at the church: Christmas Night 1973," 2.

78. Hayford, *Glory on Your House*, 63.

79. Hayford, *Glory on Your House*, 67.

80. Unless otherwise noted, the following narrative and quotation are drawn from Jack Hayford, *E Quake* (Nashville: Thomas Nelson, 1999), 66-83.

81. Stafford, "The Pentecostal Gold Standard," 28.

82. Hayford, *The Church on the Way*, 85.

83. Matthew 6:9–13.

84. Hayford, *The Church on the Way*, 85-86.

Chapter 9: The Church on the Way

1. Pastor Jack Hayford, "It's Right There in the Name," Church Bulletin, The Church on the Way, August 14, 1977, 2; Pastor Jack Hayford, "Jesus on Parade," Church Bulletin, The Church on the Way, December 19, 1978. The Foursquare denomination allowed churches to adopt a "slogan name" that differed from an individual church's legal name.

2. Hayford, "It's Right There in the Name," 24; Jack W. Hayford, "Called to Be a People Centered Work," *Acts* (n.d.), 9.

3. Hayford, "Called to Be a People Centered Work," 9.

4. For a few months, the prayer circles were not a part of every Sunday service, but eventually they became a given at The Church on the Way. Charter and Shoemake, interview, September 7, 2007.

5. Hayford, "Called to Be a People Centered Work," 9. In 1985, the church printed a booklet to address the number of people who were uncomfortable with the congregation's expressive worship and with "prayer circles." "I Like The Church on the Way, But ..." (Van Nuys: The Church on the Way, 1985). The booklet began as a left-hand-page bulletin article. "I Love It at the Church on the Way ... but oh, that Ministrytime is hard to take," Church Bulletin, The Church on the Way, January 27, 1974, 2.

6. Hayford, *Glory on Your House*, 241.

7. Hayford, *Glory on Your House*, 242.

8. Jack W. Hayford, journal entry, November 30, 1970, 1; Jack W. Hayford, journal entry, Van Nuys—1970, 1.

9. Hayford, journal entry, November 30, 1970, 1.

10. Hayford, "The Church on the Way," *Logos Journal*, 21.

11. In his journal for November 30, 1970, Hayford looks back on the three years with all its transition. He reflects on his "growth in sonship" and notices that he has not made many entries during the period. He also notes that he had not "written down the key dates and directions regarding the pastorate here in Van Nuys." He goes on to record fourteen dates, with accompanying notes, that provide near time confirmation to what he wrote in his books years later. Jack W. Hayford, journal entry, November 30, 1970, 1-2; Pastor Jack Hayford, "Exactly Seven Years Ago," Church Bulletin, The Church on the Way, January 8, 1978, 2.

12. Hayford, "Basic Guidelines received from the Lord concerning the work here at the church: Christmas Night 1973," 2.

13. Hayford, *The Church on the Way*, 30.

14. Hayford, *The Church on the Way*, 31.

15. After stepping aside as Dean of Students in the summer of 1970, Hayford not only continued to teach but for six months continued to serve as Director of College Relations, a role in which he promoted the college. This proved too much to do and he resigned that role at the end of the year. Jack W. Hayford, letter to Dr. Clarence E. Hall, December 4, 1970, private holding, 1-2.

16. Jack W. Hayford, "Why I Don't Set Goals," *Leadership*, Winter 1984, 46.

17. Hayford, "Why I Don't Set Goals," 46-47.

18. Jack Hayford, *Pastors of Promise* (Ventura, CA: Regal, 1997), 157-161. The entire narrative in the following paragraph regarding Jack's commitment to the Foursquare

Church is drawn from this book. Jack has told and written the story many times. The italics are in the source.

19. Hayford, *Pastors of Promise,* 159.

20. Hayford, *The Church on the Way,* 39-40.

21. "Worship His Majesty: That's the Root of Kingdom Life Says Jack Hayford," *Redemption,* October 1987, 46.

22. Hayford, "Basic Guidelines received from the Lord concerning the work here at the church: Christmas Night 1973," 2.

23. Hayford, *The Church on the Way,* 40.

24. Hayford, *The Church on the Way,* 41.

25. Hayford, *The Church on the Way,* 42.

26. Hayford, *The Church on the Way,* 43-44.

27. One of the promises Hayford says God gave him at the time of the confrontation was that he would give the church "a voice to many churches … in the movement." Hayford, "Basic Guidelines received from the Lord concerning the work here at the church: Christmas Night 1973," 2.

28. "Worship His Majesty: That's the Root of Kingdom Life Says Jack Hayford," 46. One example of the rising profile of Hayford and The Church on the Way was an article in the popular Charismatic periodical *Logos Journal* entitled "The Church on the Way." Although the article title made no reference to the church's legal name, The First Foursquare Church of Van Nuys, the article itself clearly states the church's denominational affiliation. Hayford, "The Church on the Way," *Logos Journal,* 20. The *Logos Journal* article became part of a book published by Logos International. Jack Hayford, "A West Coast New Testament Church," in *The New Testament Church Book* (Plainfield, NJ: Logos International Inc., 1973), 46-52. Among other authors were Dennis Bennett, Jamie Buckingham, and Dan Malachuk, each strongly connected with the Charismatic Renewal.

29. Hayford has made it clear that the Foursquare denominational leadership itself was always supportive of his leadership and the ministry of The Church on the Way. Hayford, "The Church on the Way," 20.

30. God had spoken to Jack two months earlier that He would "clothe" the church. As Jack recorded it, the Lord's promise was that He would "clothe the Body of my Church with all the facilities needed to do the work I have given her." The church would need that promise in the coming years as they grew from the hundreds to the thousands. At times it seemed as if expanding facilities was a constant but necessary focus. Hayford, "Basic Guidelines received from the Lord concerning the work here at the church: Christmas Night 1973," 2.

31. When considering the size of megachurches today, 400 hardly seems large. At the time, however, an attendance of 400 was reasonably significant. See "Test for Big Churches:

The Rise of Evangelism, Mysticism," *U.S. News and World Report*, December 17, 1973, 43-45 (44). The Church on the Way is mentioned in this article.

32. Church Bulletin, The Church on the Way, April 30, 1972, 3; Church Bulletin, The Church on the Way, June 11, 2. Sunday, June 18, was the first Sunday with two morning worship services. Only a few bulletins still exist prior to 1972. From 1972 onward, the church archived all the bulletins. It is worth noting that, aside from the Roman Catholic Church, multiple services were not a common practice in 1972.

33. Jack Hayford, "Whence Came the 'Left-Hand Page,'" Church Bulletin, The Church on the Way, July 12, 1981, 2.

34. Church Bulletin, The Church on the Way, February 27, 1972, 2.

35. Church Bulletin, The Church on the Way, March 5, 1972, 2.

36. Hayford's sermons at this time reflect a strong restorationist orientation. His restorationism mirrors the typical identification with a church history motif that sees the Reformation as the beginning of a recovery from the "Dark Ages" that continued through the Wesleyan revival and was fully expressed in the Pentecostal and Charismatic outpourings in the twentieth century. Jack W. Hayford, *My Grandmother Spoke in Tongues* (Van Nuys: SoundWord Tape Ministry, December 2, 1973), transcript, 6.

37. Church Bulletin, The Church on the Way, February 25, 1973, 2.

38. Church Bulletin, The Church on the Way, April 1, 1973, 2.

39. Church Bulletin, The Church on the Way, April 1, 1973.

40. Hayford, interview, November 13, 2007; Hayford, "Whence Came the 'Left-Hand Page,'" 2.

41. Church Bulletin, The Church on the Way, January 5, 1975, 2.

42. Jack W. Hayford, *As the Church at Antioch* (Van Nuys: SoundWord Tape Ministry, August 25, 1974), audiocassette.

43. David Di Sabbatino, *The Jesus People Movement: An Annotated Bibliography and General Resource* (Westport, CT: Greenwood-Heinemann, 1999); Edward Plowman, *The Jesus Movement in America* (Elgin, IL: David C. Cook, 1971); Robert S. Ellwood Jr., *One Way: The Jesus Movement and Its Meaning* (Englewood Cliffs, NJ: Prentice Hall, 1973); Duane Pederson, *Jesus People* (Glendale, CA: Regal Books, 1971). The two best recent histories on the Jesus People movement are Larry Eskridge, *God's Forever Family: The Jesus People Movement in America* (New York: Oxford University Press, 2013); Richard Bustraan, *The Jesus People Movement: A Story of Spiritual Revolution among Hippies* (Eugene, OR: Pickwick, 2014).

44. Jack W. Hayford, journal entry, May 19, 1973; Pat Boone, *New Song* (Carol Stream, IL: Creation House, 1972).

45. Lawson, "Pastor 'on the Way,'" 25.

46. The story of the Boones' spiritual journey is told in detail in Pat Boone, *A New Song* (Altamonte Springs, FL: Creation House, 1988).

47. Paul Davis, *Pat Boone: The Authorized Biography* (Grand Rapids, MI: Zondervan, 2001), 153; Pat Boone, interview with the author, December 20, 2018.

48. Donald E. Miller, *Reinventing American Protestantism* (Berkeley: University of California Press, 1997), 32-33.

49. Hayford, "The Church on the Way," *Logos Journal*, 39.

50. "Mushroomed" is an apt description of the church's growth in the 1970s. The 1971 yearly Sunday average attendance was 176; 1972 average attendance was 468; the 1973 average was 884; the 1974 average was 1,414; the 1975 average was 1,926; the 1976 average was 2,441; the 1977 average was 2,722; the 1978 average was 3,019. Attendance document 1969–1992, The Church on the Way holding, photocopy, 1.

51. Francis Allnutt, "A Star Is Born Again," *Logos Journal* (January/February 1977), 54. Jones went on to serve in later years on The Church on the Way's governing council and became one of Jack Hayford's closest personal friends.

52. Hayford, "Why I Don't Set Goals," 51.

53. Hayford, *Celebrating Pastor Jack's Birthday with Music and Testimony*, transcript, 6.

54. Jack W. Hayford, *An Exhortation against Half-Heartedness and Carnality* (Van Nuys: SoundWord Tape Ministry, April 20, 1975), audiocassette.

55. Hayford, *Celebrating Pastor Jack's Birthday with Music and Testimony*, transcript, 6. It is not very well known that one of Hayford's songs, "Come On Down," was recorded by Tennessee Ernie Ford and "reached 34th on the secular charts." Steven Lawson, "Pastor 'on the Way,'" *Charisma*, June 1985, 22.

56. This may seem an almost trivial struggle but any pastor knows the terrible fears and insecurities that come with the calling. American culture measures success in quantifiable terms. This creates enormous pressures on pastors. Hayford has been particularly sensitive to address this issue in his later ministry.

57. Hayford, *Celebrating Pastor Jack's Birthday with Music and Testimony*, transcript, 6.

58. Hayford has been very open in admitting that church growth does matter in the end. Growth means that people are coming to Christ, and that is the real issue. This was always a clear passion and he believed that God had promised that "many shall come to me" through his ministry at The Church on the Way. Hayford, "Basic Guidelines received from the Lord concerning the work here at the church: Christmas Night 1973."

59. Hayford's transparency about the difficulties he has faced as a leader is also part of the reason pastors are so drawn to him.

60. This transparency was not evident in Hayford's preaching notes before coming to The Church on the Way. Afterward, his teaching is far more narrative and self-effacing in character.

61. Hayford, *The Church on the Way*, 56. In the early 1970s, Hayford occasionally said that if he were forced to choose he would call himself a Calvinist. In an interview he discussed this. It seems that the typically guilt-driven Pentecostal approach to ministry he had observed, with its hyper-Arminian bent, had made him averse to calling himself an Arminian. Theologically, however, given that he believes that believers can backslide and be lost, and with his highly synergistic view of prayer, he is much more Arminian than Reformed. Hayford, interview, November 13, 2007.

62. Hayford, *The Church on the Way*, 58-59. Hayford had been taught this in college but it took on new meaning once he was in Van Nuys.

63. Hayford, *The Church on the Way*, 56.

Chapter 10: Establishing Foundations

1. Douglas Jacobsen, *Thinking in the Spirit: Theologies of the Early Pentecostal Movement* (Bloomington: Indiana University Press, 2003), 12.

2. Hayford, "'True Spirituality'—Finding the Mainstream!," Church Bulletin, The Church on the Way, February 25, 1973, 2.

3. See Jack W. Hayford, *Body Ministry: The Need to Exercise* (Van Nuys: SoundWord Tape Ministry, 1972), audiocassette; Jack W. Hayford, *Preparing for Your Ministry* (Van Nuys: SoundWord Tape Ministry, April 4, 1973), audiocassette; Jack W. Hayford, *A Survey of New Testament Ministries* (Van Nuys: SoundWord Tape Ministry, 1972), audiocassette.

4. Jack W. Hayford, School of Pastoral Nurture: Consultation II, March 2007, digital audio recording 2.24.

5. Jack W. Hayford, School of Pastoral Nurture: Consultation II, March 2007, digital audio recording 2.22.

6. Church Bulletin, The Church on the Way, July 23, 1972, 2.

7. Hayford, *My Grandmother Spoke in Tongues*, transcript, 8.

8. Hayford, *My Grandmother Spoke in Tongues*, transcript, 8. This presentation of his perspective is crude in comparison to the far more polished iterations he would later give. But it is a good early picture of how he was thinking and reshaping his views.

9. Hayford, *My Grandmother Spoke in Tongues*, transcript, 10.

10. Hayford, *My Grandmother Spoke in Tongues*, transcript, 21. He went so far as to say it might take a "sovereign work of God just prior to the rapture of the church" for every Spirit-baptized believer to speak with tongues.

11. Hayford, *My Grandmother Spoke in Tongues*, transcript, 22.

12. Hayford, *My Grandmother Spoke in Tongues*, transcript, 23-32.

13. In 1972 and 1973, Hayford frequently taught on the subject of tongues.

14. See the end of chapter 6 too for more on glossolalia.

15. In 1975, the International Church of the Foursquare Gospel made a strong reaffirmation of the initial evidence position. Though there is no documentary evidence to a direct association, one wonders, given Hayford's view on initial evidence, if the rising notoriety of The Church on the Way and Hayford's corresponding influence had anything to do with the reaffirmation. Adams, "The Development of Doctrine in the International Church of the Foursquare Gospel," 16. Jack's views on tongues and Spirit baptism were later more fully expressed in his 1996 book, *The Beauty of Spiritual Language*.

16. Robert C. Toth and Jack Jones, "Nixons Attend L.A. Wedding, John Ford Fete," *Los Angeles Times*, April 1, 1973, C3.

17. Pastor Jack Hayford, letter to the president, May 1, 1973, The Church on the Way holding, 1.

18. Richard M. Nixon, letter to Reverend Jack W. Hayford, June 7, 1973, The Church on the Way holding, 1.

19. Jack Hayford, "God Will Save America If We Pray," *Christian Life*, July 1976, 18. Prophecy for Pentecostals is a message from God spoken forth. Often it is shared in the first person. Others in the congregation judge the prophecy according to scriptural truth. If it is counter to what the Bible teaches, it is rejected.

20. Jack W. Hayford, *Our Responsibility for America's Survival* (Van Nuys: SoundWord Tape Ministry, December 5, 1973), audiocassette.

21. Church Bulletin, The Church on the Way, July 23, 1972, 3.

22. Jack W. Hayford, *Body Ministry: Fasting with Prayer for Restoration* (Van Nuys: SoundWord Tape Ministry, February 13, 1974), audiocassette; idem, *On Binding and Loosing* (Van Nuys: SoundWord Tape Ministry, March 24, 1974), audiocassette; idem, *The Meaning of Prayer and Supplication* (Van Nuys: SoundWord Tape Ministry, March 24, 1974), audiocassette; idem, *Invading the Impossible* (Van Nuys: SoundWord Tape Ministry, May 25, 1975), audiocassette; idem, *Defining Prayer Correctly* (Van Nuys: SoundWord Tape Ministry, June 1, 1975), audiocassette; idem, *How to Pray When You Don't Know How to Pray* (Van Nuys: SoundWord Tape Ministry, June 8, 1975), audiocassette; idem, *Travail: The Way to Give Birth* (Van Nuys: SoundWord Tape Ministry, June 18, 1975), audiocassette.

23. In every instance of Hayford's elaboration of the kingdom of God and prayer, he almost never interacts with the ideas of other thinkers and theologians. His concepts are expressed in exegetical and expositional forms. His most systematic presentation of his position on the kingdom in the *Hayford Bible Handbook* is presented as brief

explanations of Bible passages. Further, his exegesis and exposition are focused on pastoral perspectives and he is unconcerned with philosophical theological reflection proper. This is so even though he is very aware of the nature of the academy, as evident from interviews with him in regard to The King's Seminary. Critical reflection in the academic sense is simply not a priority for Hayford. Interestingly, he has frequently stated at leaders' gatherings that his views on the kingdom reflect an eschatology identified as "historic pre-millennialism." Usually he follows this by saying that his theology of the kingdom of God is much akin to that of George Eldon Ladd. It was then with some surprise that in a January 2003 interview Hayford said—and with some embarrassment—that he had, to his knowledge, never read anything by Ladd. His awkwardness in saying this was a result of how often he has identified himself with Ladd's theology of the kingdom of God. Hayford said he made these statements because many of his associates have told him how similar his kingdom theology is to Ladd's. Jack W. Hayford, personal interview with the author, January 10, 2003. Hayford said in another interview that the only qualification he would make is that he may have been acquainted with Ladd's kingdom theology through a secondary source at some time in the past— though he has no specific recollection. He is certain he has never read any of Ladd's books or articles. Jack W. Hayford, personal interview with the author, July 1, 2004.

24. Jack W. Hayford, *Prayer Is Invading the Impossible*, 15-16. This same basic outline remains today at the heart of Jack Hayford's theology. It has since been elaborated in other books but this early example is one of best summaries of his understanding of the kingdom of God available.

25. Jack was asked to present a paper on the kingdom of God to the faculty of Life Bible College in 1974. While most supported his views, the paper drew some resistance from a few faculty members. Jack W. Hayford, "The Message Christ Preaches," unpublished paper, April 18, 1974, The Church on the Way holding, 1-5.

26. For example: Church Bulletin, The Church on the Way, June 17, 1973, 3; Church Bulletin, The Church on the Way, May 26, 1974, 2; Church Bulletin, The Church on the Way, February 10, 1974, 2; Church Bulletin, The Church on the Way, February 10, 1974, 2; Church Bulletin, The Church on the Way, April 21, 1974, 2; Church Bulletin, The Church on the Way, May 26, 1974, 3.

27. Hayford, *Our Responsibility for America's Survival*. The message was preached on December 5, 1973.

28. Jimmy Owens, "If My People … A Call to Intercession," *Christian Life*, January 1976; Russel Chandler, "Changing U.S. Values Studied in 200th Year," *Los Angeles Times*, October 19, 1975, CC II-5. When the Lord had spoken to Jack and a group of leaders in 1972 about making the Van Nuys congregation "as the church at Antioch," they realized it would mean that many ministries to the larger church would be extended out from The Church on the Way as well. Part of the promise was that many sent out from the church would "become better known than [the] church itself." This was the case with *If My People*. Media coverage of the musical almost

never mentioned the role of The Church on the Way in supporting the production. Hayford, "Basic Guidelines received from the Lord concerning the work here at the church: Christmas Night 1973," 2. *If My People* was the second national musical production written by the Owenses. *Come Together* had toured the nation in 1973. That production emphasized unity in the body of Christ and sought to bridge doctrinal and generational barriers that separated believers. The national evangelistic campaign "Key '73" adopted the musical as part of its goal of reaching every person in the United States and Canada with the gospel. The production was videotaped and broadcast on many television stations across the nation. News coverage of the musical included the *New York Times* and *Los Angeles Herald Examiner*. The media attention focused primarily on Pat Boone and the Owenses with no mention of The Church on the Way, although the congregation was supporting the production prayerfully and financially.

29. "Prayer That Saved a Nation—an Interview with Jack Hayford," *Overflow*, December 1978, 8-10.

30. So many people were inquiring regarding the church's amazing growth that Hayford inaugurated annual pastors' conferences in 1973 that expanded over the years with thousands attending from all denominations.

31. Outside Foursquare invitations in 1973 and 1974 included events at Melodyland Christian Center, World M.A.P., and Full Gospel Businessmen's Fellowship International conferences. The majority of his travel was still within Foursquare. "Dr. Jack W Hayford's Ministry Occasions, 1972–2000," The Church on the Way holding, Van Nuys, 1-4.

32. Charter and Shoemake, interview, September 7, 2007; Jack W. Hayford, School of Pastoral Nurture: Consultation II, King's Seminary, Van Nuys, March 2007, digital audio recording 2.23; John Farmer, interview with the author, April 23, 1993. Farmer served the Church on the Way as one of its executive pastors until he retired in 2015.

33. Hayford, interview, November 13, 2007; Louie Locke, interview with the author, September 30, 2007; Hayford, *As the Church at Antioch,* audiocassette.

34. Charter and Shoemake, interview, September 7, 2007. At one point he had planned to have Paul Charter assume the role as lead pastor while Hayford went to Reno.

35. Hayford, "Basic Guidelines received from the Lord concerning the work here at the church: Christmas Night 1973," 2. In Hayford's thirty years at the church, over 300 churches and ministries were extended from Van Nuys.

36. Hayford, "Basic Guidelines received from the Lord concerning the work here at the church: Christmas Night 1973," 3; Hayford, *As the Church at Antioch,* audiocassette.

37. His sister, Luanne, had written him, encouraging Jack to stay in Van Nuys rather than move to Reno. This is just one among many factors that brought Hayford to the

conclusion that he should not go to the Nevada city. Luanne Chumley, letter to Jack Hayford, August 3, 1974, private holding, 1.

38. Hayford, *Confessions of a Wandering Pastor*, 1974.

39. Hayford, *A New Time and Place*, 87-89.

40. Hayford, *Confessions of a Wandering Pastor*.

41. Hayford, *A New Time and Place,* 89; Hayford, *Confessions of a Wandering Pastor*.

42. Darryl Roberts, letter to pastor, October 18, 1974, private holding, 1. Important issues in Roberts' letter, besides the need to cut back on his travels, were Hayford's need to be home more with his family and to carve out time to write.

43. Hayford, *Confessions of a Wandering Pastor*.

44. Space does not allow a detailed telling of the continuing influence Hayford's parents had on him after he started pastoring in Van Nuys. When the biography is expanded, this will be a part of the story.

45. This is taken verbatim from a handwritten page that Hayford recorded that night of his father's prophecy to him. Jack Hayford, "Handwritten Prophecy per Daddy," October 18, 1974, private holding, 1.

Chapter 11: Building Big People

1. Lawson, "Pastor 'on the Way,'" 20. Italics Lawson.

2. Jack Hayford, "By the Way: What Is 'Being Spiritual,'" Church Bulletin, The Church on the Way, February 9, 1975.

3. Ruth Senter, "Jack & Anna Hayford: When Words Were Not Enough," *Partnership*, November–December 1985, 24-29, 59-60 (25).

4. Hayford, *Pastors of Promise*, 113-14.

5. John Archer, "On the Way with Jack Hayford," *Release Inc*, April/May 1996, 10-14 (13).

6. Hayford, *The Church on the Way*, 74-75.

7. Hayford, "The Church on the Way," *Logos Journal*, 22.

8. Jack W. Hayford, *I Wish You a Mary Christmas* (Van Nuys: Living Way Ministry, 1973); *The Conceiving and Bearing of Life* (Van Nuys: Living Way Ministry, 1975); *Having a Baby Will Stretch You* (Van Nuys: Living Way Ministry, 1975); Jack W. Hayford, *The Mary Miracle* (Ventura, CA: Regal Books, 1994). The book is now distributed under the title *The Christmas Miracle*. See my recent essay: S. David Moore, "Discerning the 'Spirit' of the Word: The Holy Spirit in the Hermeneutics and Preaching of Jack W. Hayford Jr." in Jon Huntzinger and S. David Moore, eds., *The Pastor and the Kingdom: Essays Honoring Jack W. Hayford* (Southlake, TX: TKU Press/Gateway Academic, 2017), 291-313. Part of this section was edited and adapted from my essay.

9. Steven Land has mentioned this same analogy as it relates to a Pentecostal understanding of the function of Scripture. Land, *Pentecostal Spirituality*, 100.

10. Hayford, *Carrying a Miracle*.

11. Hayford, *Carrying a Miracle*.

12. Hayford, *The Mary Miracle*, 18.

13. Hayford, *The Mary Miracle*, 20-21.

14. Hayford, "The Church on the Way," *Logos Journal*, 22.

15. Virgil Megill, "Profile: Jack Hayford, Worship: A Way of Balance," *Religious Broadcasting*, April 1988, 36-37 (37).

16. The concept of feeding and leading the church and its relationship to pastoral teaching and preaching is a major aspect. Hayford's School of Pastoral Nurture: Consultation II.

17. Jack Hayford, "Developing Spiritual Manhood: The Key to Vitality in the Church," *Ministries Today*, September/October 1994, 35-42 (35). The call to train men dates back to February 1972.

18. Hayford, *The Church on the Way*, 126-27; Pastor Jack Hayford, "Attention Ladies and Gentlemen," Church Bulletin, The Church on the Way, September 30, 1984.

19. Hayford, *The Church on the Way*, 122. The monthly meetings were later regularly attended by as many 1,200 men.

20. Jack Hayford, "Seeking to Shape a 'Spirit-Formed' Church," School of Pastoral Nurture: Consultation I, May 2007.

21. Hayford, "Seeking to Shape a 'Spirit-Formed' Church."

22. The term "durable disciples" wasn't used in the 1970s but still describes what Jack was pursuing.

23. He called these "Concepts Basic to New Testament Church Living." When Jack developed his School of Pastoral Nurture, he was to lecture on how essential these concepts were to discipling a congregation. Jack Hayford, "Concepts Basic to New Testament Church Living" Handout, 1996.

24. Jack Hayford, "Pastor's Heart: Dissing Discipleship," *Ministries Today*, July/August 2007, 98.

25. Jack Hayford, *Grounds for Living* (Lancaster, England: Sovereign Word, 2001), 68.

26. Jack discusses his concerns about total depravity as taught by some Calvinists. In an undated transcript taken from a session of the School of Pastoral Nurture, he presents his counterview that he calls "total dependence," a perspective emphasizing there is no salvation except through Jesus Christ's atoning work. He makes clear, however, his concern that total depravity is an overly disparaging view of humanity's inherent worth as God's image bearers, however diminished that image is as a consequence of sin. Jack Hayford, "TULIP Theology Calvinism," n.d., n.p.

27. Jack Hayford, *The Kingdom of God Part 1* (Van Nuys: SoundWord Tape Ministry, September 12, 1973), audiocassette.

28. I've left this quotation punctuated in a manner that reflected Hayford's phrasing and word choice. Although grammatically awkward, it best captures the pace of proclamation. Hayford, The Kingdom of God Part 1.

29. Stormie Omartian with Jack Hayford, *The Power of Praying Together* (Eugene, OR: Harvest House, 2003), 13-14.

Chapter 12: Pastor *and* Apostle

1. "Seven Days of Prayer and Fasting," Church Bulletin, The Church on the Way, August 4, 1974, 2. Church Bulletin, The Church on the Way, February 19, 1978, 3.

2. That the church was the fastest-growing church in the movement for many years is difficult to document given the way the denomination charted the attendance of churches through paper forms during the 1970s and early 1980s. Without question, the Church on the Way was perceived as the fastest-growing church. Documentation is available in the denomination archives that shows the Church on the Way gave more money to the denomination than any other single congregation from 1977 through 2000, which lends credence to perception. Steve Zeleny, email to S. David Moore, November 1, 2019. Zeleny is the archivist for the Foursquare Church.

3. In Jack's memory, it was in the fall of 1974.

4. Hayford, interview, April 22, 1993, transcript, 36-37.

5. The church was receiving growing media coverage that continued throughout the 1970s. John Dart, "Miracles an Everyday Event to the Pentecostals," *Los Angeles Times*, January 11, 1976, B1-3; Pat Anderson, "3 Valley Churches Beat Odds, Study Shows," *Los Angeles Times*, April 10, 1977, A1, A6; "Religious Cults: Is the Wild Fling Over?," *U.S. News and World Report*, March 27, 1978, 44-45. In the *U.S. News and World Report* article, Hayford and the Van Nuys church are mentioned favorably as examples of a recovery of "old time religion" (45).

6. Certainly part of this was simply a matter of attendance but it also had to do with the increasing notice Jack's teaching ministry was getting. Attendance document 1969–1992, the Church on the Way holding, photocopy, 1. 1982 attendance averaged 4,139.

7. Hayford, "Basic Guidelines received from the Lord concerning the work here at the church: Christmas Night 1973," 3.

8. John Farmer, phone interview with the author, August 19, 2008; Max Lyle, interviews with the author, August 19, 2008.

9. Hayford, interview, April 22, 1993, transcript, 39. Jack didn't give a specific date for this but it would have been sometime in the 1970s.

10. I'm an example of this. I was pastoring an independent Charismatic church in California, and after being invited by Jack to be a part of the church's extension ministries, joined the denomination.

11. Jack Hayford, Don Basham, and Derek Prince, "Forum: Holiness," *New Wine* magazine, March 1975, 29-31; Jack Hayford, "'From My Experience …' I Was Right to Admit I Was Wrong," *Pastoral Renewal* 2, no. 6 (December 1977), 48; Jack Hayford, "The Giving Gift," *Logos Journal* (September/October 1979), 23-29; Jack W. Hayford, "A Third Viewpoint on Homosexuality," *Logos Journal* (November/December 1980).

12. Jack Hayford, "Conciliation without Compromise," *Logos Journal* (November/December 1975), 26-32; Bob Mumford, letter to Jack Hayford, August 25, 1975, private holding, 1; Pastor Jack Hayford, letter to Rev. Robert Mumford, April 23, 1976, private holding, 1-2; Pastor Jack Hayford, letter to Kevin Ranaghan, April 23, 1976, private holding, 1-2.

13. Dr. Jack W. Hayford's Ministry Occasions, 1972–2000, The Church on The Way holding, Van Nuys, 5-24. One of the most interesting relationships Hayford has had is with Paul and Jan Crouch. They claimed Hayford as their pastor, a relationship he acknowledged. The Crouches' ministry is eccentric and fits some of the caricatures of Pentecostalism.

14. Although it was not played down, the connection to the Charismatic movement was sometimes in the forefront. Various messages at the Church on the Way's first annual pastors' conference in 1973 show the conscious identification with contemporary revival in the renewal as a primary connection. Jack W. Hayford, *The Structure of the Church* (Van Nuys: SoundWord Tape Ministry, June 1973), audiocassette; idem, *The Kingdom of God* (Van Nuys: SoundWord Tape Ministry, June 1973), audiocassette. To this day, receptionists for the Church on the Way answer the phone with "The First Foursquare Church of Van Nuys."

15. Dr. Jack W Hayford's Ministry Occasions, 1972–2000, the Church on the Way holding, Van Nuys, 5-24.

16. There were a few exceptions to this, but for the most part Hayford only spoke at conferences and leadership events from 1975 onward. Dr. Jack W Hayford's Ministry Occasions, 1972–2000, the Church on the Way.

17. Jack W. Hayford, journal entry, January 31, 1978, private holding, 1. Hayford wrote: "Since you have built this congregation—'done a great work … in this place'—you are responsible for the fact that my voice has been raised."

18. Hayford, interview, April 22, 1993, transcript, 35.

19. Hayford, interview, April 22, 1993, transcript, 35-39.

20. Hayford assumed the role in August 1977. Furlong, "Viewpoint: Looking Over Three Decades of Change," *Foursquare World Advance*, 4.

21. Jack E. Hamilton, "A Presidency of Achieved Purpose," President's Dinner, February 25, 1982, 1. It should be noted that the process for accreditation was in place before Hayford became president. See also Van Cleave, *The Vine and the Branches*, 213-14. The accrediting association has since been renamed the Association of Biblical Higher Education.

22. Hamilton, "A Presidency of Achieved Purpose," 2.

23. Jack W. Hayford, "A Generation of Dreamers," transcript of an address at the 1982 Los Angeles Presidential Dinner, Life Bible College, 1982, 1-6.

24. Jack E. Hamilton, letter to Pastor Jack Hayford, April 7, 1982, private holding, 1-2; Jack E. Hamilton, letter to Dr. Jack Hayford, June 8, 1982, private holding, 1. Jack Hamilton succeeded Hayford as president of Life Bible College. His letters reflect his appreciation for Hayford's leadership at the college.

25. Hayford, *The Church on the Way*, 135.

26. Jack W. Hayford, *Ministry to the Multitudes* (Van Nuys: SoundWord Tape Ministry, May 1978), audiocassette. These small groups were part of a growing trend in the later 1970s toward "cell" groups, home groups, and house churches. Yoido Full Gospel Church in Seoul, South Korea, was gaining attention, as was the cell group approach of the shepherding movement. There is no evidence of any direct influence by any of these groups on the Van Nuys' church home group ministry. Moore, *The Shepherding Movement*, 4, 11, 181; C. Kirk Hadaway, Stuart A. Wright, and Francis M. DuBose, *Home Cell Groups and House Churches* (Nashville: Broadman, 1987); David Yonggi Cho, *More Than Numbers* (Dallas: Word Books, 1984).

27. Hayford, *The Church on the Way*, 137.

28. John Wilkin, "Syllabus on Home Ministries at 'the Church on the Way,'" Van Nuys, the Church on the Way, n.d., 1-60.

29. Lawson, "Pastor 'on the Way,'" 24.

30. Dennis Easter, personal interview with the author, March 6, 2019; Lawson, "Pastor 'on the Way,'" 26.

31. Lawson, "Pastor 'on the Way,'" 26.

32. Jack Hayford, "On Setting Our House in Order: A Message and Report to the Congregation from Pastor Jack Hayford" (Van Nuys: the Church on the Way, November 4, 1985), 1-6 (5); Jack Hayford, *Congregation Meeting: On the Setting of Our House in Order* (Van Nuys: SoundWord Tape Ministry, November 4, 1984), audiocassettes A & B.

33. Dennis Easter, *Starting Over without Starting Over* (Van Nuys: SoundWord Tape Ministry, January 6, 1985), audiocassettes A & B.

34. Interestingly, Jack had written in his journal just a week before Easter's installation. He expressed his sense that what they were doing with the transition was God's will. He wrote, "I have followed your voice & leading to the moment." But he also acknowledged "questions, fears, and uncertainties which surround the entire transitioning." He went on to write a prayer he called a "covenant": "I commit to you everything and ask you to overrule by providence what I unwittingly fail to respond to of my will and understanding." He went on, "I will to do your will. If a Gethsemane is necessary (let such a cup not be required if possible), I will do your will." Jack W. Hayford, journal entry, December 30, 1984, private holding.

35. Jack Hayford, memo to John and Dennis Regarding: Concern over "signs of confusion," private holding. There is a handwritten note on the typed memo with the date of February 27, 1985, but the text of the memo refers to March 1 as the date; Jack's son-in-law, Scott Bauer, married to Jack's older daughter, Rebecca, had written Jack a letter in February with concerns over the transition. He never criticized Dennis Easter directly but shared things with Jack about the leadership challenges he felt the church faced in the midst of the transition. Scott Bauer, personal letter to Dad, February 14, 1985, private holding.

36. Much of the following narrative is drawn from audio of the June 2, 1985, congregational meeting where Jack told of the Edinburgh encounter and what followed. Dennis Easter also read an edited version of the letter he read to Jack. Jack Hayford, *Structuring for the Future: Congregational Meeting* (Van Nuys: SoundWord Tape Ministry, June 2, 1985), audiocassette.

37. Jack W. Hayford, journal entry, May 10, 1985, private holding.

38. Chuck Shoemake, personal interview with the author, June 22, 2018.

39. Through all the years pastoring the church, Jack never wanted to clutch his position as its senior pastor, wanting always to live in availability for whatever plans God had for his life. It kept coming up again and again in his thirty-year pastorate. He was asking Dennis to serve as co-pastor as a matter of obedience to God's plan for his life; and in one sense, despite continuing ostensibly as senior pastor, he was, as Abraham had offered Isaac as a sacrifice, offering the Church on the Way. Yet while Jack was in Edinburgh, God was giving the church back to him much as God had given Isaac back to Abraham. He realized that, as he had in the past, although he was called to minister beyond the Church on the Way, his ministry outward was based on his role as pastor to the congregation.

40. Hayford, *Structuring for the Future*. The emphasis is mine and reflects the emphasis in the voice of Dennis Easter as he read the revised letter at the congregational meeting. A number of church bulletins in September highlighted the faithful service of Dennis and Patsy Easter to the congregation. Jack wrote a lengthy tribute to Dennis in the special bulletin insert that reflected on the whole process of his appointment of co-pastor and what had transpired since. Jack especially affirmed his trust for Dennis throughout the

process that eventually led to his departure. Pastor Jack Hayford, "I Know No Higher Tribute," The Church on the Way, September 29, 1985, bulletin insert.

41. It was referred to by Jack as an earthquake. See Pastor Jack Hayford, "Shake-Up, Shakedown, Shakeout," Church Bulletin, The Church on the Way, September 8, 1985.

42. Under his leadership, the small Ventura church grew and Easter went on to have a number of significant leadership roles within the Foursquare denomination.

43. Easter still affirms his love for Jack and honors him to this day. He does think that the co-pastor ordeal was as much about Jack seeing loyalties in the church changing and that he consequently felt the need to reassert his leadership. As is clear in the narrative, Jack saw it as more a matter of God testing his willingness to stay committed to serve as pastor of the Church on the Way. Easter, interview with the author.

44. Jack Hayford, "October Notes from a Shepherd," Church Bulletin, The Church on the Way, October 13, 1985. Jack wrote among a number of announcements that the Bauers had rejoined the pastoral staff.

Chapter 13: Pastor to Pastors

1. Bulletin insert referencing the sending of the Chumleys, Church Bulletin, The Church on the Way, November 28, 1976.

2. Jack Hayford, "Small World? Maybe. Maybe Not," Church Bulletin, The Church on the Way, February 27, 1977. In an undated letter sent to supporters of the Chumley family written late in 1977, the story of the cancer battle to that point is detailed. The Chumley family, letter to supporters, n.d., n.p.

3. Jack Hayford, "To Write an Epitaph," Church Bulletin, The Church on the Way, August 20, 1978; "Our Sister Luanne," Church of the Hills, August, 16, 1978; Jack Hayford, Assigned to Be River of Ministry (Van Nuys: SoundWord Tape Ministry, August 16, 1978), audiocassette.

4. Lawson, "Pastor 'on the Way,'" 26.

5. "Thankful for Extension Ministries," Church Bulletin, The Church on the Way, November 28, 1982.

6. Jan Burmeister, personal interview with the author, October 21, 2019.

7. Gary Curtis, phone interview with the author, November 1, 2019.

8. Hayford, The Church on the Way, 1982.

9. The story of writing "Majesty" has been told in many places. The two most detailed are Jack W. Hayford, "The Story behind the Song: Majesty," Psalmist Magazine, February/March 1990, 25; Hayford, Worship His Majesty, 9-14. See also Jack Hayford, "The Birth of Majesty," Jack Hayford Ministries, www.jackhayford.org /teaching/articles/the-birth-of-majesty (accessed April 14, 2020).

10. Jack W. Hayford, "The Story behind the Song: Majesty," *Psalmist Magazine*, February/March 1990, 25.

11. Hayford, *Worship His Majesty*, 13.

12. Jack Hayford, "The 'Birth' of 'Majesty,'" Jack Hayford Ministries, www.jackhayford .org/teaching/articles/the-birth-of-majesty/ (accessed November 15, 2019).

13. Jack Hayford, "Majesty," Rocksmith Music, 1981.

14. Representing 120 publishers, the Christian Copyright Licensing International (CCLI) was established in 1988 to ensure proper copyright use of songs by churches. CCLI quickly grew in membership and today serves more than 200,000 churches worldwide in worship. With CCLI's ability to track usage of songs by its members, it was possible to have a public record of what songs were being used most often in churches. Christian Copyright Licensing International, http://us.ccli.com/about/ (accessed March 3, 2016).

15. Hayford had written other books on worship before this, and many more would follow.

16. The most concise presentation of Hayford's theology on worship and views on expressive worship is found in a compact pamphlet drawn from one of his messages to the church. Jack Hayford, *The Priority of Worship* (Van Nuys: The Church on the Way, 1981), 1-4.

17. Hayford, *Worship His Majesty*, appendix 2, 225-30.

18. I personally heard Ron Mehl, longtime pastor of the Beaverton Foursquare Church, say this at the 1985 pastors conference at the Church on the Way.

19. After the founding of The King's College and Seminary in the late 1990s, the pastors' seminars were renamed the Autumn Leadership Conference and primarily hosted by the college but were still presented very much in partnership with the Church on the Way. During the building of the Living Room, the 2,200-hundred-seat new sanctuary completed in 1981, seminars were not held in 1979 and 1980. "Tapes for Pastors," Van Nuys: Living Way Ministries, 1990.

20. Gary Curtis, telephone interview with the author, November 1, 2019.

21. Jack's opening message at the 1984 pastors' seminar is an example.

22. Jack Hayford, "Megachurch Malaise," *Ministries Today*, July/August 2002, 22-23 (22).

23. Hayford, "Megachurch Malaise," 23.

24. Over the sixteen years of off-and-on research I've conducted, I had dozens of impromptu interviews with pastors and leaders, asking them what factors made Jack so appealing. His ability to articulate convictions and concepts they held about life and ministry, things they could not adequately express, was a consistent factor mentioned.

25. Parts of the following paragraphs are edited and adapted from a previously published essay. See Moore, "Discerning the 'Spirit' of the Word."

26. Some prefer to follow E. D. Hirsch and others in arguing for meaning being confined to the biblical author's intention to the original audience and to refer to a text's contemporary meaning as its significance. I prefer to think of meaning encompassing both authorial intention and a text's contemporary voice. This remains a significant hermeneutical issue for evangelicals and many Pentecostals. See Millard Erickson, *Evangelical Hermeneutics* (Grand Rapids, MI: Baker, 1993), 11; Kevin J. Vanhoozer, *Is There a Meaning in This Text* (Grand Rapids, MI: Zondervan, 1998). For a Pentecostal discussion on the issues of where to locate meaning, see Kenneth J. Archer, *A Pentecostal Hermeneutic for the Twenty-First Century* (London: T & T Clark International, 2004); Bradley Truman Noel, *Pentecostal and Postmodern Hermeneutics* (Eugene, OR: Wipf & Stock, 2010); Kevin L. Spawn and Archie T. Wright, eds., *Spirit & Scripture: Examining a Pneumatic Hermeneutic* (London: T & T Clark, 2012).

27. By now the reader likely recognizes that I am following Hayford's practice of using teaching and preaching interchangeably.

28. Hayford is fond of quoting Titus 2:1 and pointing out that for Paul sound teaching was fundamentally more ethical than propositional. Jack Hayford, *The Manifestation of the Word: A Proposition* (Van Nuys: SoundWord Tape Ministry, 1984 Pastors Seminar), audiocassette.

29. Clark Pinnock's words resonate here with what Hayford is saying. "The biblical text is quantitatively complete (that is, not requiring additions) but can always be more deeply pondered and grasped at a deeper level. The Spirit is always able to cause what has been written to be revealed in a new light." Clark H. Pinnock, "Biblical Texts—Past and Future Meanings," *JET*, March 2000, 80.

30. Hayford, *Preaching and Teaching*, 5.

31. Hayford, *Preaching and Teaching*, 6.

32. Robert Morris, pastor of Gateway Church, one of America's largest congregations with 39,000 members, recently said this almost word for word at The King's University annual gala, "An Evening at The King's" where Jack Hayford was honored on October 22, 2019.

33. Jack Hayford, *Pastors of Promise* (Ventura: Regal, 1997), 138; Hayford, *"DayBreak": Integrity, Infilling, Insight*; Hayford, "All My Earthbound Senses," *Ministries Today*, May/June 1993, 8-9.

34. Hayford, *Pastors of Promise*, 137. For other perspectives from Hayford on integrity and character, see Jack W. Hayford, "Practicing What We Preach," *Ministries Today*, November/December 2003, 22-23; idem, "It's Not about 'Office'—It's about Character," *Ministries Today*, January/February 2004, 85-86.

35. Hayford, *Pastors of Promise*, 135.

36. What makes Hayford's emphasis on "integrity of heart" distinctly Pentecostal is the role he gives to the Holy Spirit in the "affairs of the heart." Hayford, *Pastors of*

Promise, 136. It reflects what Steven Land calls "the epistemological priority of the Holy Spirit in prayerful receptivity." Land, *Pentecostal Spirituality*, 38.

37. Unless otherwise noted, quotations in the following narrative are from Hayford's message *Integrity of Heart*. Jack Hayford, *Integrity of Heart* (Van Nuys: SoundWord Tape Ministry, September 9, 1979), audiocassette.

38. Jack Hayford, "We're Incomplete without a Heart of Integrity," *New Wine* magazine, May 1983, 24-27 (25).

39. Hayford, "We're Incomplete without a Heart of Integrity," 26.

40. Jack Hayford, "The Landmark Sermon," *Leadership*, Winter 1993, 34-40 (34).

41. Jack Hayford, *The Sin of Suicide* (Van Nuys: SoundWord Tape Ministry, October 28, 1984), audiocassette.

42. Jack Hayford, *Comfort for Shock-Weary Souls* (Van Nuys: SoundWord Tape Ministry, January 23, 1994), audiocassette.

43. Jack Hayford, *How to Think about Earthquakes and Other Disasters* (Van Nuys: SoundWord Tape Ministry, October 23, 1989), audiocassette.

44. Pastor Jack Hayford, "Somewhere to Go," Church Bulletin, The Church on the Way, August 5, 1979, 2.

45. Hayford, School of Pastoral Nurture: Consultation I, May 2007, 1.21.

46. Jack Hayford, *Where Have All the Flowers Gone?* (Van Nuys: SoundWord Tape Ministry, n.d.), audiocassette. The message was later published as Jack W. Hayford, *Restoring Fallen Leaders* (Ventura, CA: Regal, 1988).

47. Jack Hayford, *A Case of New Testament Discipline* (Van Nuys: SoundWord Tape Ministry, n.d.), audiocassette.

48. Jack Hayford, *Solo Sex—Release or Rejection* (Van Nuys: SoundWord Tape Ministry, April 24, 1983), audiocassette; Hayford, *Why Sex Sins Are Worse Than Others* (Van Nuys: SoundWord Tape Ministry, April 23, 1989), audiocassette.

49. Jack Hayford, *Ex-Rated Sex Part 1: The Difference between Soil and Dirt* (Van Nuys: SoundWord Tape Ministry, March 2, 1986), audiocassette; Hayford, *Ex-Rated Sex Part 2: Heavenly Sex and How to Find It* (Van Nuys: SoundWord Tape Ministry, March 9, 1986), audiocassette; Hayford, *Ex-Rated Sex Part 3: Married' Questions about Sex* (Van Nuys: SoundWord Tape Ministry, March 16, 1986), audiocassette; Hayford, *Ex-Rated Sex Part 4: Transmitting Sexual Health* (Van Nuys: SoundWord Tape Ministry, March 23, 1986), audiocassette.

50. A few examples are Jack Hayford, *Divorce and the People of God* (Van Nuys: SoundWord Tape Ministry, April 18, 1982), audiocassette; Hayford, *Short Circuited into Eternity* (Van Nuys: SoundWord Tape Ministry, January 7, 1979), audiocassette; Hayford, *Evolution—Christian Nonsense and Cultural Blindness* (Van Nuys: SoundWord Tape Ministry, November 12, 1989), audiocassette; Hayford, *The*

Problem of Profanity (Van Nuys: SoundWord Tape Ministry, November 5, 1983), audiocassette.

51. See Kevin J. Vanhoozer and Owen Strachan, *The Pastor as Public Theologian: Reclaiming a Lost Vision* (Grand Rapids, MI: Baker Academic, 2015).

52. Gerald Hiestand, "The Pastor as Wider Theologian, or What's Wrong with Theology Today," *First Things* online edition, www.firstthings.com/web-exclusives/2011/01/the-pastor-as-wider-theologian-or-whats-wrong-with-theology-today (accessed May 1, 2016). For an exploration of Hayford's role as a pastor-theologian, see S. David Moore, ed., "Jack Hayford, the Security of the Believer, and the Need for Pentecostal Pastor-Theologians" in Vinson Synan, *The Truth about Grace* (Lake Mary, FL: Charisma House, 2018), 7-20.

53. The words in the quotation are from Jim Tolle, longtime pastoral associate and senior pastor of the Church on the Way from 2004 to 2010. Stafford, "The Pentecostal Gold Standard," 28.

54. Jack Hayford et al., *Mastering Worship* (Portland, OR: Multnomah, 1990); Leith Anderson et al., *Who's in Charge? Standing Up to Leadership Pressures* (Portland, OR: Multnomah, 1993).

55. Jack Hayford, *The Leading Edge* (Lake Mary, FL: Charisma House, 2001); Hayford, *Sharpening the Leading Edge* (Lake Mary, FL: Charisma House, 2001).

56. Brad Greenberg, "A Pastor's Pastor," *Los Angeles Daily News*, January 4, 2007, www.dailynews.com/2007/01/04/a-pastors-pastor/.

Chapter 14: Becoming a Pentecostal Statesman

1. Stafford, "Jack Hayford: The Pentecostal Gold Standard," 25.

2. Jack Hayford, "Lessons I Have Learned in Ministry," *Equipping the Saints* (Third Quarter, 1995), 21-24 (22-23).

3. Stafford, "Jack Hayford: The Pentecostal Gold Standard," 25.

4. Hayford, "Lessons I Have Learned in Ministry," 23.

5. Lloyd John Ogilvie, "The Peacemaker," in Jon Huntzinger and S. David Moore, eds., *The Pastor and the Kingdom: Essays Honoring Jack W. Hayford* (Southlake, TX: TKU Press/Gateway Academic, 2017), 314-24 (315).

6. Ogilvie, "The Peacemaker," 316.

7. Ogilvie, "The Peacemaker," 316.

8. Ogilvie, "The Peacemaker," 318.

9. Ogilvie, "The Peacemaker," 317.

10. Jack Hayford, Church Bulletin, The Church on the Way, May 10, 1992, 2; "Wonderful to Imagine ... Wonderful to Have It Here," Church Bulletin, The Church on the Way, May 24, 1992, 2.

11. John Dart, "His Way: Valley's 'Pastor Jack' Revives Church," *Los Angeles Times*, December 15, 1991, B1, B16 (B1). In the *Los Angeles Times* article, Ogilvie called Hayford "one of the great spiritual leaders of our time whose ministry spans denominational lines"; Jack Hayford, "Shepherds Loving L.A.," *Ministries Today*, July/August 1997, 23-24. See also Ted Haggard and Jack Hayford, *Loving Your City into the Kingdom* (Ventura, CA: Regal, 1997), 11-22, 195-204.

12. Jack Hayford, "We Want You to Be Sure You're Not Alone ...," Church Bulletin, The Church on the Way, January 30, 1994, 2; "Earthquake: Judgment or Mercy?," *Ministries Today*, May/June 1994, 8-9.

13. K. Connie Kang, "Faith in Prayer Unites 400 Pastors," *Los Angeles Times*, January 18, 1998, B9; Jack W. Hayford, "A Watershed Moment," *Ministries Today*, March/April 2004, 58-59.

14. Dr. Jack W. Hayford's Ministry Occasions, 1972–2000, 77.

15. Hayford, *The Beauty of Spiritual Language*, 13-16.

16. It was not so much that the content of the message was new. He had shared the ideas in various ways before this. The Robison event brought special attention to the way he expressed it with an eye to those whom he could likely expect to question glossolalia. Hayford, *The Beauty of Spiritual Language*, 16.

17. Carolyn Stedman, personal interview with the author, November 5, 2003. Stedman supervised the tape ministry of COTW for many years.

18. Hayford, *The Beauty of Spiritual Language*, 15.

19. Hayford, *The Beauty of Spiritual Language*, 91.

20. "The Foursquare Church Faces the 21st Century," *Charisma*, March 1993, 26; Hayford, *The Beauty of Spiritual Language*, 93-94.

21. Hayford, *The Beauty of Spiritual Language*, 97.

22. Hayford, *The Beauty of Spiritual Language* 95-96.

23. Jack Hayford, "Spirit Trends," personal notes from November 13, 1986, COTW Pastors Conference Session, private holding. Hayford seems to intuit what Frank Macchia says about Spirit baptism in the New Testament. The term "is a fluid metaphor surrounded by ambiguous imagery that suggests broader boundaries pneumatologically than Spirit empowerment." Frank D. Macchia, *Baptized in the Spirit: A Global Pentecostal Theology* (Grand Rapids, MI: Zondervan, 2006), 14. Having said this, Hayford still affirms Spirit baptism as a separate experience from regeneration. Jack W. Hayford, "Bothering with Tongues," *Ministries Today*, May/June 2002, 16-19 (17).

24. Hayford, *The Beauty of Spiritual Language*, 13-16.

25. Hayford, "Bothering with Tongues," 16-19.

26. Jack W. Hayford, School of Pastoral Nurture: Consultation I, King's Seminary, May 2007, digital audio recording 1.23.

27. In contrast, perhaps as high as 85 percent of the members of the Church on the Way were Spirit baptized and spoke with tongues. Hayford, "Bothering with Tongues," 17.

28. Jack W. Hayford, letter to Vinson Synan, January 13, 1993.

29. Hayford, interview, November 13, 2007. I have chosen not to provide citation information for either the denominational official's letter or Hayford's in order to prevent any embarrassment or concern for the denomination letter. Both letters are in Hayford's private correspondence files.

30. Hayford, *The Beauty of Spiritual Language*, 98.

31. Hayford, School of Pastoral Nurture: Consultation I, digital audio recording 1.23.

32. It should also be remembered that Hayford's own personal experience of Spirit baptism was not accompanied by glossolalia. It was over four years later that he finally spoke with tongues.

33. Hayford, *Invading the Impossible*, 113.

34. Jack W. Hayford, *Spiritual Language: Instrument of Deliverance* (Van Nuys: SoundWord Tape Ministry, 1973), audiocassette.

35. Hayford, *The Beauty of Spiritual Language*, 55. On the one hand, Hayford loves words and has been "roasted" for his "many words." He just as surely recognizes "the tyranny of word" and sees tongues as an escape. See Cheryl Bridges Johns, "Partners in Scandal: Wesleyan and Pentecostal Scholarship," *Wesleyan Theological Journal* 34, no. 1 (Spring 1999): 7-23.

36. Hayford, *The Beauty of Spiritual Language*, 142-47; Jack W. Hayford, *The Holy Spirit: The Great Psychiatrist*, Part One (Van Nuys: Living Way Ministries, March 11, 1979), audiocassette; idem, *The Holy Spirit: The Great Psychiatrist*, Part Two (Van Nuys: Living Way Ministries, March 18, 1979), audiocassette.

37. Hayford, School of Pastoral Nurture: Consultation I, digital audio recording 1.23. Simon Chan's "ascetical tongues" idea is interesting in that it acknowledges the prayer language value of glossolalia. Chan, *Pentecostal Theology and the Christian Spiritual Tradition*, 77-82. The way Hayford understands tongues is more than a symbolic or mystical experience. Tongues for Hayford have functionality in that the Holy Spirit inspires the believer to pray in ways that transcend human rationality. Nevertheless, something is prayed by the believer that is intelligible to God. Therefore, glossolalia should be employed whenever one feels limited by an inability to express fully one's prayers or worship to God. Further, these prayers not only bring union with God but in fact give grace to the one who prays in tongues. Hayford believes that 1 Corinthians 14:4 (NKJV) teaches this when it says, "He who speaks in a tongue edifies himself." Hayford, *The Beauty of Spiritual Language*, 134-36; Hayford,

"Prayer Is Invading the Impossible," 109-18. See also Frank D. Macchia, "Sighs Too Deep for Words: Toward a Theology of Tongues as Initial Evidence," *Journal of Pentecostal Theology* I (1992): 47-73; idem, "Tongues as a Sign: Toward a Sacramental Understanding of Pentecostal Experience," *Pneuma* 15, no. 1 (Spring 1993): 61-76.

38. John Dart, "Speaking in Tongues Declines among Pentecostal Believers," *Los Angeles Times*, October 14, 1995, 39.

39. Brian Bird, "Biblical Exposition: Becoming a Lost Art?," *Christianity Today*, April 18, 1986, 34.

40. "The Legacy of the Lausanne Movement," Lausanne Movement, www.lausanne.org /our-legacy (accessed August 31, 2019).

41. Lausanne Committee for World Evangelization, *Lausanne Covenant*, Article 14, Wheaton, IL, 1974.

42. Hayford, *A Passion for Fullness*, 16.

43. Hayford, *A Passion for Fullness*, 18.

44. Hayford, *A Passion for Fullness*, 21.

45. Hayford, *A Passion for Fullness*, 22-23.

46. The popular Reformed preacher John Piper favorably commented on Hayford's suggested term "pleromatics" in John Piper, "Thoughts from Lausanne II in Manila," July 21, 1989, Desiring God, www.desiringgod.org/articles/thoughts-from-lausanne -ii-in-manila.

47. Hayford, *A Passion for Fullness*, 20. As it relates to his worship, Hayford has been interviewed or written articles for Christianity Today Incorporated's quarterly journal, *Leadership*. Jack Hayford, "How I Prepare Myself for Worship," *Leadership*, Summer 1990, 80-85; "The Power and the Presence: A Leadership Forum," *Leadership*, Summer 1991, 14-18; Hayford, "Expressive Worship with Reluctant People," *Leadership*, Spring 1994, 36-43.

48. Dr. Jack W Hayford's Ministry Occasions, 1972–2000.

49. Larry B. Stammer, "Billy Graham Is Frail, but Mission Is Strong," *Los Angeles Times*, November 17, 2004, B1, B9.

50. Jack Hayford, "I'm Unusually Elated Today!," Church Bulletin, The Church on the Way, October 20, 1991, 2.

51. Don Moen, telephone interview with the author, February 26, 2016.

52. Moen quipped regarding Hayford's passion for thorough explanation that Hayford "tells you the reason he's going to tell you, then he tells you, and then he tells you why he told you." Moen, telephone interview, February 26, 2016.

53. Moen, telephone interview. Over the years, Jack developed personal relationships with noted worship leaders and often invited them to lead worship at the Church

on the Way or at his annual pastors' conferences (like Darlene Zschech of Hillsong). He wrote a foreword to one of Matt Redmond's books. Matt and Beth Redman, *Finding God in the Hard Times: Choosing Trust and Hope When You Can't See Why* (Bloomington: Bethany House Publishers, 2005).

54. Jack Hayford, *Stanced before Almightiness* (Van Nuys: Living Way Ministries, 1995).

55. Jack W. Hayford, journal entry, September 21, 1993, private holding, 1. The journal entry mentions that Hayford was elected as vice-chairman for Charismatic Bible Ministries, a group Oral Roberts organized that was seeking to bring Pentecostals and Charismatics together in greater unity. For other examples of his role as a facilitator, see Jack W. Hayford, "A Watershed Moment," *Ministries Today*, March/April 2004, 58-59; Hayford, "Practicing What We Preach," *Ministries Today*, November/December 2003, 23-24, 27.

56. One of Jack's most visible involvements was with Ted Haggard after his homosexual affairs brought his resignation from his megachurch, New Life Church in Colorado Springs. See www.denverpost.com/2006/11/19/haggard-headed-on-long-journey/ (accessed October 16, 2019).

Chapter 15: "Ministry on the Way"

1. "The West Campus Story," The Church on the Way, Van Nuys, September 1990, 3.

2. "The West Campus Story." Although some conversation about the property had taken place between the two churches in the two and a half years preceding 1986, nothing ever came of it before this.

3. "The West Campus Story," 2.

4. "The West Campus Story," 2.

5. Ira Rifkin, "A Holy Alliance," *Los Angeles Times*, February 18, 1988, F1, F13. With the acquisition, the Church on the Way had two separate campuses. In the 1990s, services were simulcast between the two campuses. The West Campus was not officially dedicated until June 2, 1991, nearly four years after the purchase.

6. Moody had succeeded Harold Fickett in 1976 as the First Baptist Church of Van Nuys' senior pastor.

7. Unless otherwise noted, the following paragraphs are referencing Jack Hayford, *Out Racing the World* Part 1 (Van Nuys: SoundWord Tape Ministry, October 10, 1993), audiocassette; Hayford, *Out Racing the World* Part 2 A&B (Van Nuys: SoundWord Tape Ministry, October 24, 1993), two audiocassettes.

8. Hayford specifically mentions the term "systemic racism" in one of his Pastor's Heart columns in *Ministries Today* magazine. Jack Hayford, "Pastor's Heart: Let's 'Race' to Reconcile," *Ministries Today*, January 1996, 18-19 (18).

9. Hayford, *Out Racing the World* Part 2, B.

10. The March 19, 1984, service in Washington, DC, where this occurred was at the Inner-City Pastors' Conference at Evangel Temple. Jack's message was entitled "Reconciliation: A Personal Beginning Point." Dr. Jack W. Hayford's Ministry Occasions, 1972–2000, 60.

11. Vinson Synan, "The 'Memphis Miracle,'" *Ministries Today*, January/February 1995, 36-42, 66-72.

12. David Rudolph, "Count Zinzendorf, Pastor Jack, and the Messianic Jewish Revival," in Jon Huntzinger and S. David Moore, eds., *The Pastor and the Kingdom: Essays Honoring Jack W. Hayford* (Southlake, TX: TKU Press/Gateway Academic, 2017), 92-116 (103).

13. The quote that follows is taken from Rudolph, "Count Zinzendorf," 103-4.

14. Hayford, "Seeing Israel and the Jews through the Eyes of God," 31. Cf. Hayford, "Allowing the Spirit to Refocus Our Identity," 22-23.

15. Hayford, "Seeing Israel and the Jews through the Eyes of God," 34.

16. Rudolph, "Count Zinzendorf," 113.

17. Jack Hayford, "Ready for the Wedding" (2014), 1. Online: www.jackhayford.org.

18. David Rudolph, "Count Zinzendorf," 92-116 (113).

19. Marty Waldman, conversation at PCCNA Unity Commission meeting, March 20, 2019.

20. The quote is from Rudolph, "Count Zinzendorf," 108; "Who We Are," Toward Jerusalem Council II, http://tjcii.org/about-us. See also Peter Hocken, *The Challenges of the Pentecostal, Charismatic and Messianic Movements: The Tensions of the Spirit* (Burlington, VT: Ashgate, 2009), 111-12; Hocken, *Azusa, Rome, and Zion: Pentecostal Faith, Catholic Reform, and Jewish Roots* (Eugene, OR: Pickwick, 2016), 133-61, 199; Daniel C. Juster, "Messianic Gentiles and the Gentile Christian World," in *Introduction to Messianic Judaism*, 139-42.

21. Jack W. Hayford, "The Blessings of Autumn," *Ministries Today*, September/October 2001, 18-19.

22. Hayford, interview, September 1, 2007. Hayford believes he may have been conceived on September 21 and so for him this was possibly the beginning of his sixtieth year of life. Jack W. Hayford, journal entry, September 21, 1993, private holding, 1.

23. John Dart, "Pastor Puts Energy into Mentors," *Los Angeles Times*, August 29, 1998, 1. The first Jack W. Hayford School of Pastoral Nurture was offered in June 1997.

24. "The School on the Way," Church Bulletin, The Church on the Way, January 23, 1972, 3.

25. "The King's Institute" (Van Nuys, the Church on the Way, 1997), 1-8.

26. See Promise Keepers, https://promisekeepers.org/promise-keepers/about-us/. The original link, www.promisekeepers.org/about/pkhistory, gave the cited stats, but the web page is no longer available.

27. Jack W. Hayford, interview with the author, January 26, 2016.

28. Hayford, interview, September 1, 2007; Dr. Jack W. Hayford's Ministry Occasions, 1972–2000, 164.

29. Hayford, King's College/Seminary Chapel, Van Nuys, n.d., transcript, 1; Jack W. Hayford, letter to Fellow Servants and Shepherds, July 2006, The King's College and Seminary, 2.

30. Hayford, interview, September 1, 2007.

31. John Dart, "Church to Launch Pentecostal Seminary," *Los Angeles Times*, March 29, 1997, B1, B8.

32. In 2000, the SPNs were shortened to a five-day schedule.

33. There were four distinct consultations: Consultation I, Consultation II, Consultation III, and Consultation IV, each with a different focus. The consultations were designed to follow each other and had to be attended in order. Consequently, Consultation I was held most frequently each year.

34. Steven Lawson, "The Foursquare Church Faces the 21st Century," *Charisma*, March 1993, 16-26. When the Charismatic publication *Charisma* carried a cover story on the Foursquare Church, Jack Hayford's picture was on the cover under the banner "The Changing Face of the Foursquare Church."

35. Lawson, "The Foursquare Church Faces the 21st Century," 17; Van Cleave, *The Vine and the Branches*, 219-20.

36. Dart, "His Way: Valley's 'Pastor Jack' Revives Church," B1.

37. Hayford, interview with the author, April 13, 2003.

38. Jack W. Hayford, *The Unending Trial of Aimee Semple McPherson* (Van Nuys: Living Way Ministry, 1990), transcript of September 9, 1990 message, 1; Van Cleave, *The Vine and the Branches*, 237-38.

39. Hayford, *The Unending Trial of Aimee Semple McPherson*.

40. Hayford, *The Unending Trial of Aimee Semple McPherson*, 3. As recently as 2005, Hayford wrote an article affirming Aimee in his *Ministries Today* column. Jack W. Hayford, "Lessons from Aimee," *Ministries Today*, September/October 2005, 69-70.

41. Pastor Jack Hayford, "On the Question of a Woman's Place in Church Leadership" (Van Nuys: The Church on the Way, n.d.), 1-10.

42. Jack Hayford, "Men First: But for the Right Reasons," *Ministries Today*, July/August 1993, 8-9 (9).

43. His views on women in ministry are complicated and it would take a small book to adequately address them.

44. Jack W. Hayford, confidential letter to The Church Council, June 17, 1996, 1-11 (2).

45. Memorandum to the Servant Leadership, Saturday, January 23, 1999, 1-4.

46. Church Bulletin, The Church on the Way, April 19 and 27, 1992, 4.

47. "The role and responsibility of leadership in understanding and partnering with us as we advance our pastoral leadership," memorandum to the Servant Leadership of the Church on the Way, January 23, 1999.

48. Jack W. Hayford, journal entry, October 30, 1999, private holding, 1.

49. Jack Hayford, "Why I Stepped Aside," *Ministries Today*, May/June 2000, 20-21.

50. The Church on the Way, *Jack Hayford Leads Church in 'Transferring' the Flag*, 1999.

51. Scott G. Bauer, *The New Church on the Way* (Van Nuys: the Church on the Way, 2002).

Chapter 16: Serving the King

1. Jack W. Hayford, *Hope for a Hopeless Day* (Ventura, CA: Regal, 2007), 9-12. I have chosen to correct Hayford's account in his book because of a couple of inaccuracies. For example, Jack says on page 13 that he was 68 in October 2003. He was actually 69 at the time. Also, sunrise in Los Angeles was 7:05 a.m. on October 24, 2003.

2. Hayford, *Hope for a Hopeless Day*, 13. Hayford has always said that the fall is his favorite time of the year. Jack Hayford, "A Heart of Thanksgiving," *Ministries Today*, November/December 1998.

3. Hayford, *Hope for a Hopeless Day*, 13.

4. Hayford, *Hope for a Hopeless Day*, 14.

5. Hayford, *Hope for a Hopeless Day*, 15.

6. Hayford, *Hope for a Hopeless Day*, 16.

7. Hayford, *Hope for a Hopeless Day*, 113.

8. "Obituaries: Scott Bauer, Pastor Led the Church on the Way," *Los Angeles Times*, October 29, 2003, B13; "Church on the Way Pastor Dies Unexpectedly," *Ministries Today*, January/February 2004, 12.

9. Jack Hayford, memorandum to the Combined Staffs of all COTW Ministries, October 23, 2003, the Church on the Way holding, 1-3.

10. Jack W Hayford, *In the Wake of a Shepherd's Sudden Call Home* (Van Nuys: Living Way Ministries, October 26, 2003), compact disc.

11. Rebecca Bauer, "Run to Him," Church Bulletin, The Church on the Way, n.d., insert.

12. Jack W. Hayford, journal entry, January 4, 2003, private holding.

13. Jack W. Hayford, journal entry, October 25, 2003, private holding; Jack W. Hayford, journal entry, November 29, 2003, private holding.

14. Selimah Nemoy, "It Could Have Only Been God," *Spectrum*, Fall 2004, 19.

15. "The King's Seminary Opens Its Doors to First Students," *Spectrum*, Spring 1999, 1.

16. Jack Hayford, "Answering the Call: To Train Spirit-Filled Leadership for a New Century until Christ Returns," unpublished brief, n.d.

17. Jack Hayford, "The King's Seminary," brief, April 22, 1997.

18. "Conversation with Paul Chappell," minutes, June 6, 1996.

19. Josh Morris, son of Robert Morris, who pastors in Austin, Texas, specifically mentioned that Jack Hayford's acknowledgment of legitimate alternatives to young earth creationism was particularly appealing to younger evangelicals. Josh Morris, telephone interview with the author, November 15, 2019.

20. Jim Hayford, letter to Jack Hayford, April 17, 1987, the Church on the Way holding, 1; Hayford, interview, January 10, 2003.

21. Christiana Sciaudone, "Keeping the Faith and Credibility*," Los Angeles Times*, Saturday, September 11, 2004, B2.

22. Christiana Sciaudone, "Keeping the Faith and Credibility," B2.

23. "Jack Hayford to Lead Foursquare Church," *Ministries Today*, September/October 2004, 12. There were three candidates before the convention floor. Don Latton, "Popular Evangelist Elected to Head Foursquare Church," *San Francisco Chronicle*, Saturday, June 5, 2004, B3. In early 2005, Hayford discussed—in his regular column in *Ministries Today* magazine—his new role as president of the Foursquare Church and appealed to readers to see the viability of denominations in the face of the tendency of many Pentecostals and Charismatics, notably "third waver" C. Peter Wagner, to dismiss denominations as "an ecclesiastical artifact." Jack W. Hayford, "Denominations: Alive and Well," *Ministries Today*, January/February 2005, 64, 66.

24. See chapter 12.

25. Hayford, "Denominations: Alive and Well," 64, 66.

26. Hayford, interview, May 10, 2006. Hayford, "Denominations: Alive and Well," 64.

27. Jack Hayford, personal interview with the author, June 16, 2009; Jack Hayford, personal interview with the author, May 18, 2010; Jack Hayford, personal interview with the author, September 2010; Jack Hayford, personal interview with the author, April 16, 2013.

28. Jack W. Hayford, "An Announcement from the President," The International Church of the Foursquare Gospel, May 26, 2009, 1-4.

29. Jack's journal does reflect questions about whether he'd be ratified, but he thought the doubts were coming from the "Adversary." Jack W. Hayford, journal entry, May 17, 2009, private holding.

30. Jack W. Hayford, journal entry, June 12, 2009, private holding.

31. Jack W. Hayford, journal entry, March 12, 2014, private holding.

32. Jack W. Hayford, journal entry, May 25, 2010, private holding.

33. The following paragraphs are drawn from two interviews: Robert Morris, personal interview with the author, December 5, 2018; Jack Hayford, interview with the author, November 11, 2014.

34. David Rudolph, "Count Zinzendorf," 92-116 (113).

35. Rudolph, "Count Zinzendorf," 114.

36. "Jewish," Gateway Church, https://gatewaypeople.com/ministries/jewish-ministry (accessed October 17, 2019).

37. See Jack Hayford Digital Library, www.jackhayfordlibrary.com (accessed August 12, 2019). Michael Lynch, who was the director of Jack Hayford Ministries, oversaw the project and helped raise funds for the creation of the digital library.

38. Jack Hayford, "To Write an Epitaph," Church Bulletin, The Church on the Way, August 20, 1978, 2.

39. Anna Hayford, "Carried by the Body of Christ," *Advance*, July/August 1988, 6-7, 21.

40. Jack and Anna Hayford, "Taking the Shield of Faith," Church Bulletin, The Church o the Way, February 14, 1988, 3.

41. Jack Hayford, "Faith, Prayer, and Going Home," *Ministries Today*, March/April 1998, 19-20.

42. Ruth Senter, "Jack & Anna Hayford: When Words Were Not Enough," *Partnership*, November/December 1985, 26.

43. The letter is undated, but from where it was located in Jack's files, it was likely sometime in the early 1970s. Anna Hayford, letter to "Dear Jack," n.d., private holding.

44. Senter, "Jack & Anna Hayford," 27.

45. Senter, "Jack & Anna Hayford," 27.

46. Jack W. Hayford III, telephone interview with the author, November 6, 2019; Doug and Christa Anderson, telephone interview with the author, October 31, 2019; Rebecca Bauer, personal interview with the author, June 18, 1019.

47. Jack Hayford, journal entry, June 18, 2011.

48. Jack Hayford, journal entry, June 27, 2011.

49. Jack W. Hayford, letter concerning "A Personal Word from Pastor Jack Hayford," The King's University, August 18, 2011.

50. R. Morris, interview with the author.

51. Steven Strang, "What's Kept Us Strong," *Charisma*, July 2014, Jack Hayford Special Section, 4-10 (5).

52. Hayford's way of seeing the world offers a "reenchantment" that challenges the reductionisms that have characterized modernity. In many ways his brand of Pentecostalism is also a recovery of the Christian mystical tradition that harmonizes with a more medieval, premodern sensibility See Alan Hirsch and Mark Nelson, *Reframation: Seeing God, People, and Mission through Reenchanted Frames* (100 Movements, 2019); Charles Taylor, *The Secular Age* (Cambridge: Harvard University Press, 2007); Daniel Castelo, *Pentecostalism as a Christian Mystical Tradition* (Grand Rapids, MI: Eerdmans, 2017); Hans Boersma, *Heavenly Participation: The Weaving of a Sacramental Tapestry* (Grand Rapids, MI: Eerdmans, 2011).

53. The Van Nuys church has committed to provide the parsonage until Jack's death.

54. Jack W. Hayford, "Jesus My Savior," Rocksmith Music/Word Music, Inc., 1984 (sung to tune of "Morning Has Broken").

Appendix: An Uneasy Alliance

1. For a helpful discussion on the issues related to the estimates of adherents in global Pentecostalism, see Allen Heaton Anderson, *An Introduction to Pentecostalism*, 2nd ed. (New York: Cambridge University Press, 2014), 1-7.

2. The non-Wesleyan Pentecostals, or "Finished Work" Pentecostals, would include William Durham and his Chicago mission as an essential part of their genealogy.

3. Phillip Jenkins, *The Next Christendom: The Coming of Global Christianity*, 3rd ed. (Oxford: Oxford University Press, 2011); Phillip Jenkins, *The New Faces of Christianity: Believing the Bible in the Global South* (Oxford: Oxford University Press, 2006). Estimates of 600 million or more adherents is only possible if all the varied groups are counted together as a whole despite their considerable variances and diversity.

4. Hayford, *A Passion for Fullness*, 118. Throughout the book, Jack makes clear his belief in the need for definite conversion, the centrality of Jesus' death and resurrection, his regard for biblical authority, and the need for active evangelization.

5. Sutton, *Aimee Semple McPherson*. Sutton convincingly presents McPherson as a leader in mainstreaming Pentecostalism even before World War II and the formation of the National Association of Evangelicals (NAE).